John Liggins

**The Great Value and Success of Foreign Missions**

Proved by Distinguished Witnesses....

John Liggins

**The Great Value and Success of Foreign Missions**
*Proved by Distinguished Witnesses....*

ISBN/EAN: 9783337209575

Printed in Europe, USA, Canada, Australia, Japan

Cover: Foto ©Lupo / pixelio.de

More available books at **www.hansebooks.com**

# THE GREAT

# VALUE AND SUCCESS

—OF—

# FOREIGN MISSIONS.

## PROVED BY DISTINGUISHED WITNESSES:

BEING THE TESTIMONY OF DIPLOMATIC MINISTERS, CONSULS,
NAVAL OFFICERS, AND SCIENTIFIC AND OTHER
TRAVELERS IN HEATHEN AND MO-
HAMMEDAN COUNTRIES;

### TOGETHER WITH THAT OF

ENGLISH VICEROYS, GOVERNORS, AND MILITARY OFFICERS IN
INDIA AND IN THE BRITISH COLONIES:

### ALSO

## LEADING FACTS AND LATE STATISTICS OF THE MISSIONS.

———————

## BY REV. JOHN LIGGINS

Author of "One Thousand Phrases in English and Japanese;" "England's Opium
Policy," &c., &c.

WITH AN INTRODUCTION BY

## REV. ARTHUR T. PIERSON, D. D.

——— — ———

NEW YORK:

THE BAKER & TAYLOR CO.,

740 AND 742 BROADWAY.

# INTRODUCTION.

THIS most timely book fits the need of the day, as ball fits socket, or tenon fits mortise.

To decry, or even deny, the good work done by heroic missionaries does not disprove it; the logic of events will convince any candid mind, and this book is simply a grand massing and marshalling of testimony.

Nehemiah, the model reformer and organizer, met manifold forms of antagonism. But, in face of apathy and lethargy on the part of Jews, and derisive ridicule and malicious enmity on the part of Horonite and Ammonite and Arabian, he held his tongue, kept his temper, minded his own business, and moved right forward, till the wall was built, the gates hung, and law and order were reestablished.

That ancient "repairer of the breach, and restorer of paths to dwell in," was not alone in his experience of opposition in doing his great and good work. "A light word is the Devil's keenest sword." There are many who are "willingly ignorant;" and if all that they do *not* know were put in print, the world itself could not contain the books that would be written. With a sublime disregard for the pin-point of ridicule, and even the sharp shaft of sober and serious assault, we must carry on both the work of missions, and the kindred work of informing and enlightening those who do not shut their eyes to the light. Let us give the people the facts in abundance. To some they may become the fingers of God.

In this valuable volume, the high character and grand influence of Christian missions are established beyond a doubt. Hundreds of representative men and women, whose very names carry the weight of authority, from every class in the community, here take the stand as witnesses; and in the high court of the Judgment, command and compel a hearing. They speak what they know and testify what they have seen, and only those whom prejudice blinds, or hostility hardens, will refuse to receive such concordant witness.

Modern missions have nothing to fear from the harsh or hasty words of a few like Dr. Oscar Lenz, Winwood Reade, Sir Lepel Griffin, J. J. Monteiro, Mrs. Scott Stevenson, or even J. A. Froude and Canon Taylor; while such as R. H. Dana and J. P. Donovan, James Russell Lowell and Alfred Russell Wallace, R. N. Cust and James B. Angell, William Elliot Griffis and William Fleming Stevenson, Sir Bartle Frere and Sir Richard Temple, Lords Lawrence and Loftus, Northbrook and Napier, Generals Edwards, and Haig, Wallace and Wilson, Taylor and Gordon, Admirals Wilkes and Sullivan, Foote and Gore ; nay, where Darwin no less than Dufferin, and

Keshub Chunder Sen no less than Constance Gordon-
Cumming, feel constrained to testify to the priceless
value and great success of Christian missions.

The days of supernatural signs have not passed
away. God's Word does not return to Him void.
Instead of the thorn comes up the fir-tree; instead of
the brier comes up the myrtle tree; and this dis-
placement, in the soil of society, of noxious and offen-
sive growths of sin, by useful and fragrant trees of
righteousness, is the unanswerable proof and sign of
God's Husbandry—the planting of the Lord, that He
might be glorified. Such individual, social, spiritual
tranformation shall be to the Lord for a name, for an
everlasting sign that shall not be cut off. The
Church of Christ has only to go forth and preach
everywhere. The Lord will work with and confirm
the word with signs following. Amen.

ARTHUR T. PIERSON.

2320 *Spruce St.*, *Philadelphia*,
   *November*, 1888.

# CONTENTS.

INTRODUCTION............ iii

THE SUBJECT GENERALLY...... 1

Misstatements Concerning Foreign Missions.—A Repentant
Slanderer.—A Noted African Traveller.—Skeptical Residents
and Travellers.—The Course of the London *Times*.—James
Russell Lowell on the Skeptics.—Skeptics Who Do Not Sneer
at the Missionaries.—Commending the Civilizing Influence of
the Missions.—Uninformed Travellers and Residents.—An Uninterested Clerical Gentleman.—What Many Tourists Fail to See
and to Do.—Noble Exceptions.—An Anecdote, by Dr. Bliss.—
An Uninformed American Statesman.—What Has Come to
Pass.—Prejudice Changed to Praise.—Testimony of Dr. Stevenson.—The Rev. Mr. Bainbridge and Dr. Prime.—Bishop Foster
and Dr. Abel Stevens.—Refuting Laymen by more Distinguished Laymen.—A Telling Reply to a Major-General.—Testimony
of Eminent Scientists.—An American Traveller Answered.—Sir
Lepel Griffin's Speech.—Men of a Very Different Stamp.—
Jaunty Travellers in Africa.—An American Lady and Miss Gor-
don Cumming.—The Remarkable Letter of Colonel Denby.—
Mrs. Scott Stevenson and Sir Thomas Tancred.—James A.
Froude and Charles Darwin.—Some of the Great Results of
Missions.

AFRICA................ 31

Missionary Enterprise in Africa.—Famous Explorers as Wit-
nesses.—The Governor of Natal and the Consul of Mozambique.
—General Gordon and Emin Bey.—A Distinguished Linguist's
Testimony.—Self-Sacrificing Devotion of Church of England
Men and Women.—The Same Self-Sacrificing Spirit of Other Men
and Women.—Independent Testimony as to the Results.—The

London *Times* on Drs. Moffatt and Livingstone.—Sir Charles Warren on Some of the Results He Has Seen.—The Success in South Africa.—Testimony of a Minister for the Aborigines.—The Martyrs of Uganda.—A Chivalrous Knight of the Cross.—Gen. Haig on the American Mission in Egypt.—Dr. Lenz and Archdeacon Farler.—What Can No Longer Be Maintained.

## BORNEO.................. 49

A nation of Head Hunters.—Numerous Head Takers Become Members of the Church.—Mr. Hornaday on the Great Change in the Fierce Dyaks.

## BURMAH................ 52

Dr. Judson, the Great Missionary.—Five Hundred Churches and Twenty-six Thousand Members.—Administration Report on the Debt to the Missionaries.

## CELEBES.................. 54

Celebes is Now a Christian Island.—Alfred Russell Wallace's Remarkable Testimony.

## CHINA................ ... 55

Great Missionary Progress Since 1843.—Miss Gordon Cumming's "Wanderings in China."—Her Testimony to the Great Success.--Consuls as Witnesses.—Mr. J. P. Donovan and a London *Times* Correspondent.—Minister Denby on the Immense Good Which is Being Done.—Secular and Political Results.—President Angell on What Has Been Accomplished in a Lifetime.—Action of the Viceroy Li Hung Chang.—Extensive Medical Missions in China.—The Large Hospital, Dispensary and College at Canton.—Prestige Gained By the Missions.—Opium Refuges.—A Formidable Obstacle in China.

## FIJI.................. 70

Formerly the Darkest Place on Earth.—Sir Arthur Gordon on the Wonderful Transformation.—Sir Charles St. Julian's Testimony.—Miss Gordon Cumming on the Mighty Change Which Has Been Effected.—Thrilling Stories of the Missionaries' Courage.—The Fijian Church Has Become a Missionary Body. —Testimony of Administrators McGregor and Thurston.

# GREENLAND................ 76

Sublime Faith and Patience of the Missionaries.—Testimony of Drs. Kane and Brown to Their Great Success.

# INDIA................ 79

The Three Principal Religions of India.—The Misrule of the East India Company.—A Disgraceful Memorial of the Company. —Dr. Butler on Some of the Misdeeds of the Company.—Anti-Christian Policy.—The Iniquitous Opium Traffic.—Sir John Lawrence's Superior Policy.—Major-General Edwardes on the Bad Policy Pursued.—The Earlier and Later Records of the Company.—The Only Policy of Hope.—The Policy of the Present Governing Council.—No Christian Need Apply.—Denouncing Tremendous Evils.—How One Iniquity Was Suppressed.—Two Great Native Evils.—Two Great Government Evils.—The Success of Christian Labors.—Testimony of the Earl of Northbrook and Others.—Lord Lawrence on the Popularity of the Missionaries. —Lord Napier on the Attractive Pictures of Missionary Life.—Sir Bartle Frere on the Great Changes Effected.—Sir William Muir on the Work of the American and Continental Missionaries.—Sir Richard Temple on the Bright Example of the Missionaries.—Sir Richard Temple on the Missions Being Failures.—Sir. Charles Aitcheson on the Startling Leavening Process.—Sir William Hunter's Remarkable Lecture.—Enormous Increments.—Testimony of Prince Harnam Singh.—Native Admissions as to Success. —Testimony of a Watchful Brahmin.—A Large Number of Brahmins Baptized.—Liberal Giving by Foreign Residents in India. —Native Princes Contributing.—Unsalaried Missionaries in India.—The Natives Trust Only the Missionaries.

# JAPAN ................ 111

The First Protestant Mission in Japan.—The Wonderful Changes in Less Than Thirty Years.—A Noble Body of Cultured Ladies and Gentlemen.—Miss Isabella L. Bird's Testimony.—Professor Rein on the Missionaries and Their Hinderers.—Mr. Maclay on the Work of Yokohama.—The Missionaries and the Foreign Community.—A Thoroughly Characteristic Story.—A Young Officer's Legacy.—Captain Brinkley on the Once Formidable Difficulties and the Present Success.—U. S. Minister Hubbard on this Urgently Inviting Field.—A Native Minister's Testimony.

—Mr. Arthur L. Shumway as a Witness.—Consul Seymour and Dr. Kerr.

## JAVA. ................. 126

The Island and its Inhabitants.—Progress of the Missionary Work.

## MADAGASCAR ............. 128

Remarkable Results in Madagascar.—Testimony of the Hon. N. F. Graves.—The People Raised and Purified.—Gen. J. W. Phelps on Madagascar's Passage from Barbarism to Christianity.

## MICRONESIA... ...... .... 131

The Results After About Thirty Years' Work.—The Spanish Seizure of the Caroline Islands.

## NEW GUINEA............... 134

The Island and its Inhabitants.—Captain Spry on the "Challenger's" Visit to New Guinea.—The Tragic Beginning of the Missionary Work.—The Change in Torres Straits.—Testimonies of Lord Loftus and Others as to the Change on the Mainland.— A Missionary's Great Influence.—Strange Proofs of Regard.— What the Gospel of Christ Has Done.—A Letter From a Naval Officer.

## NEW HEBRIDES ............. 144

Great Difficulties and many Martyrs.—The Outlines of a Glorious History.—Women in the Holy War.

## NEW ZEALAND ............. 148

Sublime Scenery but Barbarous People.—"The Standing Miracle of the Age."—Bishop Selwyn Founds the Melanesian Mission.—Perils Encountered.—Mr. Darwin and the Enchanter's Wand.—Mr. Froude's Statement in "Oceana."

## NORTH AMERICAN INDIANS ...... 154

Our Nation's Dishonorable Conduct Toward the Indians.— Dr. Sunderland on the Outrageous Treatment of the Indians. —A Brave Government Agent.—President Seelye on the Government's Failure to Solve the Indian Problem.—The Results of Christian Missions.—A Few Telling Facts.—Testimony of Commissioner Rhodes and Mr. Herbert Welsh.—The Change at White Earth Reservation.—"A Student of Civilization" on Bishop Hare and His Work.—The Last Lake Mohonk Conference.—An Unparalleled Government Order.—The Wonderful Change at Metlakahtla.—Commendations of Lord Dufferin and Others.—Mr. Duncan and his Indians are now in Alaska.—The New Mission in Alaska Welcomed by the Government.

### PERSIA..... ........ ..... 171

U. S. Minister Benjamin on the Growth and Power of the Missions.—Col. E. C. Stewart on the Striking Contrast in Thirteen Years.—Mark of Distinction from the Shah.

### POLYNESIA—The field generally..... 174

Some of the Great Results of Christian Missions.—What the Missionaries Have Given the Natives.—Missions have been the Preservation of the Polynesians.—The Life of a Savage.—Captain Macdonald on Safety of the Shipwrecked.—Living in a New World.—Civilization Without the Gospel Does Not Civilize —The Wonderful Result of a Loving Act.—Cheering Scenes.— Roman Catholic Aggressions.

### SAMOA................183

La Perouse on the Babarism of the Samoans.—Dr. Turner on Some of the Great Results.—Captain Erskine on the Change Effected.

### SANDWICH ISLANDS..... .... 187

The Early Navigators on the Savage Character of the Natives —Hon. Richard H. Dana on the Remarkable Change.—Miss Gordon Cumming on Hawaii Without and With the Gospel.— Summary of a Great Work.—Hon. Elisha H. Allen on the Missionaries Saving the Nation.—Mr. M. D. Conway's Experiences in Honolulu.

### SIAM ............... .. 192

Hon. David B. Sickles on the Great Work Which has been Accomplished.—The Favor of the King and Queen.

## SIBERIA ...... ... ...... 195

The Work of Dr. Lansdell and Others.—Dr. Lansdell's Latest Book.—A Letter From the Convicts.

## TAHITI........... ... ....... 198

Admiral Wilkes on the Value of Missionary Labors.—Faithful Native Christians.—Mr. Charles Darwin on the Morality and Religion of the Tahitians.—Testimony of Captain Harvey.

## TERRA DEL FUEGO... ........ 201

European Government Representatives Commend the Work. —Admiral Sullivan Writes to Darwin on the Wonderful Change.—Lieut. Bove's Testimony.—A Christian Fuegian Village.

## TONGA ISLANDS............ ... 204

The Results of a Long and Perilous Struggle.—The Fearless Energy of the Native Christians.

## TURKISH EMPIRE............. 206

Summary of the Missions of the American Board.—Sir Austen Layard on the Judicious and Earnest Efforts of the Missionaries.—Lord Redcliffe on their Discretion Tempered with Zeal.— The Earl of Shaftesbury on their Common Sense and Piety.— Deserving of Unlimited Praise.—Hon. G. P. Marsh on the Vast Significance of the Facts.—Testimony of Gen. Lew Wallace.— Gen. Wallace's Prejudice Changed to High Regard.—Lieut. Col. Mark S. Bell as a Witness.—What a British Consul at Aleppo Writes.—Mrs. Charles on the Entire Consecration of the Missionaries.—Sir Thomas Tancred on the Missions in Asia Minor.—Missions of the Church Missionary Society in Palestine. —The Moravian Hospital for Lepers at Jerusalem —The Presbyterian Mission in Syria.—The Syrian Protestant College.

## APPENDIX...... . ...... 213

The Enrichment of Occidental Science by the Missionaries. —Enriching the Orient with True Science and Philosophy.—The Awakening in the East.—The Statesmanship of Missions.

# THE GREAT VALUE AND SUCCESS OF FOREIGN MISSIONS.

## THE SUBJECT GENERALLY.

SCARCELY a month passes without an article appearing in a leading newspaper or periodical, or without a book being published, in which Foreign Missions are declared to be failures. These unfounded statements are from residents or travellers abroad, who are either hostile to missions, or who are uninformed upon the subject.

While among American and European residents in heathen and Mohammedan countries, there are many estimable persons, and some noble Christian men and women, yet there is a larger proportion of the sensual, the skeptical, and the unprincipled, than is the case among those of similar education and position at home.

Arthur Collins Maclay, who is not a missionary, says, in his "Budget of Letters from Japan," that the foreign communities in that country are very immoral, and that many of the American and European residents and visitors, "are leading lives they would not think of leading at home." He further says that the opposition to missionaries and their work comes not from the Japanese, but from these evil-living foreigners. Similar is the testimony of Prof.

Rein in his great work on Japan, and of William Elliot Griffis in his " Mikado's Empire."

J. P. Donovan, Esq., who has held important positions in China, says : " Missions are not only not a failure—they are a grand success. Many of our countrymen in China are too indifferent to inquire, or to examine for themselves the work that is being done ; the character and conduct of others is such that they studiously avoid missionaries." If the studious avoidance was accompanied by silence on the subject, it would not be so bad ; but these men speak against the missionaries and their work to the natives, and to foreign visitors, and they write against them to their friends at home, and to the newspapers and periodicals.

The Hon. Richard H. Dana, on his visit to the Sandwich Islands, wrote: " The mere seekers of pleasure, power, or gain, do not like the missionary influence ; " and, unhappily, they are greatly influenced by their dislike, in what they say against the missions abroad, and in what they write for publication at home. We have the testimony of the late Mr. Charles Darwin, in his " Voyage of the Beagle," that the foreign travellers and residents in the South Sea Islands, who write with such hostility to missions there, are men who find the missionary to be an obstacle to the accomplishment of their evil purposes.

### A REPENTANT SLANDERER.

A missionary in one of the Pacific Islands was greatly slandered in some articles which appeared anonymously in a Sydney paper. A few years afterward he received a letter from the author of the articles, of which the following is an extract : " Those newspaper articles were written by me. The regret and shame which has since possessed me for having written them will lose somewhat of its bitterness, since I know that you will rejoice that God, in the infinity of His mercy, has, during the past year, opened to me also a door of deliverance from the bondage of selfish obduracy and vice, and has given to me also (renegade, reprobate, and enemy of His Gospel as I have life-long been) some glimpses of a better hope, and poured into the dark prison-house of a mind previously impenetrable to every good thought, and hardened to all sympathy with every good work, some rays of the light of the everlasting Gospel which yourself and your fellow-laborers have toiled to spread abroad in Pagan lands."

The letter finishes thus :—

"Trusting that you may be long spared to continue your ministry, and that the blessing of God may abundantly follow the labors of your scholars, some of whom I have lately come to know, and have cause to love and admire, I remain, yours most respectfully,

"(Signed)     H——— S———."*

### A NOTED AFRICAN TRAVELLER.

Some years ago a noted English traveller and author stated in one of his books that the missionaries at a certain place in Africa accomplished nothing, and that their station was quite useless. In reply, the Rev. Alfred Saker, the leading missionary at the station referred to, wrote that his station could hardly be considered entirely useless, as it had been a refuge for the native women from the drunken attacks of the travelling companions and friends of this censor. And yet the many thousands who read, and were more or less influenced by his book, were ignorant of the character of the author.

Wilmot, the infidel, when dying, laid his trembling, emaciated hands upon the Sacred Volume, and exclaimed

---

* *The Chronicle* of the London Missionary Society for January, 1888.

solemnly, and with unwonted energy, " The only objection
against this Book is a bad life." We will not say that all
of those who declare that the work commanded and blessed
by the Divine Author of the Book is a failure are men of
evil lives, but the evidence is abundant that a great many
of them are.

Says the distinguished Archdeacon Farrar : " To sneer
at missionaries—a thing so cheap and so easy to do—has
always been the fashion of libertines and cynics and
worldlings. So far from having failed, there is no work of
God which has received so absolute, so unprecedented a
blessing. To talk of missionaries as a failure is to talk at
once like an ignorant and like a faithless man."

### SKEPTICAL RESIDENTS AND TRAVELLERS.

The word " faithless " well describes another class of
objectors to, and depreciators of, evangelistic labors, the
skeptics, or, as they at present are pleased to style themselves, the agnostics. A witty Irish Bishop says that the
reason why some heads are shaken at the Bible is that they
are empty, and that the exact meaning of agnostic is igno-
ramus. But many of these men are very far from considering themselves as real agnostics, and from their supposed
heights of knowledge they look with disdain upon all who
do not accept their notions. Some years ago a correspondent in Japan of the London *Times*, said that missions in
Japan, as everywhere else, were failures ; but he is a man
who says he believes that Christianity is no better than
Buddhism, and that both alike are false. The Rev.
George Ensor refuted his statements as to the alleged non-
success in the making of Christian converts in Japan. He
said : " Fourteen years ago I landed, the first representative of the mission spirit of the Church of England in
Japan. There was not then a single professed Protestant

convert in all the land. To-day there are nigh or over
six thousand, and none of these are historic Christians."

On the 23d of August, 1882, the *Times* contained a letter from a correspondent at Singapore, containing similar
sweeping assertions concerning the non-success of Christian labors among the Chinese at that city, and in China
itself. Dr. Burdon, the Anglican Bishop of Hongkong,
replying to it in the *Church Missionary Intelligencer*, said:
" When I went out to China as a missionary of the Church
Missionary Society, in 1853, Protestant missionary work
was in its infancy. Only ten years before that time, in
1843, there were but five or six converts; at the present
time there are between 15,000 and 20,000 communicants."

A few months ago Dr. Oscar Lenz returned to Germany
from his travels in Africa, and announced that missions
there were failures, and his statements were telegraphed to
this country, and were doubtless published in the greater
part of the secular papers in all parts of the civilized world,
and in the local papers published for the foreign communities in all parts of the uncivilized world. Yet few of the
many millions who read his statements were informed that
Dr. Lenz had not been near any mission stations in Africa
except a few of the more recently established ones, and
that he is a man who condemns the missionary's whole
object in life.

### THE COURSE OF THE LONDON " TIMES."

Other depreciating letters from various parts of the
heathen and Mohammedan world have appeared in the
London *Times*, though their appearance of late has not
been as frequent as formerly. The wonder is that they
should be allowed to appear at all, as the conductors of
the *Times* are not so wanting in intelligence and good
sense as these anti-mission correspondents, as seen in their

treatment of Dr. Lenz ; their unstinted praise of Moffatt, Livingstone, Selwyn, Patte son, Hannington, and other missionaries ; their laudation of the work in Uganda, South Africa and other places, and in the expression of such sentiments as the following, from an editorial : " Europeans have spread themselves over the world, following everywhere the bent of their own nature, following their own gain, too generally being and doing nothing that a heathen will recognize as better than himself. These preach something, and have their own mischievous influence. They preach irreligion, and the views that go with it. Their gospel does its work, and reaps its fruit."

And here it is in place to ask, Why are these irreligionists, who work evil abroad, permitted to do the same at home in the columns of the *Times ?* Great evil results from the insertion of their articles, even when refutations of their statements are inserted from other correspondents, and they are commented upon unfavorably by the editors of the *Times ;* for the average secular newspaper editor is more hostile to Foreign Missions than the conductors of the leading paper appear to be, and he publishes with pleasure the attacks on missions, while he is very careful not to give the refutations or the comments of the *Times.*

### JAMES RUSSELL LOWELL ON THE SKEPTICS.

James Russell Lowell, ex-American Minister to England, just before leaving the latter country for the United States, attended a meeting in London to do honor to the poet Browning. Some of those present made addresses in which they aired their skepticism, and said that they could get along without any religion. They did this, though they knew that by so doing they would give offence to many who were there. Mr. Lowell, having the courage of his convictions, paid some attention to these men in his address,

and among things equally pertinent and forcible, he said :
" The worst kind of religion is no religion at all ; and
these men who live in ease and luxury, indulging themselves in ' the amusement of going without religion,' may
be thankful that they live in lands where the gospel they
neglect has tamed the beastliness and ferocity of the men
who, but for Christianity, might long ago have eaten their
bodies like the South Sea Islanders, or cut off their heads
and tanned their hides like the monsters of the French
Revolution. When the microscopic search of skepticism,
which has hunted the heavens and sounded the seas to disprove the existence of a Creator, has turned its attention
to human society, and has found a place on this planet ten
miles square, where a decent man can live in decency,
comfort and security, supporting and educating his children, unspoiled and unpolluted ; a place where age is rev-
erenced, infancy respected, manhood respected, womanhood
honored, and human life held in due regard—when skeptics
can find such a place ten miles square on this globe, where
the gospel of Christ has not gone and cleared the way, and
laid the foundations, and made decency and security possible, it will then be in order for the skeptical *literati* to
move thither and then ventilate their views. But so long
as these very men are dependent upon the religion which
they discard for every privilege they enjoy, they may well
hesitate a little before they seek to rob the Christian of his
hope, and humanity of its faith, in that Saviour who alone
has given to man that hope of life eternal which makes life
tolerable and society possible, and robs death of its terrors
and the grave of its gloom."

## SKEPTICS WHO DO NOT SNEER AT THE MISSIONARIES.

But not all skeptically inclined men sneer at the missionaries or belittle the results of their work. Mr. Joseph

Thomson, who has travelled much more extensively in Africa than Dr. Lenz, and who argues that Christianity should be brought down to the level of Mohammedan teaching, in order to more easily win the natives, utterly ignoring the Divine command to "preach *the Gospel* to every creature," and the words of the great missionary, St. Paul, "woe is me if I preach not the Gospel," has nevertheless felt constrained to eulogize the missionaries, which he has done as follows in a letter to the London *Times :*

"No one is a more sincere admirer of the missionary than I; no one knows better the noble lives of many, the singleness of purpose with which they pursue the course they think the only true one. They seem to me the best and truest heroes which this nineteenth century has produced. Nobody has more reason to speak well of them than I, and rejoice that they have spread over the waste places of the earth. In the heart of the Dark Continent I have been received as a brother, I have been relieved when I was destitute, I have been nursed when I was half dead, and time after time I have been sent on my weary way, rejoicing that there is such a profession of men as Christian missionaries."

Mr. Charles Darwin, too, has written in admiration of the Christian missionary, and he became a regular contributor to the funds of the South American Missionary Society, because of the transformation in the character of the natives of Fuegia, effected through the instrumentality of missionaries of this Society.

## COMMENDING THE CIVILIZING INFLUENCE OF THE MISSIONS.

Some who attach little value to the religion propagated by the missionaries, commend, in warm terms, the benefits to science from their residence and labors abroad, and the civilizing influence they exert upon the natives. Mr. H. H. Johnston, who has travelled in Africa, is one of these. In an article in the November (1887) number of the *Nineteenth Century*, he says:—

"Indirectly, and almost unintentionally, missionary enterprise has widely increased the bounds of our knowledge, and has sometimes been the means of conferring benefits on science, the value and extent of which itself was careless to appreciate and compute. Huge is the debt which philologists owe to the labors of British missionaries in Africa! By evangelists of our own nationality nearly two hundred African languages and dialects have been illustrated by grammars, dictionaries, vocabularies, and translations of the Bible. Many of these tongues were on the point of extinction, and have since become extinct, and we owe our knowledge of them solely to the missionaries' intervention. Zoology, botany, and anthropology, and most of the other branches of scientific investigation have been enriched by the researches of missionaries who have enjoyed unequalled opportunities of collecting in new districts; while commerce and colonization have been so notoriously guided in their extension by the information derived from patriotic emissaries of Christianity, that the negro potentate was scarcely unjust when he complained that ' first came the missionary, then the merchant, and then the man-of-war.' "

An English traveller, who pretends to no sympathy for evangelistic work, and no personal regard for Christianity, writes as follows of some of the changes which have been effected through missionary labors in some parts of West Africa: " Old sanguinary customs have to a large extent been abolished; witchcraft hides itself in the forests; the fetich superstition of the people is derided by old and young; and well-built houses are springing up on every hand. It is really marvellous to mark the change that has taken place."

He says that he does not at all understand how these changes have been brought about, and that to him they seem "abnormal." Abnormal they must appear from the skeptic's standpoint, but not to him who can say with St. Paul, "I am not ashamed of the Gospel of Christ, for it is the power of God unto salvation, to every one that believeth," and godliness "has the promise of the life that now is, as well as of that which is to come."

Even these more candid skeptics see not the shining of the Sun of Righteousness, but only what has been called the "afterglow" of His shining. They perceive not that the great work of the commissioned servants of Christ, is, as Longfellow has well expressed it:

> "To rescue souls forlorn and lost,
> The troubled, tempted, tempest-tost,
> To heal, to comfort, and to teach;
> The fiery tongues of Pentecost
> His symbols were, that they should preach
> In every form of human speech,
> From continent to continent."

### UNINFORMED TRAVELLERS AND RESIDENTS.

Other travellers and sojourners abroad who do much injury to the missionary cause, either directly or indirectly, are those who are uninformed, and who do not care to be informed concerning the work and its results. The number of this class is legion. They have no particular antipathy to missionaries and their work—they simply have no interest in the subject.

Mr. Griffis, in his work on Japan, referring to the foreign residents, says: "It is hard to find an average man of the world in Japan who has any clear idea of what the

missionaries are doing, or have done. Their dense ignorance borders on the ridiculous." (Page 345.)

The Rev. Robert A. Hume, of Ahmednagar, India,
gives in the *Missionary Herald* for February, 1886, the
following specimen case : "In Ahmednagar, 150 miles
east of Bombay, where I have lived the past eleven years,
the grounds of the collector — that is, the chief English
official—and of the American mission touch at one side.
Not a collector who ever took the trouble to visit our
church and schools has failed to express wonder and delight at the results which he saw. But collectors have
lived there who knew almost nothing of our work. Some
years ago, when Sir Richard Temple, then Governor of the
Presidency, came to Ahmednagar, he visited our church,
accompanied by the collector. When the latter saw a large
church in a small city, filled with about eight hundred
Christians, he said to me : ' Here I have been living next
door to you for months, and had no idea of what your mission had accomplished.' "

Had this man returned to England before the visit of
Sir Richard Temple, he would, no doubt, have said that he
had not seen that the missionaries were doing much in India. Among these uninterested persons are many church
members, and, we are sorry to say, some Christian ministers. Certain clergymen, at home, to their shame be it
said, take little or no interest in the evangelization of the
heathen and Mohammedan world. They read no missionary magazine, preach no missionary sermon, have no missionary meeting, and take up no collection for missions.
They are disobedient to the last and great command of
Him whose ministers they profess to be, and when they go
abroad they do not visit the missions to see what is being
done.

### AN UNINTERESTED CLERICAL GENTLEMAN.

The Rev. B. C. Henry, in his valuable book on China, and the missionary work in the southern part of the empire, entitled "The Cross and Dragon," says : "One clerical gentleman, not a missionary, held a chaplaincy in Canton for three years, but at the end of that period was as ignorant of the status of mission-work as when he came. Having occasion to visit Japan, he became the guest of a missionary there, and was actually brought into contact with his host's work, in which he became interested. Returning to Canton, he dilated upon what he had seen in Japan, and criticised the course of the Canton missionaries. Close inquiry revealed the fact that the state of things which in Japan called forth his admiration not only existed in Canton, but in a much more advanced and wide-spread form ; the fact being that he had never taken the trouble to inquire into school work, hospital work, or any of the dozen branches of Christian effort constantly carried forward ; and was about to return to his native land after three years' residence,—and would of course be regarded as an authority on such subjects,—without knowing in the least the condition of things."

### WHAT MANY TOURISTS FAIL TO SEE AND TO DO.

If it is true that the great majority of the foreign residents in heathen and Mohammedan countries are uninformed concerning the evangelistic work done in them, it is of course still more true of the great majority of mere tourists. These are eager to see the sights, but they do not include in their desire the best sights of all. They visit Mohammedan mosques and minarets, heathen temples and pagodas, and such famous structures as the Taj, the Kootub Minar, the palace of the Mogul Emperors at Delhi, &c., but they do not visit the mission churches, schools, printing presses, &c. They are very desirous of making the acquaintance of foreign diplomatic ministers, consuls, and merchants, and of being introduced to natives of distinction or of wealth, but they do not desire to become acquainted with the ambassadors of the Lord Jesus Christ, or with the native ministers and teachers. They go to see the performances of Moslem priests and dervishes, of heathen priests, fakirs, serpent charmers, mountebanks, &c., but they do not go to the services and the preaching where men, women and children are being turned from dumb idols, and other debasing superstitions to serve the living God. Many travellers of both sexes have abundance of money to spend on Turkish rugs, Indian shawls, Chinese and Japanese silks, bronzes and lacquer ware, but they have nothing to give to the missionaries and native ministers to enable them to enlarge their work, and multiply their means of usefulness.

## NOBLE EXCEPTIONS.

Of course there are exceptions to all this. There are many who, in their travels or sojournings abroad, ever keep the most important things foremost in their minds and hearts. They desire above all things to see the Gospel of Christ triumphing in the lands they visit, and they do all they can to aid in bringing this about. As one illustration of this we might state that no less than $300,000 are given yearly to missions in India, by the foreign residents and tourists. The late Judge Tucker, of Fettepoor, India, gave $200 per month to missions. After the duties of his office were fulfilled, he preached Jesus to the natives. To those who remonstrated, he replied: "If every hair of my head were a life, I would give them all to Him." Other similar cases are mentioned in this book.

But these are exceptions to the rule, and it is of the rule

which we are now speaking; and it is too sadly true that even some travellers, as well as residents, whose special duty it is to inform themselves about, and to aid the work, fail to do so.

### AN ANECDOTE BY DR. BLISS.

In a speech delivered at an annual meeting of the Turkish Missions Aid Society, in London, the Rev. Dr. Bliss told the following anecdote:

"He knew an American clergyman, who, in visiting Syria, met a friend of his, the Rev. Mr. Washburn, one of the American missionaries. This clergyman remarked to Mr. Washburn that he did not think it was worth while for missionaries to be employed in Syria, as they did not seem to be accomplishing anything. Mr. Washburn said to him: 'Did you hear Mr. Thomson preach this morning? 'No,' was the reply, 'I did not know that there was any service.' 'O! yes, there was,' said Mr. Washburn; 'he preached in English this morning.' 'Indeed!' said the clergyman, 'I should like to have heard him.' The conversation was concluded as follows: 'Did you hear Dr. Vandyke preach in Arabic this afternoon?' 'No. You don't mean to say that he has preached in Arabic?' 'Yes, and he has a congregation of two hundred persons every Sunday morning. Did you visit any of the schools at Beyrut?' 'Schools! Do you mean to say that you have got schools here? I am glad to hear that you are going on so well.' 'Did you see the printing press?' 'Printing press! Have you got one?' 'O yes; we have a printing establishment in which as many as twenty persons are employed.' Thus but for the conversation, that clergyman might, when he got back to America, have told people there that the missionaries had never done anything."

The Rev. Mr. Henry, in the book already referred to,

says : " A clergyman from Singapore spent two weeks in Canton ; but in that time he had not made the acquaintance of a single missionary, or seen the inside of one of the fifteen chapels, or heard of one of the fourscore schools. He had, however, seen the execution ground, and secured the skull of a criminal as a memento, and announced his purpose of writing a book on Canton, which coming from the pen of a clergyman, must, of course, contain authentic accounts of missions. Such indifference and wilful ignorance on the part of Christian men is culpable in the extreme."

## AN UNINFORMED AMERICAN STATESMAN.

In the *New York Observer*, we find the following mention of a case of inexcusable ignorance on mission topics : " A few years since an eminent American statesman made an extended tour in the Eastern world, and on his return prepared a volume, giving his impressions of what he saw and learned. It was only through the remonstrance of some judicious friends, who knew far more upon the subject than he did, that he was induced to leave out of his book the expression of an opinion that Christian missions had proved an entire failure in Oriental lands. The explanation of his ignorance was that on his travels he had been entertained and feted by a class of men who cared little about religious things, and who had probably spoken lightly in his presence of missionaries and their work. He had learned much about the political affairs of the countries he had visited, but he was profoundly ignorant of their moral and religious state, and especially of the signal success that has attended the efforts to promote the spiritual renovation of those lands." Well would it have been if many other travellers had been persuaded by their friends to omit their animadversions upon that which they knew nothing about.

### WHAT HAS COME TO PASS.

And thus it has come to pass that through the misrepresentations of those who are hostile to missionaries and their work, and those who are ignorant of what has been accomplished, the impression very extensively prevails that the results are very much smaller than they are; and even members of the Church say, " I do not believe much in foreign missions." Some clergymen, too, are impressed by these unfounded reports. We have been surprised at the admissions which have been made to us in this respect. If these clergymen would imitate the Rev. Dr. Falding, of Rotherham, England, who, in a public address has acknowledged that he was influenced by them, but decided to visit the principal mission stations in India, China and Japan, and see for himself whether they were true or not, they would, as he says he did, see abundant evidence that they were utterly unworthy of credence, and that a great and glorious work was being done.

### PREJUDICE CHANGED TO PRAISE.

Laymen are more impressed by these false reports than clergymen, and some of them become greatly prejudiced against Foreign Missions; but the more fair-minded of such of them as have gone abroad and learned the real facts, have had their prejudice changed to admiration and praise. Cases of this kind are given in this book. A more recent case is alluded to as follows, in *The Chronicle* of the London Missionary Society, for January, 1888:

At the annual meeting of the Rhenish Missionary Society, a Dutch gentleman, Graf O. L. H. Limburg-Hirum, gave an interesting report of a visit he had paid to the stations of the Society in Sumatra. He had been travelling for four years in the Dutch East Indies, and at first allowed himself to be prejudiced against missionary work by what Europeans living here told him concerning it. He was accustomed, indeed, to write home, and in the mildest way say that the missionaries were enthusiasts. But having at last met with a missionary, he went to see some of the stations, and at once his views were entirely altered. He says that the results of the missions to the Battas are so striking that the worst enemy of missions must be compelled to rejoice in them. Among other places he visited, was the valley of Silindung—a region rather difficult of access, but lovely in the extreme. Looking down into it from the pass by which it is approached, the traveller sees a river winding through it with many islands, and here and there groups of houses, the brown roofs of which rise among the bamboo hedges, and, best of all, church towers are seen in many directions. Here, too, is a land into which advanced (?) civilization has not as yet introduced opium and brandy. Pushing on further, across a level district, called by the missionaries the *steppe*, and where also are mission stations, the Count came at last to the Toba Lake, which, he says, was one of the loveliest sights he beheld in all his Indian travels. Along the shores are rice fields, with numerous villages, and on an eminence rises the church tower of Balige, the limit of his journey As he drew near his ear caught the sound of church music. As he says: "To be welcomed in the land of cannibals by children singing hymns, this, indeed, shows the peace-creating power of the Gospel."

In these days of easy travel, many distinguished home clergymen have made the tour of the world, and have esteemed it a great privilege to make the acquaintance of the missionaries and become informed concerning the results of their work, and their testimony is most emphatic as to the present success and the bright prospects.

2

## TESTIMONY OF DR. STEVENSON.

The Rev. William Fleming Stevenson, D. D., the author of " Praying and Working," " The Dawn of the Modern Mission," &c., after his tour of the world wrote :

" Almost the whole of Polynesia is Christian. Every coast of Africa is seized. Greenland and Patagonia have their churches. The feet of them that publish the Gospel of Peace traverse the roads from the Himalaya to Cape Comorin, from Burmah to the Yellow Sea. A survey of missions has become a survey of the world. And what obstacles have been overcome to reach this result ! Within our generation China was inaccessible to the Gospel ; Japan was impregnable ; the heart of Africa was untrodden and unknown. Now, look a little deeper into the figures. It may be only a handful of missionaries at a single point ; but they are translating the Bible, pouring Christian thought into the literature of a whole race. These hundred years of modern missions have placed the Bible within intelligible reach of perhaps 500,000,000 of the race. Their light is gone out through all the earth, their words to the world's end. We see the plans of God unrolled before our eyes. And what are they ? That the whole world may be touched by the Gospel ; that it may not only touch the individual, but penetrate the tribal life and the national life in every place, and mould the proudest and most populous races by its teaching."

## REV. MR. BAINBRIDGE AND DR. PRIME.

The Rev. W. F. Bainbridge, in his excellent book, " Around the World Tour of Christian Missions," says, " We have only a joyful report to render. There is encouragement all along the line."—p. 15. " We cannot mistake the sun that shines at mid-day in a clear summer sky ; we cannot mistake the evidence that bathes the whole round world in its glowing light, that the age of universal missions, on which we have entered, will ultimately be crowned by the universal triumph of Christianity."— p. 24.

The Rev. Dr. Eusebius Prime, one of the editors of the *New York Observer*, and the author of " Around the World," is cited by the Rev. Dr. Ellinwood, as having said : " After having embraced every opportunity for becoming acquainted with the Christian laborers from every land, and with their work, I return with a higher estimate than I ever had before of the ability, learning and devotion of the missionaries as a class and as a whole; with an enlarged view of what has already been accomplished, and with a profounder conviction that through this instrumentality, or that which shall immediately grow out of it, the kingdom of our Lord and Saviour is to be established in the whole earth more speedily than the weak faith of the Church has dared even to hope." He adds: " The success of Christian missions nothing but ignorance or prejudice could call in question. What has actually been accomplished can be fully appreciated only by those who have been upon the ground, and who have witnessed the condition of Pagan nations."

### BISHOP FOSTER AND DR. ABEL STEVENS.

Bishop R. S. Foster, who has visited the missions in Japan, China, and India, says in the *Gospel in all Lands*, for January, 1888 : " The eyes of heathenism are turned to the centres of Christendom. The heathen world, dissatisfied with its religion and civilization, not less than with its poverty and misery, is looking toward Christendom for help. They are waiting for deliverance without knowing what it is they are waiting for. Heathenism cowers and shrinks away in conscious weakness before Christian thought and Christian institutions."

Abel Stevens, LL.D., the author of "Life of Madame De Staël," "The History of Methodism," &c., writing to the *Central Christian Advocate*, from Yokohama, Japan, says: "I have been inspecting the great Asiatic battle-fields, and I report the general conviction of both foreigners and intelligent natives here that the epoch of a grand social and religious revolution has set in in India, Burmah, China and Japan—that this old Asiatic heathendom is generally giving way before the continually increasing power of Western thought and Christian civilization. The present is the most propitious hour that has ever dawned on Asia since the advent of Christ. Let us hail it, and march into these great, open battle-fields with all our flags uplifted. I am not carried away by the enthusiasm of the heroic men I have met in these fields; I know well enough the difficulties that still remain, and can criticise as well as anybody grave defects in the campaign; but I feel sure that the hoary paganism of this Asiatic world is tottering to its fall; that the final Christian battle is at hand here."

### REFUTING LAYMEN BY MORE DISTINGUISHED LAYMEN.

But our purpose is not so much to give the testimony of clerical travellers, however eminent, or of missionaries, however distinguished (though we have given in the following pages statements of some of the latter which are of great importance), as it is to present as witnesses laymen who are noted for their position, their character and their fullness of information as regards missionary operations and their results. And so we refute some laymen's testimony by that of others more noted and less biased; some military and naval officers' statements by those of others of higher rank and more experience; some jaunty traveller's assertions, by the testimony of less presuming but

more distinguished travellers and explorers; some uninformed men's errors, by well-informed men's facts; some
hostile men's sneers and misrepresentations, by candid and
impartial men's judgments and truthful statements. If a
member of the English House of Lords says, as was the
case not long since, that "missionaries are a deplorable
failure," much better than to reason or argue with such a
man, will be to present him with the testimony of his
peers, Lord Redcliffe, of Constantinople, Lords Lawrence,
Napier, and Northbrook, of India, Lord Loftus, governor
of New South Wales, concerning the work in New Guinea,
and Lord Dufferin, on that among the Indians in British
America.

If an undistinguished major-general returns to England
from India, and says that missions in the latter country are
failures, and that military officers generally so consider
them, as Canon Isaac Taylor says that one did so state to
him a few months since, then the best thing to do is to
bring forward the testimony of such distinguished generals
in India as the two Lawrences, Major-General Sir Herbert
Edwards, General Taylor, &c. Concerning other fields,
the testimony of General Wallace as to Turkey in Europe,
Lieut.-Col. Mark S. Bell as to Turkey in Asia, Col. C. E.
Stewart, Persia, Col. Denby, China, Capt. Brinkley, Japan, Gen. Sir Charles Wilson, South Africa, Gen. Phelps,
Madagascar, and Gen. Haig, Egypt, may be given.

## A TELLING REPLY TO A MAJOR-GENERAL.

A very telling reply to this returned major-general and
other disparagers of missions, has been made by Mr.
Eugene Stock, the editorial secretary of the Church Missionary Society. In the course of it he said : " If Indian
missions produce such poor results, why is it that Indian
officers and civilians are their most faithful and liberal

supporters ?    Why is it that almost every station has been established at their request, and in many cases with their money ?    And how is it that when they come home they form the backbone of missionary committees ?    Why do men who have governed provinces, and been the absolute rulers of millions, sit several hours a day for three and four days a week at the Church Missionary Committee table, administering all the details of its affairs ? "

Is it a naval officer who disparages missionaries and their work, silence him by the declarations of Admirals Wilkes, Foote, Sullivan and Gore, Commodores Goldsborough and Erskine, Commander Cameron, and Navy Surgeon and Arctic Explorer, Elisha Kent Kane.

### TESTIMONY OF EMINENT SCIENTISTS.

Is it a skeptical scientist who sneers at missionaries and the work of modern evangelization, bring forward as witnesses to their worth and the remarkable results of their work such men as Dr. Robert Brown, Alfred Russell Wallace, Charles Darwin and Drs. Robert Needham Cust, George Schweinfurth, G. P. Marsh and others, whose testimony is given in the following pages, or let them have the following from the seventeenth volume of " Smithsonian Contributions to Knowledge," entitled " Systems of Consanguinity and Affinity of the Human Family," by Lewis H. Morgan :

"There is no class of men upon the earth, whether considered as scholars, as philanthropists, or as gentlemen, who have earned for themselves a more distinguished reputation.    Their labors, their self-denial, and their endurance in the work to which they have devoted their time and their abilities, are worthy of admiration.    Their contributions to history, to ethnology, to philology, to geography, and to religious literature, form a lasting monument to their fame. The renown which encircles their names falls as a wreath of honor upon the name of their country."

Or take the following from Dr. Cust's great work on "The Languages of Africa:" "Let me turn away from the subject of language, and say one farewell word of the missionaries, those good and unselfish men, who, for a high object, have sacrificed careers which might have been great and honored in their own countries, and have gone forth to live in hovels, and sometimes to die; who, as it were, in the course of their striking hard on the anvil of evangelization, their own proper work, have emitted bright sparks of linguistic light, which have rendered luminous a region previously shrouded in darkness, and these sparks have kindled a corresponding feeling of warmth in the hearts of great, and to them personally unknown, scholars, working in their studies in Vienna, Berlin, or some German university, scholars who, alas! cared little for the object of the missionaries' going forth, but rejoiced exceedingly at the wonderful, unexpected and epoch-making results of their quiet labors!"

### AN AMERICAN TRAVELLER ANSWERED.

Is it an American traveller in India who writes to the New York *Tribune* that " India officials, as a class, have no faith in the work of missionaries, so far as spreading the Gospel among the natives is concerned?" Let him be reminded that there are godless officials in India as well as in Europe and America, and perhaps a larger proportion in India than in England and the United States, because nearly all Indian officials went out from England when quite young men as cadets in the civil service, and they have been subjected to greater temptations to free-thinking and evil-living in India than they would have been in

England, and many of them have yielded to the pernicious influences of their surroundings.

### SIR LEPEL GRIFFIN'S SPEECH.

These agree with the sentiments of Sir Lepel Griffin, and express themselves as he does to the natives and to foreign visitors, though few of them do it in the same public manner as he does. This official is the Governor-General's Agent for Central India, and a few months since, in a somewhat violent speech at Gwalior, he advised the Mahrattas to look askance upon those natives who had become Christians and had thrown off the shackles of caste. He said : " Cherish and observe your ancient and noble religion, cherish and observe strictly your rules of caste, which missionaries and philanthropists tell you is a bad thing, but which is really the mortar which holds together the building of Indian Society." *

From the beginning of the British conquest of India until the present day, such Anglo-Indian officials have been disproportionately large in number, compared with men in the civil service at home ; and they have not only been a disgrace to their country, but they have proved to be the greatest obstacle to the enlightenment and regeneration of India which the Christian missionaries have had to encounter.

### MEN OF A VERY DIFFERENT STAMP.

But there have always been a few men, and latterly there have been a great many men of quite a different stamp in the Indian civil service—God-fearing men, who saw in Christian evangelization the great, indeed the *only* hope for the enlightenment and true progress of India ; and these men have praised without stint the immense value, and the

---

* From *The Christian,* London, Jan. 20, 1888.

great success, both social and spiritual, of missionary labors. Among these men are some of the most distinguished viceroys, governors and other administrators which India has had. We have given their testimony at length under INDIA.

The assertion quoted above of the correspondent of the *Tribune*, was brought to the notice of that experienced administrator, Sir Charles Aitcheson, formerly the Chief Commissioner in Burmah, and for some time the Lieutenant-Governor (highest officer) of the Punjaub, and in a letter to the Rev. Dr. Stewart of Sealkote, India, he wrote: " I have not seen the article referred to ; but I, for my part, should say that any one who writes that India officials as a class, have no faith in the work of missionaries, as a civilizing and Christianizing agency in India, must either be ignorant of facts or under the influence of a very blinding prejudice." The remainder of the important letter of which this is the opening paragraph, we have given under INDIA. For our copy of the letter we are indebted to the *Foreign Missionary*, New York.

### JAUNTY TRAVELLERS IN AFRICA.

Do such jaunty travellers in Africa as Winwood Reade and Oscar Lenz, write depreciatingly of missionaries and belittle the results of their work ? Quote against them such renowned men as General Gordon and Emin Bey, and such famous explorers as Captain Speke, V. Lovett Cameron, Henry M. Stanley, Dr. Schweinfurth, and the incomparable Livingstone. The last named wrote in great praise of the results of the missions in West Africa, missions in which he and his colleagues had no part. Or give them the laudations of the editors of the London *Times* of the results of the labors of Moffatt, Livingstone and others in South Africa, and of Bishops Mackenzie, Steere and Hannington, Archdeacon Farler, Mr. Mackay and others in Central Africa. The conductors of this journal would be certain not to praise these results except upon unquestionable authority and unimpeachable testimony.

### AN AMERICAN LADY AND MISS GORDON CUMMING.

Does an American lady travelling in Northeastern China write to a San Francisco paper depreciating the Christian workers there and the results of their labors, though doubtless not becoming acquainted either with the missionaries or any of their converts, and do the editors of papers in our eastern cities copy her misrepresentations, as was the case recently? Then what better can be done than to give the testimony of that very distinguished traveller, Miss Gordon Cumming, who not only visited Northern but Southern China, and everywhere became acquainted with the missionaries and their work. She devotes no less than seventy pages of her " Wanderings in China " to these Christian workers, and their evangelistic, educational, medical and literary labors, and their results. We have given some of her testimony under CHINA. The following words of hers we have not inserted there but they are worthy of being often quoted :

" I often wish when I hear men," (she might have said women also,) " lightly quoting from one another the stock phrases which are accepted as conclusive evidence of the uselessness of mission work, and of the hypocrisy which it is supposed to foster in its converts (all of whom are supposed to be merely nominal, or attracted by gain,) that the speakers would just take the trouble to inquire for themselves as to the truth of their statements. They would learn a very different story from the lips of men who really know what they are speaking about, and who would gladly give them a thousand details of individuals who have proved the

intensity of their convictions, by voluntarily resigning lu-
crative posts in connection with idol worship, or involving
Sunday work; by enduring bitter persecutions from their
own nearest and dearest relations, deliberately giving up
all ease and comfort in life, and accepting a lot of assured
poverty and suffering, all in the one great effort to live
worthy of the light and love which has filled their hearts
—a light which in many cases has long been steadily and
bitterly resisted, ere it has thus triumphed." (Vol. I. page
204.)

We have also the laudatory testimony of United States
Minister Denby, High Commissioner Angell, Consul Medhurst and others concerning the workers and the important
results of their labors in this vast empire.

### THE REMARKABLE LETTER OF COLONEL DENBY.

The remarkable letter of Colonel Charles Denby to his
friend General Shackleford, of Evansville, Indiana, to
which we have referred in the proper place, appears complete in the number for February, of that excellent publication, the *Missionary Review*, the consent of the writer for
its publication having been obtained. The following are
extracts from it.

"Believe nobody when he sneers at the missionaries
The man is simply not posted on the work. I saw a quiet,
cheerful woman teaching forty or more Chinese girls;
she teaches in Chinese the ordinary branches of common
school education. Beneath the shadow of the 'forbidden
city' I heard these girls sing the Psalms of David and
'Home, Sweet Home.' I saw a male teacher teaching
forty or more boys. The men or the women who put in
from 8 o'clock to 4 in teaching Chinese children, on a salary that barely enables one to live, are heroes, or heroines,
as truly as Grant or Sheridan, Nelson or Farragut; and all

this in a country where a handful of Americans is surrounded by 300,000,000 Asiatics, liable at any moment to break out into mobs and outrages, particularly in view of the tremendous crimes committed against their race at home."

" I visited the dispensaries, complete and perfect as any apothecary shop at home; then the consultation rooms, their wards for patients, coming without money or price, to be treated by the finest medical and surgical talent in the world. There are twenty-three of these hospitals in China. Think of it! Is there a more perfect charity in the world? The details of all the system were explained to me. There are two of these medical missionaries here who receive no pay whatever. The practice of the law is magnificent; but who can rival the devotedness of these men to humanity?"

"I have seen missionaries go hence a hundred miles, into districts where there is not a white person of any nationality, and they do it as coolly as you went into battle at Shiloh. And these men have remarkable learning, intelligence and courage. It is perhaps a fault that they court nobody, make no effort to attract attention, fight no selfish battle."

"It is idle for any man to decry the missionaries or their work. I can tell the real from the false. These men and women are honest, pious, sincere, industrious and trained for their work by the most arduous study. I do not address myself to the churches; but, as a man of the world, talking to sinners like himself, I say that it is difficult to say too much good of missionary work in China."

### MRS. SCOTT STEVENSON AND SIR THOMAS TANCRED.

Does a Mrs. Scott Stevenson in her "Ride" in Asia Minor, write somewhat contemptuously of the missionaries of Aintab, from whom she kept clear, and of the missions which she did not visit, we can offset her sneers and misrepresentations by the facts and the praise of Sir Thomas Tancred in his " Peep at Asia Minor," for he became acquainted with the missionaries at Aintab and other cities, and examined carefully into the work and the results ; and we can also bring forward the evidence of the English Consul at Aleppo.

### JAMES A. FROUDE AND CHARLES DARWIN.

Does James A. Froude write depreciatingly of the results of missionary labor among the natives of Zealand, because of the few Maori waifs and strays which he saw in the lake tourist district south of the Bay of Plenty? His testimony can be refuted by that of Charles Darwin, who went where the Maories most abound, held intercourse with the native Christians, and wrote in admiration of the wonderful change effected in their characters, and said : " The lesson of the missionary is the enchanter's wand." Or, there can be quoted Carl Ritter, " the prince of geographers," who said that the conversion and transformation in the character of the natives of New Zealand is " the standing miracle of the age."

If then, the depreciators and enemies of missions bring forward their witnesses, let the testimony of such men as we have named, and others like them, be presented, and there need be no fear as to what will be the decision of all impartial and fair-minded persons.

### SOME OF THE GREAT RESULTS OF MISSIONS.

When we consider the condition of Heathen and Mohammedan nations, and the firm hold which superstition has of the former, and fanaticism of the latter ; the terrible evil wrought by the foreign opium traffickers in China, and the liquor traffickers in Africa, and the encouragement and support given by the British Government to the former, and the authorities of most of the European colonies and protectorates (?) in Africa to the latter; the evil example everywhere of many of the foreign residents and visitors; the comparatively small number of the missionaries; the entire lack of interest on the part of many members of the church, and the very languid interest of many others; the fact that there are no less than one million communicants connected with the missions, and three million adherents; that two thousand five hundred of the converts are ordained ministers of the Gospel, and twenty-eight thousand are evangelists and teachers, and that thousands of native churches and schools are self-supporting, we see abundant evidence that the promise of the Saviour connected with His last command has been fulfilled : " All power is given unto me in heaven and in earth.  Go ye, therefore, and teach all nations, baptizing them in the name of the Father, and of the Son, and of the Holy Ghost; teaching them to observe all things whatsoever I have commanded you; and lo, *I am with you always, even unto the end of the world.*"   It has been by His constant presence and blessing with His commissioned servants, that these great results and many others have been accomplished, and to Him be all the praise and the glory forever.   Amen.

# AFRICA.

MISSIONARY ENTERPRISE IN AFRICA.—Ten American, 12 British and 13 Continental societies are now engaged in the work in Africa. There are about 620 stations; 710 ordained missionaries; 7,500 ordained and unordained native preachers; 175,000 communicants; 300,000 baptized members of the churches; 226,000 pupils in the schools, and 800,000 adherents. The number of baptisms yearly is now about 17,000!

The letters and published articles of these 700 American, British, French, German, Norwegian and Swiss missionaries, and the books which Ellis, Shaw, Rowley, Moffatt, Livingstone, Wilson and others of them have published, have done much to awaken an interest in weird, wild Africa, while the exploits and the writings of the recent famous explorers, Speke, Cameron, Stanley, Barth and Schweinfurth, have greatly increased this interest.

FAMOUS EXPLORERS AS WITNESSES.—These explorers refer in terms of praise to missionary labors and their results. Captain Speke, the discoverer of the greatest of the African lakes, said that the African slave trade could be more economically and effectually suppressed by supporting missionary and commercial enterprise in the interior, than by maintaining armed cruisers near the east coast. When speaking in admiration of Dr. Livingstone, and of the good which he himself had received from him, Stanley, the great explorer and the founder of the Congo Free State, said: "What has been wanted, and what I have been endeavoring to ask for the poor Africans, has been the good offices of Christians." It was owing to his earnest appeal for Uganda, that the Church Missionary Society began its mission in that country.

Dr. Schweinfurth, the distinguished scientist and explorer, and the author of those two noble volumes, "The Heart of Africa," writing from Alexandria, August 5, 1885, says: "The American Mission in Egypt has done an enormous amount of good." Commander V. Lovett Cameron, R. N., C. B., in his "Across Africa," writes in commendation of the missionaries he met with, and urges Christians at home to send out worthy assistants to them (pp. 476 and 481). The German traveller, Buller, speaks in complimentary terms of the work of the Basle Missions on the Gold Coast. They have ten chief stations, the farthest of which are five days' journey from the coast. Nearly all the smiths, joiners and coopers on the West Coast are from its industrial schools.

THE GOVERNOR OF NATAL AND THE CONSUL OF MO- ZAMBIQUE.—General Sir Charles Warren, who was until quite recently the Governor of Natal, and whose special mission was the pacification of parts of Zululand and British Bechuanaland, said that "for the preservation of peace between the colonists and natives one missionary is worth more than a whole battalion of soldiers." Henry E. O'Neil, Esq., the British Consul at Mozambique, in a recent address in Glasgow on "The Ancient Civilization, Trade, and Commerce of Eastern Africa," referred as follows to the missionary work there in our own day:

"The defence, if defence were needed, of the results of missionary work, I might well leave to those who actually know the progress made among the natives by the Scottish

Established and Free Churches, and English Universities' Missions working in East Africa. I must say that my experience of ten years in Africa has convinced me that the mission work is one of the most powerful and useful instruments we possess for the pacification of the country and the suppression of the slave trade."

GENERAL GORDON AND EMIN BEY.—That heroic and altogether remarkable man, General Gordon, was, from 1874 to 1879, Governor of the vast region from the southern border of Egypt to the Albert and Victoria Lakes, and this Egyptian Soudan, as it is called, never had so able and excellent a ruler. But great pacificator and ruler though he himself was, he maintained that there could be no permanent amelioration in the condition of any pagan or Mohammedan country without the labors of Christian missionaries. He befriended and aided in various ways the missionaries who were in the country, and those who passed through it on their way to Uganda, and he wrote to the Church Missionary Society urging the sending of more men.

Such also is the belief, and similar also has been the action of his able and famous lieutenant, Emin Bey, whom he appointed as deputy governor of the southern section of his vast realm. Before the outbreak under the Mahdi, which extended also to his district, and from which he and those who have remained faithful to him have suffered so much, he, too, wrote for missionaries, and offered to pay all their expenses for the first five years. In a letter to his friend, Mr. Allen, of London, he bears a warm testimony to the value of the Church Missionary Society's work in Central Africa, and he sends two tusks of ivory, worth $275, as a donation to aid in the work.

A DISTINGUISHED LINGUIST'S TESTIMONY.—Robert Needham Cust, LL. D., the distinguished linguist, in his

3

important work, " The Languages of Africa," bears testimony to the self-sacrificing devotion of the missionaries,
and to the many important results of their labors.  As a
linguist he naturally takes special delight in recounting
the large number of languages which they have reduced to
writing, and into which they have translated the whole, or
portions of the Word of God, and prepared other books.
In his more recent " Languages as Illustrated by Bible
Translation" (London, 1887), he thus refers to benighted
Africa, and to what is being done by some to destroy, and
by others to save, the many millions of the descendants of
Ham :—

"We turn to Africa, the Dark Continent, where ever
since the days of Aristotle there has been found always
something new, something strange, something unexpected
and unique, pyramids and obelisks, snow-capped mountains
on the equator and imperial rivers; in one part of the
Continent language so diverse that near neighbors cannot
understand each other, in another part one great family of
more than a hundred congeners, marvellous in symmetry,
and capable of expressing from their own word-store every
shade of human thought.  In that Continent we find pop-
ulations cheerfully flourishing under oppression, which
would have extinguished any other; boundless prairies,
unlimited capabilities; thousands of miles of water-way;
cannibalism, human sacrifices, deadly sorcery, grotesque
customs and abominable crimes.  Last century Europeans
were content to play the part of man-stealers, and traffickers in black ivory; in this century the scramble for Africa
itself has commenced, the most shameful spoliation and
heartless conspiracy to destroy the souls and bodies of
millions by the boundless import of spirituous liquors, arms
and gunpowder.  It is well indeed that the religious world,
of every Protestant sect and denomination, has striven to

supply the same antidote, the Bible, and give the negro a chance of education, civilization and salvation, physically as well as spiritually."

SELF-SACRIFICING DEVOTION OF CHURCH OF ENG-LAND MEN AND WOMEN IN WEST AFRICA.—The Society which carries on the most extensive missionary operations in Africa, is the English Church Missionary Society. It has large missions at Sierra Leone, the Niger Territory, the Yoruba country, and in Eastern Equatorial Africa, from Mombasa to Uganda. Soon after the organization of the society missionaries were sent to West Africa, and when Sierra Leone became an English colony, it was made the principal field of the society's operations on that coast. The living cargoes of the slave ships which English cruisers captured were taken to this colony, and to them the climate was not unsuited, but it proved to be so fatal to Europeans that the expressive title, the " White Man's Grave," was given to the region. Missionaries dropped in the first rank, but others came forward to take their places, and fell in their turn.

In a work entitled " The English Church in Other Lands," it is stated that " in the first twenty years of the existence of the Mission, fifty-three missionaries, men and women, died at their posts ; " but these losses seemed to draw out new zeal, and neither then, nor at any subsequent period, has there been much difficulty in filling up the ranks of the Sierra Leone Mission, or of the others established on the same coast. The first three bishops—Vidal, Weeks, and Bowen—died within eight years of the creation of the See, and yet there has been no difficulty in keeping up the succession.

The present results are a sufficient reward for all the self-sacrificing devotion. There is now at Sierra Leone a self-sustaining and self-extending African Church. The only white clergyman in the colony is Bishop Ingram, the whole of the pastoral work being in the hands of native clergymen.  Many native missionaries, both clerical and lay, have been furnished for the Niger and Yoruba missions. A very recent publication of the Church Missionary Society, says : "The Society's work in West Africa is now represented by 25,000 adherents, under 7 European missionaries, 40 native clergymen (one of whom is an honored bishop of many years standing), 9,000 communicants, 7,000 scholars in 90 schools and seminaries, and by 1,228 baptisms in the last year."

THE SAME SELF-SACRIFICING SPIRIT OF OTHER MEN AND WOMEN.—At the Basle Mission on the Gold Coast, during fifty-eight years, ninety-one missionaries—sixty-one men and thirty women—have fallen victims to the climate. But there are now 7,000 Christians, and the yearly baptisms are about 700.

Equally great, or even greater, has been the number of men and women of the English Wesleyan Missionary Society, who have been cut down by the West African fever in Sierra Leone, Lagos, Ashanti, and Dahomey, but there are no less than 12,300 church members connected with these vigorously sustained Wesleyan missions.

Similar self-sacrificing work has been done by the English Baptists at Fernando Po, Victoria and the Cameroons, by the Scotch Presbyterians at Old Calabar, the American Presbyterians at the Gaboon, the United Brethren at Sherbro, and the American Episcopalians at Cape Palmas, Cape Mount and other parts of Liberia.*

---

* Equal missionary zeal has been shown in the lately established missions of the English and American Baptists, and the American Methodists on the Congo.  Many of the agents have been stricken down, but there is a continued increase in the number of missionaries going from England and the United States,

INDEPENDENT TESTIMONY AS TO THE RESULTS.—Mr. McCants Stewart, formerly a professor in the South Carolina Agricultural College, and now a lawyer practicing in New York city, has visited Liberia, and in a recently published volume entitled " Liberia : The Americo-African Republic," he has given his impressions of this country, and his experiences while there. It is an able and candid work. Of the American Episcopal Mission in Liberia, Mr. Stewart says : " The Episcopalians have prosecuted work in Liberia with amazing persistency and great results. Recently a scholarly and pious colored clergyman, Rev. Samuel D. Ferguson, was elected Bishop of Cape Palmas and parts adjacent, thus practically establishing Liberia as a diocese."

Along the West African coast there are now about 200 churches, 35,000 converts, 100,000 adherents, 275 schools, 30,000 pupils ; thirty-five languages or dialects have been mastered, into which portions of the Scriptures and religious books and tracts, and general educational books, have been translated and printed, and some knowledge of the Gospel has reached about 8,000,000 of benighted Africans.

As an illustration of the beneficent changes which have been effected from the Gambia to the Gaboon, a distance of 2,000 miles, take the following from an English traveller, who pretends to no sympathy for evangelistic work, and no personal regard for Christianity : " I do not at

---

and the native converts already number 1,500. The latest missionary carried off by the fever is the Rev. J. T. Comber. A pioneer of the mission, he had seen a brother and a sister fall in the service. Long before he became known his letters had kindled a flame of missionary zeal in the hearts of his younger brothers and his sister, and one after another followed him to Africa. One brother remains at his post.

all understand how the changes at Cameroons and Victoria have been brought about. Old sanguinary customs have to a large extent been abolished; witchcraft hides itself in the forest; the fetich superstition of the people is derided by old and young; and well-built houses are springing up on every hand. It is really marvellous to mark the change that has taken place."

THE LONDON TIMES ON DRS. MOFFATT AND LIVINGSTONE.—The following tribute to Drs. Moffatt and Livingstone is from the London *Times:* "It is the fashion in some quarters to scoff at missionaries, to receive their reports with incredulity, to look at them at best as no more than harmless enthusiasts, proper subjects for pity, if not for ridicule. The records of missionary work in South Africa must be a blank page to those by whom such ideas are entertained. We owe it to our missionaries that the whole region has been opened up. Apart from their special service as preachers, they have done important work as pioneers of civilization, as geographers, as contributors to philological research. Of those that have taken part in this, Moffatt's name is not the best known. Moffatt, it may be said, has labored, and other men have entered into his labor. Livingstone has come after him, and has gone beyond him and has linked his memory forever with the records of the South African Church. The progress of South Africa has been mainly due to men of Moffatt's stamp. In him, as in David Livingstone, it is hard to say which character has predominated, that of the missionary proper or that of the teacher and guide. Certain it is that, apart from the special stimulus they felt as proclaimers of the Gospel message, they would never have thrown themselves as they did into the work to which their lives were consecrated. It was by no zeal for the spread of civilization on its own account that they passed weary years laboring and teaching among savage tribes, amid dangers of every kind, amid privations of which they themselves made light, but which only a sense of their high spiritual mission could have prompted them to face and undergo."

SIR CHARLES WARREN ON SOME OF THE RESULTS HE HAS SEEN.—At the last annual meeting of the Wesleyan Missionary Society, London, General Sir Charles Warren said : " With regard to results, there are many ways of forming an opinion. Take the Basuto Mission. I had the privilege of being in the chair at the Wesleyan Hall in Kimberly in 1878, when Mr. Colliard gave an account of his missionary work up to the Zambesi. He had previously been French Missionary in Basutoland, and he told us of the natives who were so anxious for the spiritual welfare of distant relatives of the Basutos, on the other side of the Zambesi, that they subscribed, and sent Mr. Colliard and some native missionaries to go and evangelize on the other side of the river. That I consider a fair criterion of the results of missionary work. Missionaries were first sent out to Basutoland, and then the Basutos pushed on evangelization farther themselves. Again, I have seen the same thing in Bechuanaland. The people get evangelized, and then they build churches farther afield, and ask white missionaries to assist them, and so the work goes on, and it is impossible not to think that these results are for good."

" Now I may mention another point. In travelling over South Africa I have often heard in the evening hymns rising up from the mountain side—often our revival hymns, beautifully sung, and I have ridden over to hear whence they have come, and have come to a Kaffir kraal, and here were these people sitting together, not knowing that any white man was near—there was no humbug about it—and I have found them earnestly praying and singing hymns. Now, I feel convinced that when these things take place, mission work is of the greatest benefit and service to the country. Before I conclude there is one point I wish to allude to. It always strikes me that where there may not be a sufficiently-formed public opinion, there may still be great good accomplished. On the one hand you find people very demoralized, but on the other hand you find people in a high state of spiritual life, and leading very beautiful lives, such as are not often met with in this country. It has often struck me that when you have on the one side a very great depth, you have on the other a very beautiful height in regard to spirituality." *

THE SUCCESS IN SOUTH AFRICA.—Inspector Schreiber, of the Rhenish society, says in his annual report for 1886 : " There are laboring in the region of the different colonies of South Africa and adjoining lands 350 missionaries of at least 15 different European and American societies, and some 1,500 native helpers of all sorts. The number of church members (including all baptized persons, doubtless) is 200,000, the communicants 56,000, the scholars about 38,000. The four German societies—Berlin, Hermannsburg, the Moravians, and our Rhenish—number in South Africa 182 European missionaries, and the churches contain about 55,000 members, of whom 21,400 are communicants, and there are 11,500 scholars. In other words more than half of all the missionaries laboring in South Africa are Germans. To this great number Hermannsburg and Berlin contribute most, the former 60, the latter 59 missionaries. As to adherents, the Berlin and our Rhenish society, with its 16,000, take the first place."

TESTIMONY OF THE MINISTER FOR THE ABORIGINES.— The whole Bible has been translated into the language of the

---

* Wesleyan Missionary Notices, Anniversary Number, 1887 pp. 13, 14.

Zulu Kaffirs. There are 10.000 church members among these people, with 50,000 or 60,000 under the influence of Gospel teaching. The work has been equally successful among their brothers, the Amakosa Kaffirs of the Cape Colony frontier. The following very important testimony we find in a recent number of *The Missionary Review :*

" In South Africa there is among the whites a great deal of contemptuous hatred of the Kaffirs, and a disposition to believe them incapable of either intellectual or moral improvement. Various travellers take occasion of this to discredit the missionary work. In answer to such opinions Mr. Charles Brownlee, who lately, on retiring from the office of Minister for the Aborigines, was granted by the Cape Parliament his whole salary as retiring pension, entirely without precedent, as a mark of esteem, says : ' I once asked à heathen who complained that some goats of his were concealed in a mission station by the Christian natives, whether in fifty years, he, a great man and privy councillor, had ever known a Christian Kaffir convicted of theft? He owned he had not. Had he ever known cattle-tracks traced to a mission station ?' 'No.' That is saying a good deal for a people among whom cattle-stealing seems to be the principal crime. Again: ' In one of the wars 3,000 Christian militia-men camped for two years on Brownlee's station, and during this whole time it was never needful to station a single policeman there.' Particular umbrage is taken that the Government makes grants to the mission academy of Lovedale. It is declared that the scholars, once dismissed, forthwith revert to heathenism, grease and red ochre. Mr. Brownlee says : ' Baron von Hübner makes much of it that out of 2,058 scholars 15 are known to have reverted to heathenism. Fifteen !' ' The question, says he, has been proposed : Where are the young people trained in Lovedale, and what is now their occupation? Again I refer to 'Lovedale Past and Present,' from which I find that four have gone as missionaries to Livingstonia, of whom two have died. We find them strewn over Natal to the farthest end of the Transvaal Republic, in Mashona, Bechuana, Basuto and Pondoland, and over the whole of the Cape colony, employed as pastors, evangelists, teachers, mechanics, as policemen, justices, interpreters and clerks in the service of the Government, and of merchants and lawyers, while the greater part stay at home honestly earning their living. The most of them —excepting the fifteen returned to heathenism—exercise a wholesome influence among their countrymen, requiting the Government double and treble for the support which it has contributed out of the public funds toward their instruction."

THE MARTYRS OF UGANDA.—The painful intelligence of the massacre of the native Christians in Uganda, by King Mwanga, who murdered the excellent and devoted Bishop Hannington, has been confirmed by later accounts. The first victim was speared to death, partly by the king himself; another was hacked to pieces, and another was clubbed to death; but the greater part of the victims, after being tortured in various ways, were burned. Some of these martyrs died confessing their faith, and exhorting their executioners to repent of sin and believe on the Lord Jesus Christ.

After the massacre the head executioner reported to the king that he had never killed men who showed such fortitude and endurance, and that they had prayed to God in the fire. The wicked persecutor replied: "God did not rescue them from my power." More native Christians are in hiding than those who have been put to death; but a number of these are specially marked for fire if they can be found, and the tyrannical and cruel king seems determined that all who have become Christians shall suffer, with the exception of a very few who are exceedingly useful to him as artisans. Some of the martyred ones could have escaped, but they preferred to seal their testimony with their blood. A number of those who have fled could not be persuaded to escape until after the missionaries had said that it was right to do so, and that even St. Paul, when persecuted in one place, escaped to another.

Even while the fierce persecution was raging in the capital of Uganda, the missionaries were visited at the dead of night by one and another not yet baptized, seeking further instruction and pleading to be admitted into the Christian Church by baptism ; and while the massacres were going on no less than twenty persons were baptized in secret in the night time. So the anguish of the missionaries at the slaughter of some, and the burning of others of the Christians, was mingled with rejoicing and thanksgiving at their faithful witnessing for Christ, and at the eager desire of others, even at such a time, to become the baptized followers of our Lord. About two hundred in all have been put to death by this African Nero, though not all of them were professing Christians. Some were only inquirers and readers of Christian books.

That there are many possessing the true martyr spirit in the old Church of England as well as in this infant church in Africa, is evident from the fact that within a few weeks after the intelligence of the massacre of Bishop Hannington and the native Christians in Uganda reached London, the Church Missionary Society received the offer of upwards of fifty men for the same field, and a new bishop and about a dozen new missionaries have already been sent out.

A CHIVALROUS KNIGHT OF THE CROSS.—The London *Times*, referring to the martyr-Bishop, Hannington, says :

" Careers and deaths like Bishop Hannington's remind a prosaic and artificial generation that the instinct of Christianity remains what it was at its foundation. There is a simplicity about men of his stamp such as there was in the leaders of the primitive church. In their faith there is no mixture of doubt. The one enemy they know is the darkness of heathenism. The one vocation they claim to exercise is war to the death against that. If their own life stand in the way, or be a missile they can wield, they are willing and eager to part with it. The homage of King Mwanga's court or the stocks in Usoga, life or death, they are equally ready to take, as one or the other comes."

The Rev. Gideon Draper, D. D., a Presbyterian clergyman, writes as follows from London to the *New York Observer*, concerning the " Life of Bishop Hannington," by the Rev. William Dawson, which is having an exceptionally wide circulation : "The biography of this latest martyr for Africa's redemption will interest all lovers of adventure, all admirers of heroism. It will hold the attention of the young, unsurpassed by record of travel or military hero. It will stir with warm, healthy impulse the heart of Christendom. His coolness and bravery, hardihood and enthusiasm, the magnetic influence that drew all to him, savage and Christian, the born leader and chivalrous knight of the cross, are portrayed throughout the volume. The tragic, triumphant end, the translation of the hero-martyr, the muscular frame weakened by exposure, by fever, by partial starvation, a subject of mockery, a spectacle of derision, his courage and cheer to the last makes a recital that infinitely eclipses fiction."

GEN. HAIG ON THE AMERICAN MISSION IN EGYPT.— There is greater religious liberty in Egypt than in Turkey. Sixty Mohammedans are among the 1200 members of the churches of the American United Presbyterian Mission in the former country. These 1200 members contribute at the rate of $18 a member a year, and that is without reckoning the difference between the value of money there and here. Major Gen. Haig wrote from Egypt as follows, concerning this mission to the *Church Missionary Intelligencer* (April, 1887): "The great Mission in Egypt, that which is, and has long been, doing effective work on a scale which is now, I feel sure, beginning to tell most powerfully upon the population, is the American. That Society has occupied the field in comparative force, and having been now more than thirty years at work, it has many centres, and a large native as well as American agency employed. It has nine ordained missionaries, and eight ordained native ministers. It occupies seventy different stations, most of them on the Nile south of Cairo, between it and Assiout, and in fifty-seven of these has distinct native congregations numbering 3300, of whom 1800 are communicants. It has sixty-five schools with 5414 scholars, and no less than fifty-seven of these schools are entirely supported by the fees and the native congregations. In the Delta the Mission has stations in Cairo, Boulac, Kafr-el-Misht, Zagazig, Tanta, Mansourah, Damanhoor, Alexandria, and other less important places. Its converts are indeed mostly from among the Copts, but the Mohammedans are not neglected. There are 600 Mohammedan boys, and in Cairo and its suburbs, at least 350 girls in its schools. If its converts from Mohammedanism are few, we have to remember the enormous difficulties in the way of an open profession of Christianity.

But the truth has been widely spread, at least at Cairo and other centres, and prejudices have been broken down to a remarkable degree. In illustration of this, I may mention that I was present one evening in Cairo at a meeting which is held every week in one of the large class-rooms of the magnificent Mission building. It was for the discussion of some secular subject of interest. A Protestant Copt, a man of great ability, was in the chair, and after he had given an address on Temperance (a favorite subject with the Mohammedans), two papers were read, one by a Copt, the other by a Mohammedan, on the question, "Have animals minds?" These were followed by a very lively discussion, there being several speakers, and a good deal of cheering from time to time. The language used was Arabic. The meeting, which was hearty throughout, lasted one and a half or two hours, and of the 250 persons present, nearly all young men, two-thirds were Mohammedans, and the remainder mostly converts of the Mission. That such a meeting should be held in Cairo every week (and there are others like it at one or two places in the Delta) is a most remarkable proof of the great diminution of prejudice. Not many years ago every one of these Mohammedans would have scorned to sit in the same room with a native convert, still more to take part in such meeting.

"I may also mention, as an interesting fact, that in several instances, native Christian congregations in towns in which the weekly market had always been held on the Sunday, have, by memorializing the local Governor, got the day changed. This shows that the native Church is beginning to be recognized as a distinct body of a certain social importance in the country."

DR. LENZ AND ARCHDEACON FARLER.—Dr. Oscar Lenz, a German traveller, on his return to Europe about six months ago, found fault with the missions in Africa, and said that their results are very meagre. His statements were given extensive currency in the secular press of Europe and America, but nothing was said about his not having been near any missions except a few on the Congo, and those on Lakes Tanganyika and Nyassa, all of which have been recently established—too recently for great and varied results, especially as they are in exceedingly malarious regions, and the death rate of the missionaries has been unusually large even for Africa. This German censor, too, has in a very majesterial manner, condemned the missionary's whole object in life, and he is, therefore, far from being an unprejudiced and impartial witness. The London *Times* (Aug. 26, 1887,) has published an admirable reply to Dr. Lenz's charges, written by Archdeacon Farler, of the English Universities' Mission to Central Africa. Commenting upon the subject, the *Times* says that independent and unimpeachable testimony is quite opposed to that of this German traveller, and that " there are mission villages in Central Africa that would compare favorably in conduct with many English hamlets. The picture Mr. Farler draws of his own station is corroborated by a body of independent testimony. It demonstrates the accomplishment of marvellous results in a dozen years."

Archdeacon Farler contrasts the reckless statements of the German traveller with the facts which have come under his own observation in Africa. Twelve years ago the station with which he is himself associated, consisted of a mud hut, the residence of the missionaries, a few sheds, and a small iron building used as a church. " The natives," he says, " were always fighting; no man could travel alone safely. They clothed themselves in goat skins, and their only means of exchange were strings of beads or Amerikano, *i. e.*, cotton sheeting. Now the excellent granite of the country has been quarried, lime has been burnt, a large and beautiful church, capable of holding 700 people, with nave, aisles, and arches, has been built in granite ; a large hospital has been erected, with schools, house for the missionaries, dormitories over for boarders, and dining-hall— all have been built by our native converts, in granite, under the superintendence of a young English-working mason. There is now perfect peace and safety in the land; a child can travel alone. The natives dress now in well-made garments, sewn by themselves, after the coast fashion. Trade has been introduced; a large market has been established close to the mission station, attended by 2,000 to 3,000 traders every market day. * * I can see from my window a young native Christian, who is being trained as a doctor, busily attending to a crowd of patients, sitting in a piazza near the dispensary, binding up their sores and giving medicine for their sicknesses. Finally, all our translations, some of which are now done by our native teachers, and our other literary works are printed, in the first instance by our native Christians, who have been taught printing." These native industries not only exist, but they are the fruits of the new Christian life of the people.

WHAT CAN NO LONGER BE MAINTAINED.—Dr. Christlieb, the distinguished professor at Bonn, Germany, well says: " To-day the Portuguese can no longer maintain that the Hottentots are a race of apes, incapable of Christianization. You can no longer find written over church doors in Cape Colony, 'Dogs and Hottentots not admitted,' as at the time when Dr. Vanderkemp fought there for the rights of the down-trodden natives. To-day no one could be found to agree with the French Governor of the island of Bourbon, who called out to the first missionary of Madagascar, ' So you will make the Malagasy Christians? Impossible! They are mere brutes, and have no more senses than irrational cattle; ' since there are hundreds of evangelical congregations established there which have now, counting those only of the London Mission, 386 ordained native pastors, 186 native evangelists, and 3,468 lay preachers and Bible readers."

# BORNEO.

A NATION OF HEAD HUNTERS.—The island of Borneo, called by the natives, Broonai, is next to New Guinea in size, being about 1,000 miles long and 750 wide. On a part of the coast country there are many Mohammedan Malays, Arabs and Bugies, about a million in all. There are also large settlements of Chinese. The aborigines, or Dyaks, of whom there are several millions, were before the advent of the missionaries, and the able and wise rule of Rajah Brooke, behind no nation in barbarism, and rude ignorance. Like the present pagan aborigines of Formosa, their delight was in head taking, and their constant aim was to strike off the heads of their real and supposed enemies, and to this every stranger was exposed without ceremony Skulls were their offerings to the gods they worshipped, and were the ornaments of their houses, their tombs, &c. In many of the provinces no one was allowed to marry who could not show a certain number of human heads which he had recently struck off, and this is the case to-day among the still barbarous portion of the aborigines of Formosa.

NUMEROUS HEAD TAKERS BECOME MEMBERS OF THE CHURCH.—In that portion of Borneo claimed by the Dutch, missionaries from the Netherlands have long labored, and also agents of the Rhenish Missionary Society, and they have converts from among the Dyaks, and also from among the Malays and Chinese.* In Northern and Western Borneo the Society for the Propagation of the Gospel has had an efficient mission, first under Bishop McDougall, and now

---

* The Rhenish missionaries have, in Southern Borneo, 4,000 church members.

4

under Bishop Chambers. In "The English Church in Other Lands," (pp. 198, 199) there is the following mention of the English mission and some of its results :

"In answer to the appeal of Rajah Brooke, two clergymen went to Borneo in 1848, of whom one, the Rev. F. T. McDougall was in 1855 consecrated Bishop of Labuan. Mr. McDougall was a medical man, and his skill was soon put into operation, a dispensary, which grew into a hospital, being at once opened. Other missionaries joined Mr. McDougall, who in the mean time had acquired Malay and Chinese, had translated much, and had made visits of inquiry into the interior, that he might know where to place men as they came out. From time to time, when the missions were hopefully growing, outbreaks occurred, which for a time put a stop to everything.

"In 1857 the Chinese attacked the English, killing some of the Rajah's officers, and driving the Bishop with his family and the converts into the jungle. This roused the passions of the Dyaks, who under the influence of the missionaries, had adopted a peaceful mode of life. Their old love of head-taking was nevertheless strong, and it was long before they again settled down. In 1859 a Mohammedan plot was hatched, and two Englishmen were killed. Prospects brightened when in 1863 a notorious pirate, having met with some Christian Dyaks, voluntarily placed himself under instruction. The next year he brought his wife and child, and then returned to persuade the people of his tribe. In 1867 a missionary visited this people, who had been notorious for piracy and head-taking, and baptized 180 persons. Of the various tribes of Dyaks, living on several rivers and speaking several dialects, at least 3,000 are now members of the English Church."

MR. HORNADAY ON THE GREAT CHANGE IN THE FIERCE DYAKS.—The following paragraphs give the opinion

of Mr. W. D. Hornaday, an American traveller, of the
Dyaks since they have been brought under the rule of
Rajah Brooke, and now of his nephew, and the labors of
the missionaries:

"At times I am almost afraid to write anything about
the Dyaks, lest I overdraw my account of them, and make
them out better than they are. I could not have believed
so much of the Dyaks myself if I had not seen them. I
encountered many strange beasts and birds and creeping
things in the East Indies, but none were to me half so
wonderful as the Dyaks of Sarawak.

"It is almost a misnomer to call them any longer by their
old familiar name, 'head-hunters,' for now that is only.
an empty name for people who are innocent of head-taking
and all similar crimes against humanity. Their war-shields
and jackets have been used up as playthings for the children; the deadly *parong latok*, which could easily cut off a
man's head at a single sweep, has become a rusty heirloom,
and their immense *bangkongs*, or war-boats, large enough to
hold seventy-five men, have fallen to pieces, and totally
disappeared from the rivers of Sarawak.

"The only trophies of their head-hunting days, which
they preserve with great care, and refuse to part with either
for love or money, are the head trophies themselves. They
are to be found only in the larger villages, to which they
have descended from the past generation.

"Nowhere in the world, so far as I know, is life and
property so secure and so sacred as among the once fierce
head-hunters of Sarawak. I have been robbed by white
men in the United States, by black men in the Indies,
both East and West, by red men in South America, and by
yellow men in the far East; but amongst the Dyaks, with
no protection to either person or property, I never lost a
pin's worth by theft. Had the Sibuyau Dyaks been like

the negroes of Barbadoes, or the Mexicans of the Rio Grande, they could have stripped me of all my movables, with perfect safety to themselves. But their honesty afforded my property more impregnable security than the average bank vault does here."

## BURMAH.

DR. JUDSON, THE GREAT MISSIONARY.—Mission work in Burmah was begun by Mr. Felix Carey, a son of the celebrated missionary to India, Dr. Carey. Dr. Adoniram Judson, one of the greatest missionaries of modern times, was the pioneer of the American Baptist Missions among the Burmese.

" He arrived in the East in 1813 and 'jeoparded his life in the high places of the field.' In Burmah he found himself in a land of slaves, ruled by a tyrant, and lived amid brutal murderers and vicious robbers, close to the spot of public execution, with his noble wife, seeking to set up Christ's Kingdom in the Empire of the ' the Golden Sovereign of Land and Water.' Evangelizing the people by the wayside; preaching to courtiers and even to 'the golden ears' of the throne; enduring the terrible captivity of Ava, with Annie Judson to console and feed him; shut up with hundreds of Burmese robbers and murderers; secreting his manuscript translations sewed up in his pillow; kissing his new-born babe through the bars of his cell; marching in chains with lacerated and bleeding feet; released; after twenty years of toil giving the Bible to the Burmans in their own tongue, and in 1830, with Mason, ' The Apostle to the Karens,' carrying the Gospel to that. people and seeing them converted by the thousands, till he could write: ' I eat the rice and fruit cultivated by Christian hands, look on the fields of Christians, see no dwellings but those of Christian families,'—everywhere, and from first to last—he is the same Christian divine and hero." *

Other distinguished laborers in this field have been Dr. and Mrs. Boardman, Mrs. Mason, and Drs. Kincaid, Stevens and Vinton. The last one, the Rev. J. B. Vinton, D. D., died at Rangoon, June 23d, 1887. He was very widely known in Burmah, and he knew the natives and their languages and literature thoroughly. He was a very eloquent man, and could sway great assemblies as he pleased. In the recent conflict between the British and the Burmese, Dr. Vinton rendered most important service, holding the people as only a man of high character, strong will, and indomitable energy can do.

FIVE HUNDRED CHURCHES AND TWENTY-SIX THOUS-AND MEMBERS.—There are now connected with the Baptist Mission 502 organized churches and 26,574 members among the Burmese, Karens, Shans, and other races of the country. There are 513 native preachers, 416 schools, and 10,675 scholars. For a long time the American Baptists had this field entirely to themselves, but latterly the Society for the Propagation of the Gospel has had a few missionaries laboring under the Bishop of Rangoon, Dr. Strachan. At present there are seven English missionaries, 7 native pastors, 75 native helpers, 1,849 communicants, and over 2,000 pupils in schools. The American Methodists, English Wesleyans, and German Lutherans, are also now represented in Burmah, where the facilities of missionary labor, especially in Upper Burmah, have been greatly increased during the last two years.

---

*(From " India," by the Rev. J. T. Gracey : pages 110-111.

ADMINISTRATION REPORT ON THE DEBT TO THE MIS-
SIONARIES AS REGARDS THE WORK AMONG THE KARENS.
—The Administration Report for British Burmah for the
year 1880–81, says: " Foremost in this work have been American missionaries of the Baptist persuasion. . . There are
now attached to this communion no less than 451 Christian
Karen parishes, most of which support their own church,
their own Karen pastor, and their own parish school, and
many of which subscribe considerable sums of money and
kind for the furtherance of missionary work among Karens
and other hill races beyond the British border.  Christianity continues to spread among the Karens, to the great advantage of the commonwealth; and the Christian Karen
communities are distinctly more industrious, better educated,
and more law-abiding than the Burman or Karen villages
around them.  The Karen race and the British Government owe a great debt to the American missionaries, who
have, under Providence, wrought this change among the
Karens of Burmah." *

## CELEBES.

CELEBES IS NOW A CHRISTIAN ISLAND.—In the Dutch
East India Islands there are many missions supported by
Christian people in the Netherlands.  On Java, Samatra,
Amboyna, Ki and the Aru Islands, there are large congre-
gations and many converts, and there are also converts in
Timor, Wetter, and those portions of Borneo and New Gui-
nea, to which the Dutch Government lays claim.  The
island of Celebes has become Christian, there being 199

---

* From the " Friend of India."

Christian congregations, and 125 schools. The number of adherents of the missions is no less than 80,000.

ALFRED RUSSELL WALLACE'S REMARKABLE TESTIMONY.—A book by Alfred Russell Wallace, the distinguished scientist, entitled "The Malay Archipelago, a Narrative of Travel, with Studies of Man and Nature," contains the following:

"Just opposite my abode in Rurukan in Celebes was the school-house. The schoolmaster was a native, educated by the Missionary at Tomohou. School was held every morning for about three hours, and twice a week in the evening there was catechizing and preaching. The children were all taught in Malay. They always wound up with singing, and it was very pleasing to hear many of our old psalm-tunes, in these remote mountains, sung with Malay words. Singing is one of the real blessings which missionaries introduce among savage nations, whose native chants are almost always monotonous and melancholy. The missionaries have much to be proud of in this country. They have assisted the Government in changing a savage into a civilized community in a wonderfully short space of time. Forty years ago the country was a wilderness, the people naked savages, garnishing their rude houses with human heads. Now it is a garden, worthy of its sweet native name of 'Minahata.'"

# CHINA.

GREAT MISSIONARY PROGRESS SINCE 1843.—In 1843 there were only six Christian converts in the vast empire of China. Now there are 30,000 communicants, 125,000 adherents, 300 organized churches, 600 stations, 140 ordained and

1300 unordained native evangelists and teachers. We will give a few illustrations of the progress in different parts of this great field. Forty years ago there were 10 converts in the Province of Canton, China; now there are 4,000. In the Province of Shantung there was not a professing Christian twenty-five years ago; now Christians meet regularly for worship in 300 places.

The Rev. Dr. Ashmore says that twenty-four years ago there were only two Christians in Swatow, China, while now there 1,001; but "1,001" meant twenty mobs, sacked dwellings, bushels of stones, curses by thousands, tears, heartaches; but also prayers of faith and blessed reward of toil. The Rev. Llewellyn Lloyd, a missionary of the Church of England at Foo-chow, China, has baptized 1,000 native converts since the year 1876. The number of converts there has grown in that time from 1,600 to nearly 6,000.

In connection with the English Baptist Mission in Shantung Province, China, there are 55 churches, all self-supporting, being ministered to by native pastors and teachers. During the last twelve months, 300 converts have been baptized. Formosa is getting ready to send missionaries to its heathen neighbors in the Pescadore Islands. The people have liberally responded to the appeals of the missionary. There are now thirty-eight churches, with two thousand two hundred and forty-seven members, and two native ordained and many unordained preachers in Formosa.

MISS GORDON CUMMING'S "WANDERINGS IN CHINA." —A most readable and excellent work on this country, is Miss C. F. Gordon Cumming's "Wanderings in China." Unlike some travellers, Miss Gordon Cumming does not ignore missionary operations and their results. Feeling a deep interest in the welfare of the native races among whom she travels, she examines with care the different departments of mission work, and faithfully records her impressions, and the results of her investigations.

It is cause for much gratification and thankfulness that such a keen observer and skillful and vivid writer should be visiting foreign mission fields at a time when not a few travellers and foreign residents are like those referred to in the following from Miss Gordon Cumming's book: "There is no gainsaying the fact that many persons look upon missionaries and their work as altogether a mistake —an annoying effort to bring about undesirable and unprofitable changes. What a pity it must be to such thinkers that St. Columba and St. Patrick ever took the trouble to come to Britain, or indeed, that a handful of low-born Jews should have presumed to preach in Greece or Rome—to say nothing of their little trouble with the *literati* of Judea. As regards obedience to the Master whose last commandment these troublesome missionaries are trying to carry out, *that* may be all very well in theory, but not in practice; and as to a Chinese St. Stephen, they have neither interest in nor sympathy with any such, even when his martyrdom is enacted almost at their doors."

While this is true of many foreign visitors and residents in China it is not so of all : " In the case of this first general persecution at Foo-chow, it led to the usual result of calling much attention to the new doctrine, and greatly enlarging the number of genuine inquirers, from which, one by one, arose individuals desiring Baptism. Several European merchants were so much impressed by the constancy of these native Christians under such serious persecution that they subscribed £1,000 to build a church for their use, in the heart of the city."

MISS GORDON CUMMING'S TESTIMONY TO THE GREAT SUCCESS.—Miss Gordon Cumming testifies to the great success of the missionary work, and she says that the converts are unsurpassed in self-denial, zeal and true Christian devotedness. Not a few from the different provinces of China have joined the noble army of martyrs. Here is her mention of five from one district in the Canton province : "At Christmas-time, 1879, there was a fearful persecution in a district within a hundred miles of Canton, where a wealthy Christian convert, having determined to build a church in this village, was seized and tortured, to make him forswear Christ. On his remaining steadfast, he was bound to a cross and swathed in cotton-wool saturated with oil, and so was burned alive. Four of his fellow-Christians were also fearfully tortured and mutilated, and then they likewise (since they could not be induced to recant) were tied to crosses and burnt."

CONSULS AS WITNESSES.—Wm. H. Medhurst, Esq., for many years the British Consul at Shanghai, says, in his interesting work on China, "The Foreigner in Far Cathay" :

" After the merchants of China, the missionaries next claim attention as an important element of foreign society. In approaching this part of my subject, I wish to premise that I have no sympathy with those who, for want of consideration or from mere prejudice, think lightly of the work and character of the missionary. The man who honestly devotes his life and energies to the instruction of the poor and ignorant at home, or to the conversion of benighted heathen abroad, must always merit the profound respect of every right-minded individual. It does not need my feeble testimony to sustain the assertion that there have been and now are many such devoted men of all denominations of the Christian Church laboring in China.

" I am not in a position to state definitely what are the results of Protestant missionary labor among the Chinese so far. Their practice of only reckoning as converts those adults whom they conscientiously believe to have been brought to a saving knowledge of the truth, reduces their statistics of proselytism to a very material extent; but even with this check, and taking into consideration, on the one hand, the limited number of laborers, and, on the other, the difficulty of bringing the Chinese mind to appreciate abstract religious truths independently of sensational influences, I think I am only doing the Protestant missionaries simple justice when I state that their efforts have been attended with exceptional success, and this although it is but a short while ago since they ceased to count their converts by mere hundreds."

The British Consul of Newchang, in his late communications to the Foreign Office, speaks very favorably of work done by the missionaries in Manchuria. "Their labors," he says, "indirectly benefit our merchants, manufacturers and artisans. By means of these labors," he adds, "the tone of morality among the Chinese people has, during the last twenty years, perceptibly attained to a higher platform," and to the same cause he attributes "the improved public spirit and the greater solicitude for the welfare of the people manifested by those in power."

MR. J. P. DONOVAN AND A LONDON "TIMES" CORRESPONDENT.—Another witness in China, Mr. J. P. Donovan, of Shanghai, who has filled an important position in the Empire, says: "Missions are not only not a failure—they are a grand success. Many of our countrymen in China are too indifferent to inquire or examine for themselves the work that is being done; the character and conduct of others is such that they studiously avoid missionaries. But those who will take the trouble to go and see soon discover a great work is going on. I have seen it myself in Shanghai, Tientsin, Hankow and Peking, and can speak of it from personal knowledge and observation. Indeed, the ignorance of Christian people at home about this great work amazes me."

A London *Times* correspondent, in writing from Tientsin last year upon "Missionaries in China," remarked that "the good effected by missionaries of all nationalities and all sects is by no means to be measured by a list of conversions. * * * They are the true pioneers of civilization; it is to them we have to look to carry the reputation of foreigners into the heart of the country, and it is on their wisdom, justice and power of sympathy that the renascence of China may largely depend."

MINISTER DENBY ON THE IMMENSE GOOD WHICH IS BEING DONE.—Colonel Denby, the United States Minister to China, after visiting many of the mission stations, and the churches, schools and hospitals, has expressed in a public address in China, and in letters to friends in the United States, the strongest testimony to the greatness of the work of the missionaries, and the devotedness of their lives. *The American Messenger* says that in one of his letters he wrote as follows : "The missionaries are doing immense good to China, and indirectly to all the civilized world. The tourist who sneers at the missionaries, or fails to give them his unqualified admiration and sympathy, is, if earnest, simply ignorant. He has not taken the trouble to go through their missions as I have done."

SECULAR AND POLITICAL RESULTS.—United States Minister Denby, in a paper read before the Peking Oriental Society entitled "China before the Treaties," openly declared that the missionaries precede commerce and prepare the way for it; that they are the forerunners who render possible a foreign residence; that their educational and literary labors have instructed foreigners as to China, and the Chinese as to foreigners; that their philanthropy has elicited the respect and confidence of the Chinese, and that to them and the early and, in fact, the only pioneers and translators, the legations owe a debt of gratitude. The *Interior*, in comment upon this says : " The impartial and truthful words of Minister Denby, spoken after a thorough observation, clearly indicate that the secular and political results of foreign missions have more than repaid to the United States alone all the money they have cost those who have supported them, and they have not cost our government one dollar."—*The Church at Home and Abroad, October*, 1887.

PRESIDENT ANGELL ON WHAT HAS BEEN ACCOMPLISHED IN A LIFE TIME.—J. B. Angell, LL.D., the President of the University of Michigan, and formerly a United States High Commissioner to China, said, in an address at the annual meeting of the American Board, in October, 1883:

" I wish our venerable friends, Dr. S. Wells Williams and Dr. Peter Parker, who are still living in a green and venerable old age, honored and respected by all who love China or who love Christianity,—I wish they were here to-day, that we might look upon them in the flesh, and see men who went to China when there was hardly room to put one's foot, almost sixty years ago ; and yet to-day we see all China open to our missionaries, 20,000 communicants in Protestant churches, the Bible translated into that difficult language, a large Christian literature already organized, and our missionaries everywhere familiar with the best methods of conducting the work. And this within the lifetime of our venerable president who sits here, and who doubtless remembers the whole of it. So that we have not reason to be entirely discouraged even concerning China.

" And when we remember what a magnificent prize that empire is for Christ to win, we must not be too speedily disheartened. We must expect slow but sure progress. There are none of the brilliant dashes of the Japanese in the Chinese. They are a slow, steady-moving people. They are often compared to the Saxons, and they have much of those qualities which gave the Saxons their great skill, pluck, and endurance. They have their staying qualities. They never give up. When they set their face toward an end, they go to it, if it takes centuries. I knew an old general there, the greatest living general in China. He commanded the forces that carried on the war against the Russians, away over in Central Asia; and his method of warfare was so characteristic of the Chinese character, that I must speak of it in closing. There was an almost impassable desert between China and the province where the military operations were to be carried on, hundreds of miles of sand, with here and there an oasis. They could not get provisions across to the armies that were fighting the Russians, so what did they do? Why, this old gentleman set himself to planting colonies of Chinese soldiers in these oases, and they planted crops year after year. So they pushed their way along. He wasn't in any hurry; he knew the Russians would wait there for him, and when he got his crops all ready, then he moved his armies on over these oases with a base of supplies a good deal more complete than General Sherman had in his march down to Atlanta. Then he engaged in all those hard-fought battles in which the Chinese armies did not suffer with the Russians. This is a splendid illustration of the Chinese mode of proceeding; and if at last they will give up their vanity and accept Christ, we may be assured they will wield a power which will be felt not only throughout Asia, but throughout the world."

ACTION OF THE VICEROY, LI HUNG CHANG, AND OTHER OFFICIALS.—When the Chinese Government some years ago established at Peking a college in which young men could obtain a training in foreign languages, literature and science, the Rev. Dr. W. A. P. Martin, a well-known American missionary in that city, was chosen as the principal of it, and he still holds the position. When Li Hung Chang, who is acknowledged to be the most influential man in China, needed, about a year ago, a private tutor for his two sons, he selected the Rev. Charles Tenney, an American missionary at Tientsin, and it is said that he intends to make this missionary the principal of a college he is establishing at his vice-regal city. This distinguished Viceroy gives a liberal support to the Mission Hospital and Dispensary at Tientsin, and it is stated that he has written to the King of Corea advising him to favor the introduction of Protestant Christianity into his kingdom, as it is a good religion and will be highly beneficial to the nation. *

The Chinese Governor of the large island of Formosa has chosen a Christian missionary to plan and to superintend a college he is establishing in that island. The city of Canton has been especially noted in the past for its hostility to the "outside barbarians," and to the Christian religion. But the faithful preaching and teaching of the gospel of Christ, and the patient continuance in well doing of the missionaries, combined with the exemplary conduct of the native Christians, have wrought a wonderful change in public sentiment in this city. See the strong proof of this in the following from a recent number of the *Missionary Herald* :

"Rev. Dr. Happer has received, in answer to his appeals, the $125,000 necessary for opening the proposed college in Canton. He still seeks an additional $50,000

---

* It is said that though he praised Protestant Christianity he wrote disparagingly of Romanism.

for the proper furnishing of the institution, and he proposes
to return to China in October next to spend the remainder
of his life in missionary work.  A remarkable fact connected with this movement is the request received from
more than four hundred officers, gentry and scholars of
Canton and vicinity, asking that the new Christian institution be located among them.  Of the signers of this paper
ten are members of the Imperial Academy, and more than
one hundred and twenty have the degree of A. B. or A. M.
One hundred of them hold official positions under the government.  In their request for this object these gentlemen
say they express the united sentiment of all the gentry in
the province of Canton.  They also guarantee that there
shall be as many students as the college can accommodate.
This movement in China is much like the movements
which we have recently chronicled from various parts of
Japan.  Both empires are seeking education, and while
their public men are not confessedly Christians, they can
see that the Christian education brought by the missionaries is superior to anything they now enjoy.  Hence these
remarkable requests."

EXTENSIVE MEDICAL MISSIONS IN CHINA.—There are
now 82 medical missionaries in China, the majority of
whom are from the United States.  Sixteen of them are
female physicians.  There are large mission hospitals and
dispensaries in Peking, Tientsin, Shanghai and Canton,
and smaller ones at various other cities.  At these hospitals, where many thousands are treated yearly, and at the
homes of other sick people, the teaching of the gospel of
Christ goes hand in hand with the medical treatment, and
the good accomplished is very great.  In no part of the
world is the medical missionary more highly appreciated
than within the Chinese Empire, and a great part of the
current expenses of the hospitals and dispensaries are borne

by Chinese officials, the gentry and the merchants. Foreigners residing in China also give a good deal.

THE LARGE HOSPITAL, DISPENSARY AND COLLEGE, AT CANTON.—In a recent published volume, "The Cross and the Dragon," * there is an extended account of the great hospital and dispensary at Canton, from which we glean the following facts:

For thirty years, the hospital has been under the care of Dr. Kerr, under whose able and judicious management it has been greatly developed, and now unites an extensive hospital, dispensary and medical college. There are no less than five successive lines of good substantial buildings, four of which are devoted to the accommodation of patients. There is also a very fine church, capable of seating six hundred people.

This great institution is one of the sights of the city of Canton, and is visited and inspected by intelligent Chinamen from all sections of the country, and by foreign travellers and residents. Twenty thousand persons burdened with diseases are the recipients of its benefits each year. Its great practical benevolence has so commended it to both natives and foreigners that Chinese and Parsees gladly join with Europeans and Americans in its support. The Viceroy, Hoppo and other high native officials are regular contributors. Connected with the central hospital, are branches at four cities in the interior.

Associated with Dr. Kerr is an efficient staff of native doctors and surgeons trained by him. In the course of his career he has instructed some scores of pupils, thirty of whom have taken the full course and received certificates.

---

* This very interesting and valuable book on China, and the missionary work there, is published by A. D. F. Randolph & Co., New York.

5

Most of the native doctors educated are Christians, and engage more or less in evangelistic work wherever they go. For the instruction of these medical students, and for the diffusion of true medical science in China, Dr. Kerr has prepared more than a score of valuable works in Chinese, some of them translations, and the others original works.

In the great hospital and its branches, every effort is made to impress the people who come with the importance of Christian truth. There is daily service in the chapel, special services there and elsewhere, regular visitation of the wards, in which the missionary physician is aided by native clergymen, and distribution of books and tracts. "Some come only to die, but the light of the Cross illumines their way to the grave; and from these beds of pain many a ransomed spirit has winged its flight to the fair world on high. Many, as they depart, take special pains to see the physician, the pastor and the ladies, saying, 'Thanks to you doctor; thanks to you pastor; thanks to you mistress, and thanks to Jesus, for the blessings I have received.' In every district of the country they are found, and are ready to greet the missionary in his travels, and give glad evidence of their gratitude."

Besides the many hundreds who have been brought to Christ, and the many thousands who have been cured of their diseases or have had their sufferings lessened, the good effects of this medical mission work are seen in numberless ways; in lessening the anti-foreign feeling of the Chinese; in diminishing the power of superstition which connects diseases with evil spirits, and sends the suffering to the exorcists and the idols instead of to the physician ; in giving constant proof of the unselfish character of our religion ; and in preparing the way, and making openings for direct evangelistic work, near by and far off.

PRESTIGE GAINED BY THE MISSIONS.—In many parts

of China, and in almost all parts of the heathen and Mohammedan world, special facilities for propagating the gospel have come through the healing of the sick by medical missionaries. Dr. Jeremiassen, an American missionary physician, has lately been greatly occupied with the soldiers of the garrison at his interior station in the great island of Hainan, off the south-east coast of China. He has been successful during the prevalence of a fatal epidemic, and Gen. Feng, the commanding officer, has telegraphed to the Viceroy at Canton that " but for Dr. Jeremiassen he would have had no soldiers left." The General has authorized this missionary physician to have two buildings for hospital use erected at the government's expense, and after the present military inmates have sufficiently recovered to be able to leave them, they are to be made over to the mission. The prestige thus gained for the recently established American Presbyterian mission in the interior of Hainan is very great.

Dr. Duncan Main, of the English Church Mission, in the large city of Hangchow, has recently had built a fine hospital. One of the Chinese newspapers, in referring to its formal opening, said : " At the opening of the hospital all Mandarins came to congratulate him. Chinese and foreigners all came together ; there was not a person in Hangchow that did not praise the work." Dr. Main treats more than ten thousand cases in a year, and during last year seventy-nine cases of attempted suicide by opium poisoning were brought to him, in sixty of which life was saved. Thirteen persons made a profession of faith in Christ during the year.

Hangchow is one of the most famous and important of all the cities in the Chinese empire. On account of its beautiful natural surroundings, the intelligence of its inhabitants, and its historic interest, it has been for a long time the favorite place of residence for literary men and the aristocracy, and to have gained so much prestige in this city as Dr. Main has done, is of very great importance.

The wife of the distinguished Viceroy Li Hung Chang, having been cured of a serious illness by Miss Howard, now Mrs. King, a lady missionary physician, now, in gratitude, gives very liberally in aid of the hospital for women at Tientsin, and she supports a number of young ladies who are now studying our medical practice under Mrs. King, M. D. Lady Li also occasionally visits the hospital, and bestows gifts to the poor patients.

Three years ago, during an outbreak in the capital city of Corea, a number of officers of the government were wounded, and also many soldiers. Among the wounded officers was a nephew of the king. In consequence of healing the wounds of this nephew and others, Dr. Allen, a medical missionary, has obtained special facilities in the " Hermit Kingdom." The king has established a hospital and placed it under Dr. Allen's charge, and Miss Ellis, an American medical missionary, has been made physician to the Queen of Corea.

OPIUM REFUGES.—At some of the mission hospitals in China there are wards for the treatment of the slaves of the opium vice, but a number of the medical missionaries have " opium refuges " separate from the hospitals. These asylums should be greatly multiplied, and other remedial and preventive measures should be increased, as some reparation for the terrible wrong of which England has been guilty in her enforced opium traffic with China. The irreversible verdict concerning this odious trade is that to which the great and good Earl of Shaftesbury gave utterance—" It is a nefarious traffic, and a national abomination."

The authoritative assemblies of the Church of England,

and of all the other Christian bodies in Great Britain, have denounced this traffic and the government's connection with it, and none regret the course pursued by the Indian and home governments more than true Christians in England and India.

A FORMIDABLE OBSTACLE IN CHINA.—The terrible evils of the opium traffic, and the very formidable obstacle it is to the christianization of China, continue to be referred to, not only by missionaries but also by consuls, travellers and others. Miss Gordon Cumming dwells at length upon it in her "Wanderings in China," and says that the success of the missionary work would have been much greater than it is but for the hateful traffic—a traffic forced upon China "by the persuasive eloquence of British cannon." (Vol. 2, p. 305.)

Consul Medhurst, in his book already referred to, says : " It cannot be doubted that the opium traffic has much to answer for in the way of neutralizing missionary efforts, not only in its direct effects upon the victims themselves, but in the hatred and suspicion of everything foreign which it has engendered in the minds of the natives generally."

The Rev. Horace Randle, of the China Island Mission, who has travelled extensively in the interior as well as on the seaboard, says in a recent letter, that while many of the Chinese have right ideas on the subject, yet the mass of them, especially in the interior, have an exceeding dislike and mistrust of foreigners and their religion because of England's opium wars, and the consequent spread of the opium vice in China. They make little, if any, distinction between the different nationalities or classes of foreigners.

The Rev. J. Hudson Taylor, M. D., the founder and principal director of the China Island Mission, said, at the Mildmay Conference, London, in June, 1887 : "We were listening yesterday to a description of the horrors of the slave trade—of the untold multitudes who must have perished before reaching their destination. But, having labored many years in China, my solemn conviction is that all the misery and sin and suffering caused by the slave trade are not equal to the wrongs inflicted upon China by the opium traffic. That may seem a strong thing to say, but it is not at all too strong. I could not possibly describe the incalculable misery which I have witnessed as a result of this curse which we introduced into China. As a medical missionary I have been into many homes where people were endeavoring to kill themselves by taking opium, to escape from the greater · evils they have brought upon themselves by the habit of opium smoking. If you love your country, pray God that he will raise up a standard against this horrible, awful curse, and that he will deliver us from the guilt of it." *

---

# FIJI.

Formerly the Darkest Place on Earth.—As is well-known, the Fijians were savages of the most inhuman kind, and cannibals of the worst description. Commodore Wilkes, who explored the extensive Fiji group (there are 80 inhabited islands) in 1840, says in his "Narrative of the United States Exploring Expedition": "So beautiful was the aspect of the islands that I could scarcely bring

---

* For an account of the rise and progress of the traffic, England's opium wars, and the terrible consequences, see the writer's pamphlet, entitled "Opium. England's Coercive Opium Policy, and its disastrous Results in China and India." Published by Funk and Wagnalls, New York and London.

my mind to realize the well-known fact that they were the abodes of a savage, ferocious, and treacherous race of cannibals." And yet this " darkest place on earth," has been so transformed by the Divine blessing upon missionary labors, that Fiji is one of the most Christian of countries.

SIR ARTHUR GORDON ON THE WONDERFUL TRANSFORMATION.—The instruments in this work of grace were English Wesleyan missionaries, the first of whom arrived in Fiji in 1835. By 1874 nearly all the islands were Christianized, and at the request of the principal chief, who had become a Christian, and several subordinate chiefs, Fiji was made a British colony. The first governor was Sir Arthur Gordon, and this gentleman on his return to England in 1879, said, at a public meeting in London, in regard to those who had, so short a time before, been such ferocious cannibals :

" Out of a population of about a hundred and twenty thousand, one hundred and two thousand are now regular worshippers in the churches, which number eight hundred, all well built and completed. In every family there is morning and evening worship. Over forty-two thousand children are in attendance in the fifteen hundred and thirty-four Christian day-schools. The heathenism which still exists in the mountain districts, surrounded as it is on all sides by a Christian population on the coast, is rapidly dying out."

SIR CHARLES ST. JULIAN'S TESTIMONY.—Chief-Justice Sir Charles St. Julian, of Fiji, remarks that he " had been a close observer of the Wesleyan Mission, and when he came to the Island was hardly prepared for what he saw. If the work done by that society had only been to cause the natives to cast off bad practices and customs, it would have been a very gratifying result ; but the Mission had built up a kingdom."

The statistics of the mission at present are, eleven foreign missionaries, fifty-three native missionaries, 1,877 local preachers, 44 catechists, 1,058 teachers, 1,255 churches, chapels and preaching places, 27,421 communicants and 42,651 Sunday-school pupils.

MISS GORDON CUMMING ON THE MIGHTY CHANGE WHICH HAS BEEN EFFECTED.—Miss Gordon Cumming, writing in her interesting work, "At Home in Fiji," thus describes the former character and condition of the people, and what Christianity has done for them :

"I often wish that some of the cavillers who are forever sneering at Christian missions could see something of their results in these islands. But first they would have to re-call the Fiji of ten years ago, when every man's hand was against his neighbor, and the land had no rest from barba-rous inter-tribal wars, in which the foe, without respect of age or sex, were looked upon only in the light of so much beef, the prisoners deliberately fattened for the slaughter, dead bodies dug up that had been buried ten or twelve days, and could only be cooked in the form of puddings, limbs cut off from living men and women and cooked and eaten in presence of the victim, who had previously been compelled to dig the oven and cut the firewood for the pur-pose, and this not only in the time of war, when such atroc-ity might be deemed less inexcusable, but in time of peace, to gratify the caprice or fancy of the moment.*

"Then, further, think of the sick buried alive, the array of widows who were deliberately strangled on the death of

---

* The Rev. James Calvert, who might be called the Apostle of Fiji, and who has lived and labored until there is not one heathen Fijian left, says that one wretched cannibal was wont to put down a stone for every human body of which he partook, and his horrid memorial reached the number of 872 stones.

J. L.

any great man, the living victims who were buried beside every post of a chief's new house, and must needs stand clasping it while the earth was gradually heaped over their devoted heads, or those who were bound hand and foot and laid on the ground to act as rollers when a chief launched a new canoe, and thus doomed to a death of excruciating agony—a time when there was not the slightest security for life and property, and no man knew how quickly his hour of doom might come, when whole villages were depopulated simply to supply their neighbors with fresh meat.

"Just think of all this, and of the change that has been wrought, and then just imagine white men who can sneer at missionary work in the way they do. Now you may pass from isle to isle, certain everywhere to find the same cordial reception by kindly men and women. Every village on the eighty inhabited isles has built for itself a tidy little church and a good house for its teacher or native minister, for whom the village also provide food and clothing. Can you realize that there are *nine hundred* Wesleyan churches in Fiji, at every one of which the frequent services are crowded by devout congregations, that the schools are well attended, and that the first sound that greets your ear at dawn, and the last at night, is that of hymn-singing and most fervent worship rising from each dwelling at the hour of family worship?"

THRILLING STORIES OF THE MISSIONARIES' COURAGE. Some thrilling stories are told by Miss Gordon Cumming of the courage displayed by the missionaries in their endeavors to put an end to the native atrocities. Here is one of them : In 1849 two ladies, Mrs. Calvert and Mrs. Lyth, with a single native Christian, their husbands being absent, rescued five women, nine having already been sacrificed, from the very hands of the butcher. Captain Erskine, R. N., who touched at the island a few weeks after, says : " Regardless of the sanctity of the place, it being ' tabued ' to women, they forced themselves into old Ta-noa's (the father of Thakombau, and an inveterate cannibal) chamber, who demanded, with astonishment at their temerity, what these women did there ? The Christian chief, who well maintained his lately adopted character, answered for them, that they came to solicit the lives of the surviving prisoners, presenting at the same time the two whales' teeth." After some hesitation Tanoa said : " Those who are dead are dead : those who are alive shall live." " If anything could have increased our admiration of their heroism," adds Captain Erskine, " it was the unaffected manner in which, when pressed by us to relate the circumstances of their awful visit, they spoke of it as the simple performance of an ordinary duty."

THE FIJIAN CHURCH HAS BECOME A MISSIONARY BODY.—The Fijian Church has in its turn become a missionary body, and the first effort to Christianize the savage natives of New Britain and New Ireland is being made by a party of brave Fijian teachers, who, well knowing the danger they would have to face, volunteered to accompany the Rev. Mr. Brown when he sailed on this very difficult mission. Nine earnest men (seven of whom were married and their wives true helpmates in this great work) announced their wish to go.

The English Consul deemed it his duty to summon them, and repeat in strongest terms what dangers awaited them, and the horrors of their almost inevitable fate at the hands of barbarous cannibals. They replied that they had counted the cost, and were all of one mind : that they were perfectly aware of the danger, but had determined of their own free will to go, because of the great longing they felt to teach those poor savages the holy faith which had so entirely changed their own country. So in 1875 they sailed·

Mr. Brown left his wife and children in New Zealand, and I think two years elapsed before any chance of communication presented itself. While we were living in Fiji, in 1877, he returned thither, to report that the infant mission was fairly established, and to ask for more workers. His difficulty was, not to obtain them, but to select only a few from the many willing volunteers.

A few months more elapsed, and tidings reached Fiji that four of these native teachers had been treacherously murdered and eaten by the cannibal people of the Duke of York Island, on which they, with their wives and their little ones, had settled, in the hope of forming a separate mission. This terrible news reached Fiji just as a fresh detachment of teachers was about to start for New Britain. Their determination was no whit shaken. One of the wives was asked whether she still intended to accompany her husband to a scene of so great danger. She replied, ' I am like the outrigger of a canoe,* where the canoe goes, there you will surely find the outrigger.' "—*Miss Gordon Cumming in London Sunday Magazine.*

TESTIMONY OF " ADMINISTRATORS " MCGREGOR AND THURSTON.—The progress, religious, social and moral, since the annexation of the Islands, may be gathered from the reports of Administrators W. McGregor, who made a tour of the colony in 1885. He says : " The people are, speaking generally, well governed, are contented and in comfortable circumstances, using in their houses an unusually large amount of the comforts and conveniences of civilized life." On Vanua Levu, the smaller of the two chief islands, there is a native industrial school, almost self-supporting in the matter of food. On the larger island, Uiti Levu, the houses are good and well furnished, besides

---

* Balancing Float.

being stocked with native property.    As the people are industrious, food is very abundant.    The Sabbath is so strictly observed in the interior of Viti Levu that no travelling can be done on that day."

Administrator J. B. Thurston, also writing in 1885, contrasts from personal knowledge the condition of the people then with their condition in 1865.

" During the day or two that I spent with them in 1855, war, intrigue and general insecurity was their chronic condition.    Beimana and every other town was fortified by strong fences, moats, and other earthworks.    No man stirred beyond his war fence after sunset.    The quiet of night was broken by the sounds of the ' dérua ' (a peculiar beat of the native wooden drum when some slaughtered enemy was brought in front of the heathen temple) ; and in Beimana itself three human bodies were eaten during my stay, and the ' forks ' used upon the occasion were presented to me.    It was possible for me, therefore, to dwell with force upon the altered condition of the country, and to contrast, with effect, the peace of the present with the horrors and ceaseless anxieties of the past."

---

# GREENLAND.

SUBLIME FAITH AND PATIENCE OF THE MISSIONARIES. —Sir Roderick Murchison, President of the Royal Geographical Society, in one of his anniversary addresses, said of Dr. Kane's " Arctic Explorations": " There never was a work written which more feelingly develops the struggles of humanity, under the most intense sufferings, or demonstrates more strikingly how the most appalling difficulties can be overcome by the union of a firm resolve with the never-failing resources of a bright intellect.' This high tribute was not undeserved by the author of that remarkable record of self-exile in the polar regions.

But when we turn to the annals of *missionary research* and labors in those same and other regions, we have examples of yet sublimer faith, hope and patience under sufferings. Dr. Kane's exile was but for a brief period, and his endurance of hardship was but for one, or at most, for two years at a time. The missionaries' exile and trials are generally for life, and though their privations and sufferings are greatest at the beginning of missions in the various fields, yet they continue more or less in after years.

In the life of Matthew Stack, a Moravian missionary, it is stated that, " The first missionaries to Greenland were often driven to allay the cravings of hunger with shell-fish and sea-weed : they had recourse even to the remnants of tallow candles, and thought themselves happy, when they could procure some train-oil to mix up with their scanty morsel of oatmeal. Their perseverance under these painful privations only excited the contempt of the natives.

" The Greenlanders would leave them, in the midst of their instructions, to attend a dancing match. Sometimes they told the missionaries they had heard enough already of spiritual things from abler instructors. Besides being volatile and trifling, they used all possible means to entice the missionaries to a conformity with their own dissolute practices. Failing of success in this wicked design, they would annoy them, by mocking their religious exercises, by praying with all kinds of ridiculous mimicry, or by beating drums in time of worship. The brethren bore this painful treatment with equanimity. But when the savages perceived that they could effect nothing in this way, they began to insult and abuse the persons of the missionaries. They pelted them with stones, and destroyed some of their property. Amid such appalling discouragements did the Moravians persevere in the work of evangelizing this inhospitable country."

TESTIMONY OF DRS. KANE AND BROWN TO THEIR GREAT SUCCESS.—In Western or Danish Greenland it is said that there is not a single pagan left, and a Moravian missionary who has recently returned to England after forty years active service, reports that in *all* Greenland there is but one station in the neighborhood of which there are heathen. Concerning the labors of the self-denying missionaries in this inhospitable country, Dr. Kane, in his "Arctic Explorations," says : "The missionaries have been so far successful among the natives of Greenland that there are but few of them who are not now Christians. Before missionaries came, murder, burial of the living, and infanticide were not numbered among crimes. It was unsafe for vessels to touch upon the coast ; but now Greenland is safer for the wrecked mariner than many parts of our own coast."

"The testimony of Dr. Robert Brown, a Fellow of the Geographical Society of London, who accompanied the West Greenland expedition as Botanist and Geologist, we quote from an interesting article published by him in *Mission Life :* "Mission stations are now scattered at intervals, and from being a simple missionary, the Greenland priest has become the 'parish minister;' *for there is now not one professed Pagan in all Danish Greenland.* Settlements for the trade—conducted (by the Danish Government) solely for the benefit of the natives, and so extensive that it employs seven ships, and yields a profit of £11,000—are established from Cape Farewell up to 73° north latitude, where at Kingatok, on a little islet, lives a solitary Dane, who has the eminent distinction of being the most northerly civilized man in the world."

# INDIA.

The Three Principal Religions of India.—In an address in New York in November, 1882, Sir Richard Temple, who has occupied high official positions in different parts of India for nearly thirty years, referred in the following well-chosen words, to the great need for Christianity in that country, as evidenced by the character of the three principal religions :

" I have heard in England and even in this country that many think there is not much need of Christianity in India. There is great need, as will be seen by the character of the three great religions of the land. As to Mohammedanism, it withers human character as with a blight, warps all the feelings and sentiments, crystallizes everything which it touches, and rivets all customs and opinions in a groove. It is utterly intolerant. Anything more sanguinary than its fanaticism cannot be imagined.

" As to Hinduism, I cannot give you an exact idea of the vicious orgies which occur constantly in the Hindu temples. There is a considerable amount of abominable immorality, which is practically the outcome of this false religion. As to Buddhism, however excellent and attractive the poetic accounts of it may be, as given in the well-known poem, ' The Light of Asia,' the actual Buddhism of India is as degrading as can well be imagined." *

India is pre-eminently a land of error and vice, and it is the great stronghold of the arch-enemy of mankind. Great as is the progress which has been made toward the capturing of this stronghold, it would have been still greater if the heroes engaged in this holy war had not been opposed

---

* From the report of the address in the *Foreign Missionary*.

and obstructed by some who ought to have aided and encouraged them. Many in high position and of great influence who ought to have been on the "Lord's side" in the conflict have rendered all possible aid to the enemy. This is especially true of the directors and agents of the East India Company.

THE MISRULE OF THE EAST INDIA COMPANY.—The East India Company ruled India for about one hundred years—from soon after Clive's victory at Plassy until the Great Mutiny or Rebellion of 1857–8, when it was abolished by the British Parliament, in response to numerously signed memorials recounting the misdeeds of the Company and its agents. It favored and aided the native idolatries and superstitions, a. l repressed Christian missionary effort. In its charters it succeeded in getting from Parliament the proviso that no educational or religious effort should be allowed in India.

In 1812, owing to the representations of the Company, Parliament was strongly inclined to continue the proviso when renewing the charter of the Company. It required 900 largely signed petitions presented to, and urged upon Parliament by the great and good Wilberforce and his supporters to secure even a partially tolerant charter.

When Carey and Thomas reached India in 1793, they were subjected to great trials and indignities by the agents of the East India Company, and this continued until 1798, when the missionaries took up their abode in the Danish settlement of Serampore, where they were under the protection of the Danish Crown. Judson and other American missionaries were, on their arrival in India, ordered to depart from the country, and India's loss, as regards the great missionary Judson, was Burmah's gain.

A DISGRACEFUL MEMORIAL OF THE COMPANY.— The Directors of the East India Company placed on sol-

emn record, in a formal memorial to the British Parliament,
" their decided conviction," after " consideration and examination," that " the sending of Christian missionaries into our
Eastern possessions is the maddest, most extravagant, most
expensive, most unwarrantable project that was ever proposed by a lunatic enthusiast."\* But they were compelled
to submit to the decision of Parliament obtained by Wilberforce, and his supporters, and to cease ordering the ex-
pulsion of missionaries from India. Little, however, was
gained besides this. The agents of the Company continued to favor and aid the native religions, and to discourage,
in various ways, missionary enterprise.

DR. BUTLER ON SOME OF THE MISDEEDS OF THE
COMPANY.—In one of the ablest and best books on India,
" The Land of the Veda," by the Rev. Dr. Butler, reference
is made to facts well known in India, which were recounted in one of the memorials to Parliament, " such as Lord
Clive personally attending a heathen festival at Conjeve-
ram, and presenting an ornament to the idol worth 1,050
pagodas ($1,850); Lord Auckland, another Governor-Gen-
eral, offering 2,000 rupees ($1,000) at the Muttra shrine,
and being highly praised in a native newspaper for his
piety.† Lord Ellenborough, in 1842, ordering the gates

---

\* This memorial was all the more inexcusable and disgraceful
because of the abundant evidence there was of the great good
of the labors of Ziegenbalg, Plutschau, Swartz, Kiernander and
other European missionaries in India, in the eighteenth century, and of how these men had promoted peace between the
English and the native princes and people. When the English
were alarmed at the victorious career of Hyder Ali, they sent an
embassy to treat with him, but that monarch sent them away,
saying, " Send me the Christian (Swartz), he will not deceive
me."

† We have no intention of dwelling on the disastrous war in
which Lord Auckland imperilled our prestige, beyond remark-

of the Temple of Somnath (carried off by a Mohammedan conqueror eight hundred years ago) to be carried back hundreds of miles, with military honors, and his issuing a proclamation, announcing the heathenish act, 'to all the Princes, Chiefs and people of India.' Lord Dalhousie, later still, paying reverence to an idol, by changing his dress on entering the heathen temple of Umritsur, and making an offering to it of 5,000 rupees, ($2,500). These things were done by Indian Viceroys, while Government servants were required to collect pilgrims' tax, administer the estates of idol temples, and pay allowances to officials connected with heathen shrines; and even military officers had to parade troops and present arms in honor of idol processions !"

" These things were so. The writer has seen (and could give the name of the place, and of the commanding officer responsible) British cannon loaned and ammunition supplied, to fire a salute in honor of a heathen idol, and that on the holy Sabbath day ! Christian Englishmen in India groaned over these acts, officers in the army threw up their commissions sooner than obey such orders, and men in high positions protested against them as sins of the deepest dye, fearing that God would 'visit for these things,' and appealed to the British public to stop the madness of the East India Company and their servants in India."—Pp. 403–4.

---

ing that the gods whom he strove to propitiate by his offerings paid scant heed to him. At the outbreak of the war in 1839 he visited Brindabun, where he gave 200 rupees to one idol and 700 to others; at Muttra he distributed 1,500 rupees to idols and at other places 500. The Chandrika newspaper praised him " for his holiness," and declared that a ruler who had given thousands of rupees for the service of the idols must carry all before him. But he did not.—*Church Missionary Intelligencer, May,* 1887.

Anti-Christian Policy.—The Koran and the Shasters were allowed to be freely used in the Government educational institutions, but the teaching of the Holy Scriptures, or even the answering of spontaneous inquiries respecting their contents were forbidden during school hours. No native Christian was permitted to join the Government forces, and if any one already in the army became a Christian he was expelled. Hindu priests and Moslem propagandists had free access to the native troops, but not Christian missionaries. What wonder, then, that when the infamous Nana Sahib started the mutiny, the native soldiers (Sepoys as they were called) joined him.

The Iniquitous Opium Traffic.—The iniquitous opium traffic with China was begun by Warren Hastings and other agents of the company, and England's opium wars, which, as Dr. Arnold of Rugby, John Bright, the Earl of Shaftesbury, and many other eminent Englishmen have said are among the most infamous in history, were instigated and fomented by this dishonorable company. The enforced traffic has been of incalculable injury to China, and a most formidable obstacle to the Christianization of that empire. It has also caused much demoralization and misery in India, as the opium vice is spreading there also. It has also worked much injury to India in other ways. It causes, or increases the periodic famines, owing to the perversion of such a vast area from food crops to crops of poison, and the government traffic shocks the moral sense of the better class of Hindus.*

Sir John Lawrence's Superior Policy. — Sir John Lawrence was Governor of the Punjab when the Rebellion broke out; the elements around him were as

---

* For proofs on these points see the writer's pamphlet, referred to on page 70.

energetic, and some of them as dangerous, as any in India. He had been superior to the policy of his masters, and would insist on favoring Missionaries and the Bible in the schools. What was the result of this open and candid course, even in the hour when all around them had fallen ? The missionaries waited upon him to say that, if their public preaching in the streets of Lahore was any embarrassment in the condition of the country, they were ready to pause for a season, if he thought it requisite to do so. His prompt reply, which will be a lasting honor to him, was, " No, gentlemen ; prosecute your preaching and missionary enterprise just as usual. Christian things, done in a Christian way, will never alienate the heathen." They acted on his advice, and did not preach a sermon the less for the Rebellion. Though all India around them had " gone," their Punjab stood firm, and even supplied the men and means for sustaining the siege of Delhi, till it fell, and the Government was fully restored. The East India Company was abolished, amid the contempt of all good men, and even of the candid heathen ; while this very man, Sir John Lawrence, was chosen by the Queen to be Viceroy of India.—*The Land of the Veda, pp.* 408-9.

MAJOR-GENERAL SIR HERBERT EDWARDES ON THE BAD POLICY PURSUED.—In "Our Indian Empire," a lecture delivered in London in 1860, by Major-General Sir Herbert Edwardes, one of the most distinguished of English soldiers and administrators in India, we read : " Much, it must be admitted, has been done by our English rulers in the great cause of education. Scientific and historic truth has been clothed in the languages of the country, and has shaken Hindooism to its base. But, alas ! it must be admitted also that our English Government in India, even in its schools and its colleges, has withheld the Bible and kept back Christianity. It has indeed made many infidels and deists, but it may be doubted whether it ever made a single Christian. On the other hand, it is recorded by a distinguished Hindoo Prince and scholar, Rajah Jay Narain, of Benares, that 'if Christianity were true, the British would have communicated a knowledge of it to their Hindoo subjects.' Precisely the same sentiment is also recorded by an eminent native mathematician, Ram Chundra, author of the 'Treatise on Maxima and Minima,' edited by Prof. DeMorgan, who was educated to be a Deist in the Government College at Delhi, and was converted afterwards to be a Christian through private teaching.

" The conclusions which these two native gentlemen have avowed and published, cannot fail to have been the secret conviction of all their thoughtful countrymen; for they saw the same Government which excluded the Bible from its colleges and schools, admitting the Shasters and the Koran; fostering caste in its native army; expelling a Sepoy from the ranks because he became a Christian (Prubhu Deen, 1819); preventing missionaries from coming to India as long as it could; sharing the pilgrim taxes of Juggernauth till England interfered; and even so late as 1857, disbursing £200,000 a year from its treasury to Heathen and Mohammedan temples."

SIR HERBERT EDWARDES ON THE EARLIER AND LATER RECORDS OF THE COMPANY.—" It is a remarkable thing, but only too consonant with human nature in all situations, that in the poor and humble days of the East India Company, when it came to India literally as an adventurer, it came, nevertheless, as a Christian. The charter of 1698 actually enacted that the Company should provide ministers who were to 'apply themselves to learn the native language of the country where they shall reside, the better to enable them to instruct the Gentoos, that shall be servants or slaves to the said Company, in the Protestant religion.' And the early records of the Company show them at one time (1659) sending out Bibles in several languages; at another, (1677) catechisms, ordering that ' when any shall be able to repeat the catechism by heart, you may give each of them two rupees for their encouragement.' And whatever were the faults of Robert Clive, who founded the Imperial era of the Company, he was no coward. In governing Heathens and Mohammedans, he was minded, like Sir John Lawrence in our day, to ' be bound by our conscience, not by theirs; ' and he boldly welcomed the great missionary, Kiernander, to Calcutta in 1758. What was it then that so entirely changed the policy of the East India Company ? Prosperity, greatness, increase of territory and goods, want of faith in their own destiny and in the God that shaped it ! They first dropped the desire to convert ' the Gentoos ' (corruption of a Portuguese word signifying Gentiles) then took the patronage of Juggernauth, and in their last days may be described as barely tolerant of native Christianity."

" Well was it for India, and well for England, too, that the Christian duty which the British India Government neglected, private Englishmen (and not only Englishmen, but Americans and Germans) came forward to perform, and the result of this missionary labor is from 150,000 to 200,000 Protestant native Christians in the present generation.* The number is small in comparison with the population, but I consider it large in comparison with the obstacles it had to overcome."—*Ibid.*

THE ONLY POLICY OF HOPE.—The London *Christian* for July 15th, 1887, contains an extended notice of the " Memorials of the Life and Letters of Major-General Sir Herbert B. Edwardes, K. C. B., K. C. S. I., By His Wife,"

---

* In 1887 the number is over 500,000

in which occurs the following: "In season and out of season he pleaded for the adoption of a Christian policy in the rule of India. That policy, he maintained, was the only policy of hope. His wide knowledge, varied experience, and persuasive eloquence were all brought to bear on the advocacy of this noble plea. The closing words of his splendid oration at Exeter Hall, in May, 1860, are as applicable now as then: 'If you ask me what is safe for the future—if you ask me to indicate a safe and expedient policy to the Government—I say, an open Bible. Put it in your schools. Stand avowedly as a Christian Government. Follow the noble example of your Queen. Declare yourselves, in the face of the Indian people, a Christian nation, as her Majesty has declared herself a Christian Queen, and you will not only do honor to her but to your God, and in that alone you will find that true safety rests.'"

THE POLICY OF THE PRESENT GOVERNING COUNCIL. —English authority in India is still endangered, and the progress of Christianity greatly hindered, because the policy advocated by General Edwardes is so far from being adopted. The Government Council at Calcutta, (composed mainly of "old Indians" and partly of native gentlemen,† and which Council really rules India,) has, until within about a year, discriminated against Christianity in the Government colleges and schools, and even now God is entirely ignored in the Government institutions of learning. While the Bible and books commendatory of Christianity have been excluded, those commending idolatry and containing heathen indecencies have been used.

---

† There is a similarly constituted but subordinate Council in each of the provinces having a Governor or Lieutenant-Governor.

Dr. Murdoch and other distinguished missionaries have faithfully exposed and denounced the teaching contained in some of the Government school books, and it is due to their persistent efforts that idolatrous and indecent passages no longer disgrace them.  But the Creator and Preserver of the universe is still ignored, and the tendency of the instruction is toward atheism and materialism.  European sceptics and atheists are often employed to teach young men.  Prince Harnam Singh, who attended the Queen's Jubilee, said in an address in London, that the most determined opponents of Christianity in India are the graduates of the Government colleges,* and yet these are the men who are appointed to the thousands of Government offices which are filled by Hindus !

The veteran and highly distinguished American missionary, the Rev. Jacob Chamberlain, D. D., who is now establishing a Christian college in India, said at a meeting in New Brunswick, last year: " Three millions of young men in India know English without knowing Christ.  The government universities are sending out 3,000 a year ; only three per cent. of these are Christians ; the others go forth to poison the minds of the people with naturalism, agnosticism, and to brand Christianity as a worn-out system.  They say, " Our English education has taught us that."

NO CHRISTIAN NEED APPLY.—In the old times, as was commonly said, men left their Christianity at the Cape, and often forgot to pick it up again upon their return, having apparently wholly lost sight of it during a long expatriation.  Things are altered now.  People now travel by the overland route, and take little luggage with them.  Some deeming Christianity superfluous, do not encumber themselves with it as far as Suez.  They leave it at home, hav-

---

* See his address in the *Church Missionary Intelligencer* for August, 1887.

ing no occasion for it in the East. One such gentleman, a
Mr. Cotton, has found his way to India in the Bengal Civil
Service. He has published a book called *New India; or,
India in Transitions*. It has fallen into the hands of a
native Christian, Behari Lal Chandra, who has come to
the conclusion that the author is " no better nor worse than
a positivist who knows no God and no future life, and to
whom there is no such thing as sin, and who can bind his
love to a woman, but not to his Maker." * The Bengali
Christian proceeds to argue that the " religious morality of
Government is an entire sham." According to him, on the
one hand it gags the mouths of chaplains : on the other it
" appoints to the Education Departments positivists, atheists, and agnostics, who openly sneer at Christianity, and
poison the minds of hundreds of youths entrusted to their
care." He goes on to say, " It is not religious neutrality
but irreligious antagonism to Christianity, inasmuch as it
consists only in shutting Christianity out of its schools and
colleges, and allowing positivism, atheism, and agnosticism
free entrance."

We may reasonably believe that the native Christian
has considerable facilities for knowing what has been the
character of Government teaching among his compeers.
The author quotes a remarkable instance of religious neutrality upon the part of our Christian Government which is
well worth reproducing. A native Christian gentleman
applied for employment in the Bengal Inspecting Educational Department. In reply he received the following
letter from the Inspector of Schools, Presidency Circle :—
" Memo. No. 1548. In reply to your application of this
day, the Director of Public Instruction informs me that the

---

*A few brief Remarks on Mr. Cotton's " New India," Chapter IX.
By Behari Lal Chandra. Calcutta, 1886.

order of the Secretary of State for India that no Christian
shall be employed in the Inspecting Educational Service is
still in force.—(Signed) C. B. CLARKE." It might be
worth while, if there is a Christian in the House of Com-
mons, to have a question put whether this order tabooing
Christians and Christianity is still in force, and if it is can-
celled, *when* this measure of common justice was meted out
by the servants of a Christian sovereign. So far as we
can understand, "No Christian need apply" has been,
and may now be, the order of things in India.—*Church
Missionary Intelligencer, October*, 1887.

DENOUNCING TREMENDOUS EVILS.—Canon Hole, at a
meeting in Nottingham England, June 15, 1887, said:
"Seventy years ago, I quote from a statement published in
India, in the *Indian Watchman*, the fires of Suttee were
publicly blazing in the Presidency towns of Madras, Bombay and Calcutta, and all over India, the fires of Suttee, in
which the screaming and struggling widow, in many cases
herself a mere child, was bound to the dead body of her
husband, and with him burned to ashes. Seventy years
ago infants were publicly thrown into the Ganges, as sacrifices to the goddess of the river. Seventy years ago young
men and maidens, decked with flowers, were slain in Hindoo temples before the hideous idol of the goddess Kali,
or hacked to pieces as the Meras, that their quivering flesh
might be given to propitiate the god of the soil. Seventy
years ago the cars of Juggernaut were rolling over India,
crushing hundreds of human victims annually beneath their
wheels. Seventy years ago lepers were burned alive, de-
votees publicly starved themselves to death, children
brought their parents to the banks of the Ganges and hast-
ened their death by filling their mouths with the sand and
the water of the so-called sacred river. Seventy years ago
the swinging festivals attracted thousands to see the poor

writhing wretches, with iron hooks thrust through the mus-
cles of their backs, swing in mid-air in honor of their gods.
For these scenes, which disgraced India seventy years ago,
we may now look in vain. And need I remind you that
every one of these changes for the better is due directly or
indirectly to missionary enterprise, and the spirit of Christianity. It was Christian missionaries, and those who supported them, who proclaimed and denounced these tremendous evils. Branded as fanatics and satirized as fools, they
ceased not until one by one these hideous hallucinations
were suppressed." *

But though these monstrous evils prevailed seventy years
since, they were not declared illegal so long ago as that.
Even the burning alive of widows was not suppressed
until 1829, and some of the other great evils referred to by
Canon Hole were not made illegal until long after Suttee
was.† It has always required much agitation, and long
continued, both in India and England, to get the government of India to change its own objectionable course or to
suppress native enormities, and the leaders in these necessary agitations have always been able men among the missionaries, from Dr. Carey, who gained the first victory, the
abolition of Suttee, down to Dr. Murdoch, who gained the
last, the change in the government educational text-books.

How One Iniquity was Suppressed.—As an illustration of the successful methods employed by the mission-

---

* From the *Mission Field* for August, 1887.

† An enormity not referred to by Canon Hole, is thus alluded
to by the *Church Missionary Gleaner* for August, 1887 : "In 1837
the horrible league of religious assassins, called Thugs, was in
full swing, the devoted followers of Kali, whose profession was
murder, and their livelihood plunder; and Europeans would
attend her nautches and festivals, and her priests used often
publicly to make offerings to the idol in the name of the East
India Company.

aries, take the following from the *Church Missionary Intelligencer* for September, 1887 : " In 1838 or '39 the annual festival of the goddess Yaygathal, who is supposed to protect the Black Town of Madras, was approaching. The principal of the C. M. Institution (J. H. Gray), and his assistant, (J. J. H. Elouis), fired with indignation at the grossness of the idolatry annually practiced by the East India Company, on that occasion issued forth, the former with pen, and the latter with pencil in hand, the one to describe and the other to draw the scene witnessed.

The goddess borne in procession round the Black Town was at length carried to the gates of Fort St. George, where the English were supposed to reside, and which was in consequence called the White Town. A high official of the East India Company came out, bearing a handsome cashmere shawl as a bridal present to the idol, and a thaley, or ornament, which in native marriage is bound round the bride's neck by the bridegroom. In Christian native weddings it is used instead of the ring, and the words are used, " With this thaley I thee wed," &c. The high official having presented the shawl, and tied the thaley round the idol's neck, the marriage ceremony was completed between the East India Company and the idol Yaygathal, and the idol was asked to protect the Black Town during another year.

Then pen and pencil sketches of this grossly idolatrous act were sent home to Sir P. Maitland. He took them to Bishop Blomfield, of London, and the Bishop carried them to the House of Lords, held them up to view, and declared that if the connection between the East India Company and the idol system of India was not abolished, he would send the letter and sketch broadcast through the land. The threat was sufficient. The connection was severed, and the East India Company, which used to farm the revenues of the idol temples, to collect their rents and sanction the expenditure of their moneys, handed over the whole trust to native heathen to farm for themselves, and thus washed their hands of the whole concern."

TWO GREAT NATIVE EVILS.—Two great native evils, which are still upheld by the British rulers of India, child marriage and the cruel and barbarous treatment of widows, the missionaries are now endeavoring to have suppressed, and they believe that these could be more easily abolished now, than some of the enormities previously referred to were suppressed long ago. The prime minister of Indore, a cultured but orthodox Hindu, holds that Hindu civilization is doomed, unless the women are lifted out of their " present bondage of ignorance an superstition." He says, " child marriage is no marriage at all," that " the existence of the child widow is one of the darkest blots that ever defaced the civilization of any people." A Brahmin has published a tract on infanticide. He shows that the murder of 12,542 infants has been made public during the past 15 years. This catalogue represents only a fraction of the murders committed upon helpless Hindoos. This Brahmin gentleman charges these murders upon the enforced widowhood of Hindoo women.

In some respects the rule of the great native emperor Akbar, (A. D., 1558–1605), was in advance of what the English, after more than a century of supremacy in India, have yet attained. Sir Herbert Edwardes, in the lecture already referred to, says (page 15) : " In justice to the great Akbar, it should be stated that he preceded the English Government in the following measures : —1. He forbade Suttee *against the will of widows.* 2. He allowed widows to re-marry. 3. He abolished Pilgrim Taxes. 4. He reformed the Revenue. 5. He put all religions on an equality. And he went beyond the English Government in these, that—6. He forbade child-marriage—(that infanticide of heart and home). 7. He manifested great respect for Christianity; and ordered Fyzee, the brother of the Prime Minister, to translate the Gospels."

TWO GREAT GOVERNMENT EVILS.—The missionaries are also opposing energetically the abominable opium traffic of the Government of India, and also the encouragement given to the liquor traffic by certain of the provincial governments, notably those of Bengal, Bombay and Assam. In Bengal the returns from the excise duties on liquor have increased in seven years from three millions of dollars to five millions, and in Assam the revenue has trebled itself in ten years. A few months since a resolution was passed by the Bombay government and published, that one of the prominent ends to be aimed at is " to secure to consumers a supply of raw toddy at low prices ! "

Members of Parliament like Mr. Samuel Smith and Mr. W. S. Caine, who have recently visited India, declare, as do the missionaries, the surgeons in the British army and others, that intemperance is spreading in India, because certain local governments are not only encouraging the sale of liquor, but pushing it. There is a different state of things in the Northwestern provinces (the Punjaub), because they have a truly Christian Governor, Sir C. U. Aitcheson, and there are more Christian men in the government council than is the case elsewhere in India.

THE SUCCESS OF CHRISTIAN LABORS.—Though the missionaries have not neglected their duty as regards the objectionable measures of the government, and the tolerance of monstrous evils, their main work has been the preaching and teaching of the gospel of Christ, ministering to the sick in their homes and in the mission hospitals, and translating and circulating the Holy Scriptures and other Christian books. These labors have been greatly blessed of

God. Many thousands of native converts have died in the peace and joy of true believers in Christ. There are at present more than 150,000 communicants, more than 500,000 baptized converts, and about a million of adherents. The increase of communicants between 1861 and 1871 was 61 per cent.; between 1871 and 1881 it was 86 per cent., and in the present decade, it is believed that it will be more than 100 per cent. No persons are more outspoken as to the great value and decided success of missions in India than recent Viceroys and Governors, especially the Christian men among them.

TESTIMONY OF THE EARL OF NORTHBROOK AND OTHERS.—At a meeting in London in the beginning of 1887 the Earl of Northbrook, a returned Viceroy, bore testimony from his own observation to the beneficent influence of missions in India. General Herbert Edwardes and General Taylor, two of the most distinguished soldiers of the time; Lord Lawrence, one of the best administrators which India ever had; Sir Donald M'Leod, Sir Bartle Frere, and many others—these men were not only Christian men but far-sighted men, some of the best business men in the world, and they would never have given their approval to the missionary enterprise unless satisfied that those conducting it, did so on correct principles. Speaking from personal acquaintance, he could say that he had seen many missionaries, and many mission stations of various bodies, and he had on all occasions seen that these men were doing a great work, and in every way were gaining the affection of the people.

Sir Herbert Edwardes, in a speech delivered in Exeter Hall, London, in 1868, said : " Every other faith in India is decaying; Christianity alone is beginning to run its course. It has taken root, and, by God's grace, will never be uprooted. The Christian converts were tested by persecution and martyrdom in 1857, and they stood the test without apostacy; and I believe that, if the English were driven out of India to-morrow, Christianity would remain and triumph."

Sir Donald McLeod, Lieutenant-Governor (highest officer) of the Punjaub in 1872, writes : " In many places the impression prevails that our missions have not produced results adequate to the efforts which have been made ; but I trust enough has been said to prove that there is no real foundation for this impression ; and those who hold such opinions know but little of the reality. The work may be going on silently, but when the process of undermining the mountain of idolatry has been completed, the whole may be expected to fall with rapidity, and crumble to dust."

Sir C. U. Aitcheson, the present occupant of the position formerly held by Sir Donald McLeod, writes : " The changes that are to-day being wrought out by Christian missionaries in India are simply marvellous. Teaching wherever they go the universal brotherhood of man, and animated by a faith which goes beyond the ties of family caste and relationship, Christian missionaries are slowly, but none the less surely, undermining the foundations of Hindoo superstition, and bringing about a peaceful, religious, moral, and social revolution."

Sir Augustus Rivers Thompson, K. C. S. I., C. I. E., a Lieut.-Governor of Bengal, at a meeting in Calcutta before his return to England, said : " In my judgment, Christian missionaries have done more real and lasting good to the people of India than all other agencies combined. They have been the salt of the country, and the true saviors of the Empire." The Right Hon. W. E. Baxter, M. P., in his " Winter in India," says : " The teaching of the missionaries is shaking to its very centre the whole fabric of

heathen mythology. The upper and educated classes have
no belief in the gods of their fathers."

LORD LAWRENCE ON THE POPULARITY OF THE MIS-
SIONARIES.—At a meeting in London in behalf of Foreign Missions, Lord Lawrence bore the following testimony
to the character, influence and popularity of the missionaries
in India : He believed, notwithstanding all that the English
people had done to benefit that country, the missionaries
had done more than all other agencies combined. They
had had arduous and uphill work, often receiving no encouragement, and sometimes a great deal of discourage-
ment, from their own countrymen, and had to bear the
taunts and obloquy of those who despised and disliked
their preaching ; but such had been the effect of their earnest zeal, untiring devotion, and of the excellent example
which they had, he might say, universally shown to the
people, that he had no doubt whatever that, both universally and collectively, in spite of the great masses of the
people being intensely opposed to their doctrine—he had
no doubt whatever that, as a body, they were remarkably
popular in the country.

LORD NAPIER ON THE ATTRACTIVE PICTURES OF MIS-
SIONARY LIFE.—Lord Napier and Ettrick (formerly Governor of Madras), in a speech at Tanjore, reported in the
*Homeward Mail*, Nov. 27th, 1871, said : " My travels in
this Presidency are now drawing to a close, but when I
shall revert to them in the midst of other engagements and
other scenes, memory will offer no more attractive pictures
than those which will reproduce the features of missionary
life. In Ganjam, in Masulipatam, in North Arcot, in Travancore, in Tinnevelly, in Tanjore, I have broken the missionary's bread, I have been present at his administrations
I have witnessed his teaching, I have seen the beauty of
his life. The benefits of missionary enterprise are felt in

7

three directions—in converting, civilizing and teaching the Indian people.   It is not easy to overrate the value in this vast empire of a class of Englishmen of pious lives and disinterested labors, living and moving in the most forsaken places, walking between the Government and the people, with devotion to both, the friends of right, the adversaries of wrong, impartial spectators of good and evil."

SIR BARTLE FRERE ON THE GREAT CHANGES EFFECTED.—Sir Bartle Frere (formerly Governor of Bombay), in a lecture on " Christianity suited to all forms of Civilization," delivered in connection with the Christian Evidence Society, London, July 9, 1872, said : " I speak simply as to matters of experience and observation, and not of opinion ; just as a Roman prefect might have reported to Trajan or the Antonines ; and I assure you that, whatever you may be told to the contrary, the teaching of Christianity among 160 millions of civilized, industrious Hindoos and Mohammedans in India is effecting changes, moral, social, and political, which for extent and rapidity of effect are far more extraordinary than anything you or your fathers have witnessed in modern Europe."

SIR WILLIAM MUIR ON THE WORK OF THE AMERICAN AND CONTINENTAL MISSIONARIES.—Sir William Muir, late Lieutenant-Governor of the Northwest Provinces, in a speech delivered at the Mildmay Missionary Conference, held in 1876, gave the following testimony to the work of American and Continental Societies in India : " I would say one word with reference to the exertions of the American and Continental Societies in India.   I have had the opportunity of seeing their work in Upper India, and I have tendered to them my grateful and hearty thanks for the great work which they are doing—a work which bears not only on the spiritual regeneration of India, but on the civilization, the education, the enlightenment of its people.

I think, therefore, that Englishmen are under the deepest obligations to our American and Continental friends for their exertions in that country." ·

SIR RICHARD TEMPLE ON THE BRIGHT EXAMPLE OF THE MISSIONARIES.—One of the most competent of all the witnesses which India can furnish is Sir Richard Temple, Bart., G. C. S. I., D. C. L. He has been nearly 30 years in India, and has held office in every province but one. He has been Commissioner of the Central Provinces, Lieutenant-Governor of Bengal, Governor of Bombay, and Finance Minister of India. In his very able and comprehensive work entitled, " India in 1880," he writes as follows, on the bright example of the missionaries in every good word and work :

"The natives must inevitably perceive some alloy in British virtue ; there is much which they think blameworthy in British conduct. It is well that in the religious missions they should behold something of which the merit is unalloyed, and with which no fault can reasonably be found. The missionaries themselves display an example the brightness of which is reflected on the nations to which they belong. They are to be heard preaching in every city, and almost in every large town throughout the empire. They are considerately attentive to every inquirer and listener. They are held to be among the best teachers and schoolmasters in the country, even at a time when the educational staff of the Government affords a model of organization. They receive heathen children in the mission schools, not withholding Christian instruction, and yet they retain the unabated confidence of the heathen parents. They are trusted as benevolent advisers by their native neighbors. They are known as friends in need and trouble, and as being ready to advocate temperately the redress of wrongs or the removal of oppression. In seasons of pestilence and of famine, they have been vigilant in forecasting evil consequences and instant in dispensing aid. They have been among the foremost in the voluntary bands of relief.

They have often afforded to the Government and to its officers information which could not have been so well obtained otherwise. They have done much to elucidate before their countrymen and before the world the customs, the institutions, and the feelings of the natives. They have contributed greatly to the culture of the vernacular languages; many of them as scholars, historians, sociologists or lexicographers, have held a high place in Oriental literature, and have written books of lasting fame and utility. They have, with the co-operation of their wives and daughters, accomplished much towards establishing and promoting female education, and have exemplified before the natives the sphere of usefulness that may be occupied by educated women. They have enabled the natives to note the beauty of British homes, which shed abroad the light of charitable ministration and diffuse the genial warmth of practical philanthropy." (p. 176.)

SIR RICHARD TEMPLE ON THE MISSIONS BEING FAILURES.—In a speech delivered at Lincoln, England, November 7th, 1881, Sir Richard Temple said : "I will ask you to consider in what does failure or success consist ? What would you consider to be a successful result ? What is the result ? Why, that at this moment there are 390,000 native Christians in India, of whom 100,000 are communicants. Besides these there are 200,000 boys and girls at school, who, though not all of them Christians, are entrusted by heathen parents to the missionaries, and are receiving Christian instruction. Out of these no less than 40,000 are girls. So that, with converts and scholars, there are 590,000 persons, or, in round numbers, 600,000 altogether.

Statistics, you will remember, are furnished by missionaries, and the objectors may not altogether accept missionary figures. But my figures are taken not only from the missionary reports, but verified from the official reports of the Government of India—and are particularly confirmed by the returns of the census which is periodically taken in India.

"The romance, if it be a romance, consists greatly, I might say, sublimely, of the following array of figures: We have 432 mission stations, 500 European missionaries, and 8 missionary Bishops, 4,500 native assistants, 300 native ordained clergy,* 85 training schools, and 4 normal institutions, from which are turned out 3,000 students annually. We raise £20,000 a year from poor native Christians. We have 24 mission presses, from which there issue three-quarters of a million of religious books annually, which are sold to the native public for a sum of £3,800 a year. We have 400,000 native Christians, and 200,000 boys and girls at school of whom 1,700 have at different times entered the universities established by law in India, and of whom again 700 have passed on to taking of degrees. There are 40,000 girls at school, and 1,300 classes for the Zenana missions in the apartments of the native ladies, and those classes are attended by 3,000 lady students. I feel in giving those figures as if I were reading the record of some great State Department, and not of private enterprise such as this really is. I will say that it is truly honorable to the zeal of the Protestant Church."

SIR CHARLES AITCHESON ON THE STARTLING LEAVENING PROCESS.—Among men of large and varied official experience in India is Sir Charles Aitcheson, the present Lieutenant-Governor (highest officer) of the Punjaub. In a letter written in 1886, he says:

---

* There are now about 600.—J. L.

"Missionary teaching and Christian literature are leavening native opinion in a way and to an extent quite startling to those who take a little personal trouble to investigate the facts. Out of many examples I could give, take one. I know one of the ruling princes of India who probably never saw or spoke to a Christian missionary in his life. After a long talk with me on religious matters, he told me himself that he reads the Sanskrit translation of our Bible and prays to Jesus Christ every day for the pardon of his sins. It is not too much to say that the whole Brahma movement, which takes a lead in all social and moral reforms in India, and which, although decidedly unchristian, pays to Christianity the sincere flattery of imitation, is the direct product of missionary teaching.

"Any one who wishes to appreciate what missions have done for India cannot do better than read the recent biography of Carey, by Dr. Geo. Smith (John Murray, 1885), particularly the three chapters: 'What Carey did for Literature and for Humanity;' 'What Carey did for Science,' and 'Carey as an Educator.' The same work the missionaries are doing still. They have been the pioneers of education, both vernacular and English, and they are still the only body who maintain schools for the low castes and the poor. To them we owe even the reduction of several of the vernacular languages (in this part of India, for example, Sindi and Pushtu) to written characters. The only translation opening up to us the sacred books of the Sikhs we owe to a missionary (Dr. Trumpp). To the missionaries, and the missionaries alone, we owe the movement in favor of female education; and the remarks in the last education report for the Punjaub, and the review thereof, show how efficient are the mission female schools, and how highly the labors of the missionaries are appreciated by the Government. It was at the suggestion

of the missionaries that I have this year framed and introduced a system of Government grants in aid of hospitals
and dispensaries. It is to the example set by missionary
ladies, during the last eight or ten years, in mission hospitals and in house to house visitation, that the present wide-
spreading demand for medical aid and medical training to
the women of India is mainly due. Apart altogether from
the strictly Christian aspect of the question, which is of itself so full of bright hopes that no Christian man who
reflects on what has already been achieved, can fail to
thank God and take great courage, I should, from a purely
administrative point of view, deplore the drying-up of Christian liberality to missions in this country as a most lamentable check to social and moral progress, and a grievous
injury to the best interests of the people."

SIR WILLIAM HUNTER'S REMARKABLE LECTURE.—
A remarkable lecture was lately delivered in London
before the Indian Section of the Society of Arts, by Sir
William Hunter, the accomplished author of the " Imperial
Gazetteer of India." It was on the dayspring of missionary
labor in India, and its present great development and success. Concerning the former, he said :

" English missionary work practically began in the last
year of the last century. It owed its origin to private
effort. But the three devoted men who planted this mighty
English growth had to labor under the shelter of a foreign
flag, and the governor of a little Danish settlement had to
refuse to surrender to a Governor-General of British India.
The record of the work done by the Serampur missionaries
reads like an Eastern romance. They created a prose
vernacular literature for Bengal ; they established the
modern method of popular education ; they founded the
present Protestant Indian Church ; they gave the first
great impulse to the native Press ; they set up the first

steam engine in India ; with its help they introduced the
modern manufacture of paper on a large scale ; in ten years
they translated and printed the Bible, or parts thereof, in
thirty-one languages   Although they received help from
their Baptist friends in England, yet the main part of their
funds they earned by their own heads and hands.   They
built a college, which still ranks among the most splendid
educational edifices in India   As one contemplates its
magnificent pillared façade overlooking the broad Hugli
River, or mounts its costly staircase of cut brass (the gift
of the King of Denmark), one is lost in admiration at the
faith of three poor men who dared to build on so noble a
scale.

"From their central seminary they planted out their converts into the districts, building churches and supporting
pastors chiefly from the profits of their boarding-school,
their paper mill, and printing press.   They blessed God that
during thirty-eight years of toil they were able to spend
more than £50,000 of their own substance on His work."

ENORMOUS INCREMENTS.—Concerning the   immense
progress in the missions from 1851 to 1881, Sir William
Hunter said : " In 1851, the Protestant missions in India
and Burmah had 222 stations ; in 1881, their stations had
increased nearly three-fold to 601.  But the number of their
churches or congregations had during the same thirty years
multiplied from 267 to 4,180, or over fifteen-fold.  There
is not only a vast increase in the number of the stations,
but also a still greater increase in the work done by each
station within itself.   In the same way, while the number
of native Protestant Christians increased from 91,092  in
1851, to 492,882 in 1881, or five-fold, the number of communicants increased from 14,661 to 138,254, or nearly ten-
fold.  The progress is again, therefore, not alone in numbers,
but also in pastoral care and internal discipline.  During the

same thirty years the pupils in mission schools multiplied by three-fold, from 64,043 to 196,350. These enormous increments have been obtained by making a larger use of native agency. A native Protestant Church has, in truth, grown up in India, capable of supplying, in a large measure, its own staff. In 1851, there were only twenty-one ordained native ministers; by 1881 they had increased to 575, or twenty-seven-fold. The number of native lay preachers had risen during the thirty years from 493 to the vast total of 2,856."

This distinguished Indian administrator and author says in an article in a late number of *The Nineteenth Century :* " The careless onlooker may have no particular convictions on the subject, and flippant persons may ridicule religious effort in India as elsewhere. But I think that few Indian administrators have passed through high office, and had to deal with ultimate problems of British government in that assembly, without feeling the value of the work done by the missionaries. Such men gradually realize, as I have realized, that the missionaries do really represent the spiritual side of the new civilization, and of the new life which we are introducing into India.' He also says that the confidence of the people of India in the purity and unselfishness of the motives of the missionaries is complete, and that neither the officials nor any other class of foreign residents is held in so much esteem as they are.

TESTIMONY OF PRINCE HARNAM SINGH.—Among the distinguished persons who went to London for the Queen's Jubilee was Prince Harnam Singh, of Kapurthala, a semi-independent State adjoining the Punjaub. The Prince is a Christian, having been baptized in 1873, at a serious sacrifice of his worldly interests. At a reception which was given him by the Church Missionary Society, while he was in London, he said :

" Do we look back to the work done by such eminent men as our most distinguished statesmen, Lord Dalhousie, Lord Canning, Lord Lawrence, Lord Ripon, or even the present grand representative of her Majesty in India, Lord Dufferin, for the new light that has been shed over that dark continent ? No! we look back to the time when such men as Marshman and Carey, and pre-eminently that great and learned man—that devoted servant of Christ— Dr. Duff, first introduced that mysterious volume, the word of God, which shows a man the secrets of his own heart, and tells him how he can be reconciled to an offended God as no other book does.

" They have been followed throughout India by missionaries sent out by many societies, of which this Society is one of the most distinguished, whose labors in their pulpits and their schools are beginning to bear fruit out of all proportion to their number. I feel sure that with the aid of all these valuable societies the time is not far distant when the full light will shine in India as the midday sun, and my country will throw away its idols and bow itself before the unseen God, who makes Himself known in His revealed Word, and by His Spirit which dwelleth in man."

NATIVE ADMISSIONS AS TO SUCCESS.—Hear what Keshub Chunder Sen, the Brahmin theist, says : " Who rules India ? What power sways its destiny at the present moment ? (He was writing when Lord Lytton was in the Cabinet.) Not Lord Lytton in the Cabinet, nor Sir Frederick Haines in the field, not politics, nor diplomacy, nor the bayonet or cannon. Christ rules British India. India is unconsciously imbibing this new civilization, succumbing to its irresistible influence. It is not the British army that deserves the honor of holding India ; if any army can claim that honor, that army is the army of Christian missionaries headed by their invincible Captain, Jesus

Christ." Here is the admission of the *Indu Prakash*, the native Bombay newspaper: "We daily see Hindoos, of every caste, becoming Christians and devoted 'missionaries of the cross.'"

The following is from an address recently delivered in Bombay by an educated Hindu who is not a professing Christian : "Cast your eyes around, and take a survey of the nations abroad! What has made England great? Christianity! What has made the other nations of Europe great? Christianity! What has started our present religious Somajas all over India? Contact with Christian missionaries! Who began female education in Bombay? The good old Dr. Wilson and Mrs. Wilson, of beloved and honored memory. Christians again! Christianity has not only been the saviour of man's soul, but the regeneration of man's habitation on earth."

TESTIMONY OF A WATCHFUL BRAHMIM.—A learned Brahmin, at the close of a lecture by Dr. Chamberlain, a missionary clergyman and physician, in the presence of nearly two hundred Brahmins, officials, students and others, said :

"I have watched the missionaries and seen what they are. What have they come to this country for? What tempts them to leave their parents, friends and country, and come to this, to them, unhealthy clime? Is it for gain or profit that they come? Some of us, country clerks in government offices, receive larger salaries than they. Is it for an easy life? See how they work, and then tell me.

"Look at the missionary. He came here a few years ago, leaving all, and for our good! He was met with cold looks and suspicious glances. He sought to talk with us of what, he told us, was the matter of most importance in heaven and earth; but we would not hear. He was not discouraged; he opened a dispensary, and we said, 'Let the pariahs (lowest caste people) take his medicine, we won't;' but in the time of our sickness and our fear we were glad to go to him, and he welcomed us. We complained at first if he walked through our Brahmin streets; but ere long, when our wives and daughters were in sickness and anguish, we went and begged him to come—even into our inner apartments—and he came, and our wives and daughters, now smile upon us in health ! Has he made any money by it ? Even the cost of the medicine he has given has not been returned to him.

"Now what is it that makes him do all this for us ? It is the Bible ! I have looked into it a good deal in different languages I chance to know. It is the same in all languages. The Bible ! there is nothing to compare with it, in all our sacred books, for goodness and purity, and holiness, and love, and for motives of action. Where did the English people get their intelligence and energy and cleverness and power ? It is the Bible that gives it to them. And they now bring it to us and say, 'That is what raised us; take it and raise yourselves.' They do not force it upon us, as did the Mohammedans with their Koran, but they bring it in love and say, 'Look at it, read it, examine it, and see if it is not good.' Of one thing I am convinced: Do what we will, oppose it as we may, it is the Christian Bible that will, sooner or later, work the regeneration of our land !"

A LARGE NUMBER OF BRAHMINS BAPTIZED.—Referring to a remarkable missionary event at a recent festival in India when 248 persons were baptized, the majority of them Brahmins, the *Indian Witness* says: "We cannot believe that this extraordinary movement will end with the dispersion of the people who attended the fair. A hundred thousand busy tongues will tell the story over and over again, and by this time it is known to 10,000,000 of people in North India that Brahmins and other high caste people are accepting Christianity freely." The *Missionary Review* says: " A few years ago, among the Telugus in Eastern India, so many streamed to Christ that the hands of the missionary were weary baptizing. Has the stream lessened? It has increased, till it now rolls in a volume of 200 baptisms every month."

LIBERAL GIVING BY FOREIGN RESIDENTS IN INDIA. —British and other foreign residents in India give more than $300,000 a year to the missions in that country, which shows what they think of them. The late Hugh Miller, M. D., after living many years in India, gave to the missions $100,000. Col. W. J. Martin, who died at Torquay, England, March 18th, 1886, gave more than $10,000 to the Punjaub and Peshawar Missions, and then gave himself to the work as a self-supporting lay missionary. His example of liberal money-giving, and then of personal service, has been imitated by Mr. H. E. Perkins, for many years the Commissioner of Amritsar, and others. Dr. Butler, in his " Land of the Veda," page 431, says, in speaking of Colonel Gowan: " This devoted servant of God encouraged and stood by me in all my future plans for the extension of our mission. He aided me in procuring homes for the missionaries, in establishing our Orphanage and Training School, and he built and endowed the schools in Khera Bajhera, (the village where he was so long sheltered,)* so that his liberality to our mission work up to the present, cannot be much less than $15,000."

NATIVE PRINCES CONTRIBUTING.—Some of the native princes and officials also contribute liberally to the missionary work. A recent number of the *Church Missionary Intelligencer* says: " The new Dewan, or Prime Minister, of Travancore, T. Rama Row, through not a Christian, is

---

* When wounded during the Mutiny.

a great friend of the C. M. S. Mission. ' His appointment,' writes the Rev. W. J. Richards, ' is the best thing external to the Church of Christ, which has taken place for generations.' When he was a lower official, he transferred his office establishment to Cottayam, the chief C. M. S. station, in order, he said, ' to be near the light.' The present Maharajah, also, lately sent Mr. Richards 500 rupees for his projected Leper Asylum at Allepie."

There is a girls' school carried on in Bombay by a native Christian woman. This lady, with her husband, recently visited the court of the Guikwar of the Baroda and met a hearty reception in the prince's zenana. His Highness had several interviews with the Christians himself, and was delighted with their conversation. Before they left the State his Highness gave Mrs. Kanaren four thousand rupees, or about two thousand dollars, for her school.

UNSALARIED MISSIONARIES IN INDIA.—The Rev. M. M. Carleton writes as follows to the editor of the *Missionary Review* concerning the unsalaried missionaries in India : " We find in the foreign field men and women from England who have gone out among the heathen with independent fortunes of their own. They give their wealth *plus themselves* to missionary work. During the thirty-two years I have been in India, I have known several of this class of English missionaries. They are among the best workers in the mission field. They come from old English families distinguished for generations both in Church and State. Some of them enter the mission field with private fortunes of half a million of dollars, and with this wealth they give their own lives freely to the cause of missions.

THE CONTRIBUTIONS OF NATIVE CONVERTS. — In " India," by Rev. J. T. Gracey, we read : " The contributions of the native converts themselves show most encouraging growth. The London Missionary Society said a few years since of its missions on the Malabar coast : 'Several of the churches are self-supporting : the contributions have reached $7,000 a year, which, considering what is paid for labor in that country, is equal to $40,000 at least of our currency.' The South India Mission of the Church of England Missionary Society contributed one year $13,582 in gold. The aggregated contributions of the native Christian community in India, Burmah and Ceylon rose from about 60,000 rupees in 1861, to 159,124 rupees in 1871, and to 228,517 rupees in 1881."

THE NATIVES TRUST ONLY THE MISSIONARIES.—In "Protestant Foreign Missions," by Theodore Christlieb, D. D., Ph.D., page 186, we read : "The moral influence of Christianity and of Christians in China, and also in India, is almost wholly sustained through the missionaries alone. 'But for the English missionaries,' says *The Friend of India* (a secular organ), 'the natives of India would have a very poor opinion of Englishmen. The missionary alone, of all Englishmen, is the representative of a disinterested desire to elevate and improve the people.' And a Hindoo in very high standing said a short time ago to the wife of a missionary closely related to myself, 'You missionaries are the only persons in whom we really have confidence.' Hence they are a very important bond between the little loved English government and the Indian people."

---

# JAPAN.

THE FIRST PROTESTANT MISSION IN JAPAN.—The following mention of the first Protestant mission established in Japan is from "A Historical Sketch of the Japan Mission of the Protestant Episcopal Church of the United States of America" (New York, 1883) :

" We now come to the first direct missionary movement on the part of the Protestant Episcopal Church.   Early in 1859 the Rev. John Liggins, who had been laboring for four years as a missionary in China, visited Japan for the benefit of his health, and met with an unexpectedly cordial reception from the Japanese officials.   A few days after his arrival at Nagasaki he received information that the Foreign Committee had appointed the Rev. Channing Moore Williams and himself as missionaries to Japan. Being already in the field, Mr. Liggins at once entered upon his duties, and thus was established the first Protestant Mission in the Empire of Japan.

" Mr. Williams reached Nagasaki in the latter part of June, and in September of the same year Dr. H. Ernst Schmid was appointed missionary physician.   Great interest was manifested in the church regarding the new mission, and the visit of Bishop Boone, of China, to Philadelphia, accompanied by a deputation from the Foreign Committee, was made the occasion of special services in behalf of the movement.   The first pecuniary aid was the sum of $200, contributed by St. Mark's Church, New York, toward the support of the first missionary.

" Meanwhile, Mr. Liggins found that but little could be done at first beyond learning the Japanese language (a sufficiently formidable task), teaching English to native officials, and furnishing the Holy Scriptures and scientific works to those who would accept or purchase them. Among his labors was the preparation and publication of a book entitled ' One Thousand Familiar phrases in English and Japanese,' which met with a large demand and passed through several editions.

" Mr. Liggins' visitors evinced much curiosity as to the nature of the religious views which he came to impart, but were greatly shocked to learn that he was a *Ki-ris-itan*, or

Christian, as that was the term by which the Jesuits were formerly known, and in their minds it was synonymous with all that was vile. Upon learning that the missionary sympathized with their opposition to some of the doctrines and practices of the Jesuits, they were greatly astonished, and eagerly sought further information."

THE WONDERFUL CHANGES IN LESS THAN THIRTY YEARS.—The wonderful changes in Japan which have been effected in less than thirty years, and the remarkable progress which has been made in the Christianizing of the people, are very generally known.

Missionaries from various Christian bodies in the United States, Canada, and Great Britain, have gradually joined in the work, and it has been so greatly blessed of God that there are already sixteen thousand Church members* one hundred and ninety-three organized churches, of which sixty-four are self-supporting, ninety-three native ministers, one hundred and sixty-nine preparing for the ministry, and a hundred and sixty unordained preachers and helpers. The prospect is that in one or two more decades the idols will be utterly abolished in Japan, and this " Land of the Rising Sun," be as much a Christian nation as those now generally so-called are, if not much more so.

The Buddhist priests have already dwindled from 244,000 to 50,000. " The telegraph stretches from one end of the land to the other. The mail service is admirable. Railways cross the country in various directions, and fleets of steamers ply from port to port up and down the coast. Banks and hospitals have been established. Daily newspapers abound. There is an excellent system of education culminating in a university. The army and navy are or-

---

* While this work was going through the press, we learn that the number is now 20,000, and that there is an increase of 500 a month.

ganized after foreign models.   A new code of laws, based upon those of Europe, has been adopted.   In the year 1890 there is to be a parliament."

A NOBLE BODY OF CULTURED LADIES AND GENTLE-MEN.—The most comprehensive and best American book on Japan is "The Mikado's Empire," by William Elliott Griffis, A. M., late of the Imperial University of Tokio, Japan.   New York, 1876.   On page 345 Mr. Griffis says: " It is hard to find an average man of the world in Japan who has any clear idea of what the missionaries are doing or have done.   Their dense ignorance borders on the ridiculous."   On pages 577–8 he says :

" Let us note what America has done.   Our missionaries, a notable body of cultured gentlemen and ladies, with but few exceptions, have translated large portions of the Bible in a scholarly and simple version, and thus given to Japan the sum of religious knowledge and the mightiest moral force and motor of civilization.   The standard Japanese-English and English-Japanese dictionary is the fruit of fourteen years' labor of an eminent scholar, translator, physician and philanthropist, J. C. Hepburn, M. D., LL. D. The first grammar of the Japanese language printed in English, the beginnings of a Christian popular literature and hymnology, the organization of Christian churches, the introduction of theological seminaries, and of girls' schools, are the work of American ladies and gentlemen."

" Gently, but resistlessly, Christianity is leavening the nation.   In the next century the native word *inaka* (rustic, boor,) will mean ' heathen.'   With those forces that centre in pure Christianity, and under that Almighty Providence who raises up one nation and casts down another, I cherish the firm hope that Japan will in time take and hold her equal place among the foremost nations of the world, and that, in the onward march of civilization which follows the

s'in, the Sun-land may lead the nations of Asia that are
now appearing in the theatre of universal history."

Miss Isabella L. Bird's Testimony.— The distinguished traveller and author, Miss Isabella L. Bird, in her
work, "Unbeaten Tracks in Japan " (1880), says : " Christ-
tianity is destined to be a power in moulding the future of
Japan, I do not doubt. It is tending to bind men together irrespective of class, in a true democracy in a very surprising way. The small Christian congregations are pecuni-
arily independent, and are vigorous in their efforts. The
Kobe congregation, numbering 350 members, beside contributing nearly $1,000 to erect a church, sustaining its
own poor, providing medicine and advice for its indigent
sick, and paying its own pastor, engages in various forms
of benevolent effort, and compensates Christians who are too
poor to abstain from work on Sunday for the loss of a day's
wages. At Osaka the native Christians have established a
Christian school for their girls. The Christian students in
Kioto are intensely zealous, preach through the country in
their vacations, and aim at nothing less than the Christianizing of Japan."

"The practical sagacity with which the Americans man-
age their missions is worthy of notice. So far from seeking for a quantity of converts, they are mainly solicitous
for quality. They might indeed baptize hundreds where
they are content with tens. The same remark applies to
Dr. Palm, and the missionaries of C. M. S. at Hakodate
and Niigata. There are hundreds of men and women scattered throughout this neighborhood who are practically
Christians, who meet together to read the Bible, and who
subscribe for Christian objects, but have never received
baptism."

"I have the highest respect for both the Niigata missionaries. They are true, honest, conscientious men, not

sanguine or enthusiastic, but given up to the work of making Christianity known in the way which seems best to each of them, because they believe it to be the work indicated by the Master. They are alike incapable of dressing up "cases for reports," of magnifying trifling encouragements, of suppressing serious discouragements, or of responding in any unrighteous way to the pressure brought to bear upon missionaries by persons at home, who are naturally anxious for results. Dr. Palm, for some time a childless widower, has had it in his power to itinerate regularly and extensively among the populous towns and villages contained within the treaty limits of twenty-five miles. Mr. and Mrs. Tyson offer what is very important in this land of loose morals, the example of a virtuous Christian home, in which servants are treated with consideration and justice, and in which a singularly sensitive conscientiousness penetrates even the smallest details."

Professor Rein on the Missionaries and their Hinderers.—A very elaborate work on the Sunrise Kingdom is, "Japan : Travels and Researches Undertaken at the Cost of the Prussian Government. By J. J. Rein, Professor of Geography in Marburg. Translated from the German." In the New York edition (1884) page 464, we read : "The missionaries, who are good speakers and are masters of the language, have always a large number of attentive hearers, and are forming congregations which justify the largest expectations. The greatest hindrances in the way of the preaching of the Gospel have disappeared ; and the country is more and more approximating to complete religious liberty. Yet the missionaries have no lack of difficulties with which to contend ; the greatest and most lamentable being, not so much the indifference of the heathen Japanese, or the variety of Christian confessions, as the indifference, nay, even the enmity,

6

towards Christianity of many foreigners, who gave utterance to their feeling by word and deed. The Japanese
will, however, learn to distinguish between those who
merely bear the name of Christians, and those whose
thoughts and acts are guided and ennobled by Christian
doctrine, and will no longer estimate the value of Christianity by the former."

MR. MACLAY ON THE WORK AT YOKOHAMA.—The
latest book on the Sunrise Kingdom, is "A Budget of Letters
from Japan," by Arthur Collins Maclay, A.M., LL.B., (New
York, 1884). Mr. Collins was employed for five years
as Instructor in English in government colleges in Hirosa-
ki, Tokio and Kioto. His letters may be said to describe
the halcyon days of foreign school teaching in Japan. Mr.
Collins made trips into the various parts of the country,
and at almost all times he had the benefit of the compan-
ionship of intelligent natives. His book is one of considerable interest, and it treats of some topics not referred to
by other writers on Japan. Of the missionary work in
Yokohama and its vicinity he writes (pp. 200–201) as follows :

"In addition to abundant preaching and teaching,
much good is accomplished by a well-organized medical
dispensary. There are also a number of seminaries and
foundling asylums. In no part of Japan is there such an
abundant distribution of religious literature. In various
ways at least three thousand people must hear the truth
every week. Places for preaching and instruction are rent-
ed in many of the villages surrounding Yokohama, and
there are places in the country where weekly or monthly
visits are paid. And occasionally a Japanese from the far
interior will request a missionary to accompany him to his
native village among the mountains to expound the Scriptures to his friends who are too poor to come to Yokohama.

Much good seed is thus cast. When the missionary reaches the village he puts up at a hotel. He then informs the landlord that he wishes to preach in his room. Permission is generally easily obtained. The *shojees* are then removed, thus throwing all the rooms into one. The talking then begins in a conversational way, and the crowd begins to gather until the streets and yard are packed with listeners. The exhorter then steps out on the veranda, and preaches to a respectful gathering for a couple of hours at a time.

The people are champion listeners. They wear an ordinary man out. They are insatiate. They come three or four times a day urging a continuance of the speech. I knew one missionary who began at four o'clock in the afternoon, and when he was exhausted, his native helpers carried on the exhortation until nine o'clock at night. Of course sermonizing is not resorted to. Simply the barest recital of the life, the work, the agony of our Redeemer seems to claim their attention. The people then disperse. Very few of them, perhaps, will be baptized. But curiosity has been awakened to know about this extraordinary religion; books are bought; and when the missionary makes his next visit, he will find a number of earnest inquirers after the truth. The good that will result from this kind of circuit work is incalculable. Nor are the missionaries in Yokohama negligent of their own countrymen. Through their influence a temperance hall and reading-room has been established. They preach on Sundays in English at the church in the settlement, and they are interested in other good works."

THE MISSIONARIES AND THE FOREIGN COMMUNITY.—Mr. Maclay says, on pages 204 and 205 : " The presence of missionaries is a continued rebuke to the greater portion of the foreign community, who are leading lives they would not think of leading at home. The natives are soon taught that these foreigners are living beneath their duties and privileges. They soon learn to point this fact with cutting and contemptuous observations, which gall the recipients thereof exceedingly. They naturally say that the missionaries must be of a higher caste. And they soon begin to draw a line between the two portions of the community; one portion is bent on gain; it is selfish and grasping, it abuses its servants, deals harshly with the natives, and is licentious; the other portion acts justly toward all, so that servants are anxious to secure them as masters, and the merchants are always on the *qui vive* to open accounts with them. They learn the language accurately and elegantly, and instruct the people carefully and thoroughly, and the people soon begin to love and respect them."

A THOROUGHLY CHARACTERISTIC STORY.—The following from Mr. Maclay's book (pp. 215–216) deals with a subject of great importance : "The Japanese who have been so assiduously introducing our civilization, are now startled with the discovery that they have been but the pioneers for Christian missionaries. They now see that the intellectual qualities, the animal passions, and the selfish desires of natives under Christian influences are controlled and curbed by some moral power that they had not noticed. And they also see that but for the checking force of these moral principles, the tremendous faculties of Europe and America would be dangerous to the world."

" While they have assiduously cultivated the intellectual faculties of their youth, are intensifying their appetites and passions by nourishing and stimulating food, yet they have put no guide on the road, have put no brake on the wheels, have introduced no moral power to restrain the undue exercise of these mental and physical powers. They find Shintoism and Buddhism quite powerless to do so. Nor can the copious and bitter draughts of infidelity, already freely imbibed, accomplish this end. Nothing under the sun but the gospel of Christ can do it."

"This fact was most whimsically acknowledged by the Japanese when the Mitsui Bank was started in Tokio. This is a national bank, and is backed up with the money of the Government. Young Japanese had been specially educated abroad to carry on the banking system on approved foreign principles. They were intelligent, capable and shrewd. They made excellent cashiers, tellers, book-keepers and clerks, so far as the merely executive qualities were concerned. They possessed every intellectual requirement necessary for the carrying on of a bank. But they were *too* intelligent! They were so thoroughly acquainted with financing that they understood many little methods of deflecting cash from the treasury into their own pockets. And there was no power except fear that could prevent their doing so; and fear had but little effect, as there was hardly any danger that the capitalists, composed of effete Daimios and of government officers unfamiliar with banking, could detect how the cash disappeared.

"In this predicament, one of the bank officers, with great candor and solicitude, came and explained the situation to one of the missionaries. He frankly admitted that he did not believe in any religion whatsoever. He claimed that the Japanese intellect was of too philosophical a nature to accept the Jewish myth called Christianity. 'But,' said he, 'your religion does something that our religion cannot do. *It makes men honest.* Now, we wish our employees at the bank to be carefully instructed in these principles, so that they may learn to discharge their duties with scrupulous integrity.' This story is thoroughly characteristic."

A YOUNG OFFICER'S LEGACY.—In September last year (1885), Mr. Alfred T. Knight, B. A., of St. John's

College, Cambridge, naval instructor of H. M. S. "Auda-cious," died in the naval hospital at Yokohama, Japan. He left all he possessed, about £320, to the Church Mis-sionary Society, "as likely to secure," writes his father, the Rev. T. Knight, of Woodford, Wilts, "in the most efficient way the promotion of the Gospel of the Lord and Master he so dearly loved, and so ardently desired to serve in life and death. He made it a point of honor to inquire on the spot, when possible, into any charges brought against mis-sionaries, and in no case did he find current stories to their discredit to be true; but he was enabled to testify on many occasions to the solid and truly Christian character of their work, and to their patient labor, suffering and self-denial." His desire was, when freed from official duties, to be a missionary himself.—*Church Missionary Gleaner.*

CAPTAIN BRINKLEY ON THE ONCE FORMIDABLE DIFFICULTIES AND THE PRESENT SUCCESS.—Captain T. Brinkley, R. A., in the article entitled, "A Tour in Japan," in the *Fortnightly Review* for May 1st, 1887, says:

"Now Christianity is beginning to win its way. The difficulties in its path were once very formidable. When Westerns first came to Japan they were received with open arms. In 1613 the illustrious Regent Iyeyasu made with Sir Thomas Smith, England's representative, a treaty which, in the words of the first article, gave "free license to the subjects of Great Britain for ever, to come safely in-to any of our ports of our Empire of Japan, with their ships and their merchandise, without any hindrance to them or their goods; and to abide, buy, sell and barter, according to their own manner with all nations; to tarry here as long as they think good, and to depart at their pleasure.' But this license was not long of fruitful gain. Already Jesuit intrigues and sectarian quarrels had led to disturbance and confusion. The Roman Catholic propagandists incited their disciples to destroy the temples of Buddha and to persecute the priests, while the Portuguese and Dutch traders rivalled each other in trickery and extortion. For the first time in her history Japan became acquainted with the horrors of religious feuds and intolerance.

"Her rulers at first sought by comparatively gentle means to control these abuses, but were subsequently constrained to banish the Portuguese altogether, and to adopt the severest measures of repression against the native Christians. The country ceased to be a profitable field for trade. The English settlers turned their ships homewards in 1628. Forty-five years later she tried to renew the treaty of Iyeyasu, but so vivid was the recollection of the intrigues and excesses of the early Roman Catholic propagandists, that the alliance between the royal families of Great Britain and Portugal, in the reign of Charles II., sufficed to close Japan against all Englishmen. Tradition deepened the dislike and the apprehension excited by the events of those early days. In Japanese eyes every alien became a *Bateren* (padre) and therefore an evil person harboring mischievous designs against the integrity of the empire.

" The Japanese is a patriot before everything. When foreigners came, in 1856, with ships of war, to force their intercourse upon the country, every brave man in the land believed himself bound by all the principles he respected, to expel the dangerous intruders. Happily this feeling did not long survive contact with Western civilization, but being rooted in the memory of Christian political intrigues, its last active vestiges were anti-Christian. The new preachers of the Christian faith had, therefore, a hard battle to fight. But they won their way gradually. There are now from forty to fifty thousand baptized Japanese Christians; and it is well known that several of the ablest and most influential statesmen in the empire advocate the adoption of a creed which they regard as the basis of European civilization. So far, however, as it is possible to foresee at present, absolute tolerance will be the attitude of the Government toward all faiths. There will be no State religion. When the new Civil Code, now completed and only waiting final revision—is promulgated, its first article will probably declare all creeds equal in the sight of the law. Practically they are already equal, for high official positions and chairs of learning are occupied by professing native Christians."

U. S. MINISTER HUBBARD ON THIS URGENTLY INVITING FIELD.—The Hon. R. B. Hubbard, U. S. Minister to Japan, writes to a friend in Texas, giving statistics of missionary work in Japan, and says: "A great field is 'wide open' now, and is becoming wider every year here in Japan for Christian evangelization. Here are 38,000,000 people on islands containing not much more than one-half of the area of the State of Texas! The whole country is accessible to the heralds of the Cross from all Christian lands. Within the past one-third of a century their awakening from a sleep of ages has been marvellous to the western world, and certainly without a parallel heretofore in history. In a word, they are ready and willing, in fact eagerly so, if convinced, to let the scales fall from their eyes, and to embrace new thoughts and creeds, whether of government, science or religion. Such a people, just at this special juncture, it seems to me, present the most inviting—urgently inviting—field for this great work, of all other oriental lands."

A NATIVE MINISTER'S TESTIMONY.—The Rev. Y. Hiraiwa, a native Japanese clergyman, is now temporarily in Canada. In a recent public address he said that prior to the arrival of Christian missionaries in Japan, the lower classes of Japanese were Buddhists, and they were usually very bigoted. The more intelligent people did not believe in any religion at all. Their experience of the native religions led them to regard all religion as superstition until they began to inquire into the doctrines of Christianity. The result of that inquiry was that many of them embraced the new religion ; in fact, it is from this class that the greatest number of converts to Christianity have been made. There is now a complete toleration of Christianity in Japan. The edict against Christianity has, it is true, not been repealed, but it has been allowed quietly to drop out of sight. A Japanese statesman gave a curious reason for not formally repealing the edict: " If we passed such a law it would show that Christianity was previously forbidden."

MR. ARTHUR L. SHUMWAY AS A WITNESS.—The attempt of a writer in the *Atlantic Monthly* to depreciate the character of the missionaries in Japan, has called forth a very complete vindication of their worth, and of the results of their labors, for Mr. Arthur L. Shumway, an accredited newspaper correspondent, who has travelled extensively in Japan and other Asiatic countries. In a letter in a late number of the *Christian Union*, he says he has made " a special study of the missionary's characteristics and his labor everywhere," and he asserts that this writer has " misrepresented missionary character." We give the following portion of his own testimony :

" In Japan I not only inspected the work in progress at the chief ports on the east coast, but also at Hiogo, Osaka, Kioli, Nagasaki and other points in the western half of the empire. Leaving Japan, I surveyed the work quite carefully in several cities in China, in Malaysia, in Burmah, in India, in Egypt, in Palestine, in Syria, in Greece, in Asia Minor, in Turkey, and in papal Europe. I studied the work both from without and from within. I went with

missionaries again and again on their tours of visitation. I
attended native services in missionary chapels. I visited
hospitals, asylums, homes, day-schools, Sunday-schools,
and printing stations. I inspected scores and scores of
missions, many on the beaten tracks of tourist travel and
many in the interior, far from the coast. In a number of
instances I lodged for several days at a time under missionary roofs, in places where hotel accommodations could not
be secured. What is true in Japan, I found to be true
elsewhere. . . . Missionaries are, almost without an
exception, men and women not only of the most exalted
Christian character, but also of the ripest scholarship and
intellectual culture.

" Turn to the Oriental shelves in our libraries, and you
will be amazed to find that nearly all of the brightest,
deepest and most valuable books there have been written
by missionaries. To missionary pens we are indebted for
the most reliable information that we have regarding the
far East, as well as for the most fascinating, poetical and
scholarly of the correct pictures of Oriental life that we
have. There are a few exceptions to this rule, but by their
very scarcity they only serve to prove the rule."

CONSUL SEYMOUR AND DR. KERR.—From a large
number of similarly conspicuous proofs of the worth, and
the self-denying labors of the missionaries, Mr. Shumway
selects the following reminiscence :

" One day as I was walking the streets of Canton, China,
with Mr. Charles Seymour, our American consul-general
in that great city, we met and passed a quiet, modest-man-
nered man on his way into the city. Said Mr. Seymour :

" ' Do you see that man yonder ?' pointing in the direction
of the receding stranger.

" I assented, and he continued :

" ' That is Dr. Kerr. He is in charge of the great missionary hospital yonder. The hospital was founded in 1838, and has already treated three-quarters of a million cases, I believe. I consider that he is the peer of any living surgeon in the world to-day. To my personal knowledge he undertakes, almost daily, cases which our most distinguished surgeons at home do not dare attempt, even in Philadelphia, the medical capital of our country. I suppose that humble man might just as well as not be enjoying an income of from $50,000 to $75,000 a year, instead of his present small salary, if he was only practicing in the city of New York on his own account. And I suppose he knows it, too.'

"And when we afterwards passed through the hospital, inspected the photographs of operations already performed, and viewed the array of deformities to be treated that afternoon, I could not doubt that what he had said was literally true."

## JAVA.

THE ISLAND AND ITS INHABITANTS.—The Hon. N. F. Graves, of Tennessee, who has made a tour of the world, furnishes to the *Gospel in all Lands* for September, 1887, an account of the island of Java and its inhabitants, and of the missionary work there. From his narrative, we extract the following :

Java is the most important of all the islands of the Indian archipelago. It is by no means the largest, but has a greater population than all the others together. The population is as dense as any country in Europe. The natural beauty of the country is not surpassed anywhere. The climate is mild, and the people are industrious, and the productions are very rich. The rice fields are unsurpassed in any country, and the coffee and sugar are like a gold mine, a constant source of wealth. East and west it is over 600 miles and is 120 miles wide, with an area of 52,000 square miles.

The native Javanese belong to the Malay race, and are divided into Javanese, Sundonese and the Madurese. The Javanese are vastly the more numerous, as well as the most civilized. The color of the skin in all these cases is a yellowish brown, with a hue of olive green. The eyes are brown or black. They are without beard, and small of stature. They are generally industrious, sober and peaceable. They are Mohammedans as much as anything. In former times they were Buddhists and Brahmins. They worship their ancestors, and seem to have gathered something from every system of religion with which they have come in contact.

PROGRESS OF THE MISSIONARY WORK.—The Dutch Reformed Missionary Society have the Dutch colonies for their field of labor. This society was organized in 1797, very like the London Missionary Society, being undenominational. This society has missions in many parts of the island, with twenty-nine congregations, with over 3,000 Christians, nearly all of whom have been won from the Mohammedans. The New Rotterdam Missionary Society was founded in 1859, is laboring among the Mohammedan Sudonese, and has translated the New Testament into that language. The missionaries of these societies are principally educated at Rotterdam. There are now 70,000 native Christians.

Mr. Anthing, a high officer of the Dutch government, has at his own expense established a mission of his own, and works principally in the city of Batavia, by means of native preachers trained by himself. Rev. Dr. Scheeurmann, a government chaplain, has established a large training institution at Depok, near Batavia, in which native preachers and teachers are trained. It is said the institution cost over $200,000. The Christian youths are received from Java, Borneo and other places and are trained for evangelical work. The institution is having a very great influence, and many are benefited by the instruction, and the promise for the future is very great. Some portions of Java are Christianized.—*Ibid.*

## MADAGASCAR.

REMARKABLE RESULTS IN MADAGASCAR.—In Madagascar, where as late as 1857 nearly 2,000 people were put to death for adhering to the Christian faith, there are 1,200 churches and 71,586 communicants. The native churches during the past ten years have given nearly $1,000,000 for the spread of the Gospel. No nation, with perhaps the exception of the Japanese, has made so much progress, and has shown so much vigor for development in Christianity and civilization as the people of Madagascar, during the last twenty years. The societies laboring there, in the order of the number of their missionaries and converts, are the London Missionary Society, the Norwegian Missionary Society, the Society for the Propagation of the Gospel, and the English Friends Mission.

TESTIMONY OF THE HON. N. F. GRAVES.—The Hon. N. F. Graves, of Tennessee, in the course of his tour of the world, visited Madagascar, and in one of his articles in "The Gospel in All Lands," he writes as follows:

"The Protestants are represented by about 350,000 adherents. In Imerena, the chief province, are over 1,100 schools with 151,000 pupils, and of these two-thirds belong to the London Missionary Society and the Friends' Mission.

The native Christians give largely every year to the spread of the Gospel. Antananarivo, the capital of Madagascar, is much the largest city on the island. It is said to contain a population of 100,000. It is an old town, but within a few years has been almost entirely rebuilt. The old wooden buildings have been taken down and replaced by far better ones, constructed chiefly of stone and sun-dried brick. Most of these new houses and building are on the European plan.

The ridge extending through the city is a very prominent feature, and is now covered with royal palaces with high roofs and arched verandas. The new elegant palace of the Prime Minister is on the ridge. The ridge has become an attractive place, not only on account of royalty, and royal palaces, but on account of the churches and other beautiful erections. There is a fine stone church with beautiful towers near by the spot where the Christian martyrs suffered in the early persecutions.

THE PEOPLE RAISED AND PURIFIED.—The gospel has come in Madagascar, as everywhere else, raising and purifying the people, increasing the comforts of human life, and improving their dwellings and habits. Since the re-opening of the country there has been a steady increase in the foreign trade, a stimulus has been given to the cultivation and collection of the valuable products of the island, and there is a constantly increasing demand for the calicos, prints, cloths and hardware of European manufacture. The repeal of the old law, closely connected with idolatry, forbidding the erection in Antananarivo of any stone or brick structure, has given a great impetus to building, so that the city has been almost rebuilt; hundreds of substantial and handsome houses of sun-dried brick replace those of timber or rush. And this improvement has extended far away from Antananarivo. The erection of the

9

Four Memorial Churches (1864-1874) trained up a body of artisans—stonemasons, builders, carpenters, tilers and glaziers—skilled in the building arts.

The abolition of cruel customs and laws belonging to the heathen state of society has been largely effected by the kindly and merciful spirit of Christianity. The Malagasy were formerly very cruel, and disregardful of human life ; the laws prescribing death for numerous offences, and this was inflicted in many barbarous ways. Soldiers were burned alive for trifling military offences, and people were stoned to death for petty thefts in the market. *Now*, it may be said that these cruelties have passed away ; capital punishment has for several years been inflicted only for heinous crimes, and this only in the most merciful form.— *"Madagascar."* *By James Sibree, F. R. G. S.*

GENERAL J. W. PHELPS ON MADAGASCAR'S PASSAGE FROM BARBARISM TO CHRISTIANITY.—The special envoy of the British government, Gore Jones, to the Queen of Madagascar, in 1882, stated at a public meeting in London that on reaching Antananarivo, whither he was sent as commander-in-chief of the East Indian naval station to congratulate the Queen of Madagascar, he was surprised to find what manner of people the Malagasy were. He found Antananarivo to be a really splendid city, with magnificent public buildings. The house he lodged at was as good as any in London. The Prime Minister, who was, curiously enough, husband of the Queen, and almost the most intelligent, astute and cleverest man he had ever met, occupied a splendid official residence.

By the beginning of 1883 an embassy was received in England from the Queen of Madagascar, and its members were entertained by the government and people with the most respectful and considerate attention, everything of interest being shown to them in a way to heighten their regard for the Christian civilization and power of Great Britain, as well as for the kindness and benevolence of the citizens and missionaries. The embassy subsequently visited the United States, where it arrived in the month of March, 1883, and entered into treaty stipulations with our government. Thus during the present century, and chiefly through missionary agency, Madagascar has passed from a state of pagan barbarism to one of Christian civilization, in which it has entered and taken a stand among the Christian nations of the world.—*From " The Island of Madagascar," by Gen. J. W. Phelps, pp.* 92–93.

## MICRONESIA.

THE RESULTS AFTER ABOUT THIRTY YEARS' WORK. —For about thirty years missionaries of the American Board, and native missionaries from the Sandwich Islands, have been laboring in the three eastern groups of Micronesia, the Gilbert Islands, the Marshall Islands, and the Caroline Islands. In the annual survey of the Board's missions for 1887, published in the *Missionary Herald* for November, 1887, the results of the work in eastern Micronesia are thus stated :

Though it is scarcely more than a quarter of a century since the first converts there were baptized, the mission now includes 46 wholly self-supporting churches, with 5,312 members. Six high schools for training native preachers and teachers and their wives, gather 178 pupils, and send out new and well-trained laborers every year into the widening field ; while 42 common schools, taught by natives and wholly self-supporting, give instruction to some 2,800 pupils. The Scriptures are translated wholly or in part into five different languages, and other Christian literature as well as school-books, has been provided by the missionaries. The work thus far has extended to about half the islands of the three groups embraced, and new islands are visited every year.

THE SPANISH SEIZURE OF THE CAROLINE ISLANDS. —When Bismarck was about to seize the Caroline Islands he was opposed by Spain, and the matter being referred to the Pope's arbitration, he decided in favor of Spain. Then a band of Spanish officials and priests went to the islands and aroused against the missionaries and native converts a vagabond class of natives known as "beach combers," and after a time a leading missionary, the Rev. E. T. Doane, was, under a flimsy pretext, arrested and sent to the Spanish Governor-General at Manilla, Emilio Terrero. The latter soon set Mr. Doane at liberty, assuring him that he should be protected in his work, and promised to send him back to Ponape on a Spanish cruiser. He also wrote to him a letter of which the following is an extract:

"The important labors in the field of culture performed by yourself and other missionaries cannot but be appreciated and considered of extraordinary service to humanity and civilization; as likewise the great hardship suffered by yourself in the propagation of the gospel convinces me of the faith and enthusiasm with which you have borne and overcome all sorts of obstacles and troubles in the conversion to Christianity of the savages of those islands."

Miss Fletcher, a missionary, writes at Ponape, the principal island: "Never was the island in so good a condition as when the Spanish came; the work never prospered as well as during the last year. Church work, schools, everything was in good order."

"The wreck that has been made in three months seems impossible. The public schools, with the exception of two, the governor has closed. The church services at one sta-

tion are closed and we live in hourly expectation of a
notice to close the boarding-school.  As it is, we have to
watch the girls day and night, to keep them from being
stolen and placed in houses where they will learn, to say
the least, no good."

"That Spain has to these islands the right of discovery
none will dispute; but how about those thirty-four or thirty-
five years of labor and expense which America has given?
During all this time Spain has not even looked at these
islands; and now she comes in and finds our natives well
civilized, schools, churches, all under headway, and must
we step aside and see all this come to naught?"

When the Spanish Governor came he had six Roman
Catholic priests with him.  The effects of the change Mr.
Doane sketches: "Schools were closed; congregations
thinned down; liquor flowed freely; many natives returned
to *ava* planting and pounding and drinking; chiefs, church
members, were shorn of the power they possessed to correct
evil in their own realms."

Articles have appeared in the Madrid newspapers touching Mr. Doane's arrest.  Among others the *Globo*, the paper
of Senor Castelar, the eminent Spanish statesman, gives an
admirable account of the missionary operations of the American Board in the Caroline Islands, accompanied by approving comments.  It sums up the case as follows:

"The Island of Ponape, as we see from these data,
is not an unknown and an uncultivated land inhabited by a
few savages, and without communication with the world.
Ponape and adjacent islands for many years had enjoyed many
of the advantages of modern civilization.  Against these
religious beliefs, and against these various interests that
we have recounted in this article, we have harshly flung our-
selves—whether ignorantly, or knowingly, or imprudently,
it is impossible for us now to say."

An American man-of-war has been for some time at the Islands, for the protection of American missionaries, and Spain has agreed to pay an indemnity for the wrong done Mr. Doane, and to guarantee the security of the mission work at Ponape.

---

# NEW GUINEA.

THE ISLAND AND ITS INHABITANTS.—Sixty miles north of the Australian continent lies one of the largest islands in the world—Papua or New Guinea. It is about 1,400 miles long, and 490 broad in its widest part. Its population is estimated to be about 1,500,000. The Dutch claim nearly half of the island, and the English and Germans divide between them the other half. The British portion is almost equal in size to the whole of Great Britain. It is the southern part of the vast island. The people are tattooed and unclothed, except with barbaric ornaments. Sixteen years ago they were all fierce and excitable savages, and many of the tribes were addicted to cannibalism. "They delighted in bloody deeds; each man had a tattoo mark on his chest and back, like a medal of honor, for every person he had slain, and was proud of it;"* and there was a chronic state of warfare between the different tribes. Now, through the blessing of God upon the labors of the truly heroic and self-sacrificing missionaries, European and Polynesian, peace of an enduring character has been established among the tribes on the south-east coast and the adjoining islands, and thousands of the once fierce natives show the power of the gospel of peace over their hearts and lives.

---

* Rev. James Chalmers.

CAPTAIN SPRY ON THE "CHALLENGER'S" VISIT TO NEW GUINEA.—In February, 1875, H. M. S. "Challenger," which was on a scientific voyage round the world, reached Humboldt Bay in New Guinea, where no missionaries had yet labored. Captain W. J. Spry, in his narrative, entitled "The Cruise of the 'Challenger,'" thus refers to the visit:

"This was our first view of the shores of New Guinea, and all gazed with profound interest at what seemed the portal (as it were) to the most unknown and, up to this date, the least explored region of the earth. It is well-known that but few Europeans (if any) had ever trodden the shores we gazed upon, the exploration of which appeared so flattering to the imagination, so likely to be fruitful in interesting results, whether to the naturalist, the ethnologist, or the surveyor; and altogether so well calculated to gratify the enlightened curiosity of an adventurous explorer, that all were in high spirits at the apparent prospect of getting into the interior of New Guinea, for its plants, birds, animals and inhabitants would be entirely a new study; so speculation ran high on what the next few days would bring to light as we neared the anchorage.

"As soon as we anchored all our boats were got out, as it was intended to spend a week here and make a survey of the bay; and great were the preparations among the naturalists and others at the prospect of exploring the beautiful forests, &c., stretched out around us, where altogether everything was likely to be new.

"On the first of the boats approaching the shore, it was closed upon by a number of savages in their canoes, and all that could be stolen they laid hands on. A second boat was similarly treated, and they evidently opposed any landing being made with hostile demonstrations, bending their bows and intimating their intention to shoot if we persisted in the attempt. Very judiciously we gave way, although all were fully armed, and the boats returned to the ship, every one feeling disappointed at the result."

THE TRAGIC BEGINNING OF THE MISSIONARY WORK. —New Guinea is surrounded by countless islands, some of which are of considerable size. On some of them in Torres Straits the London Missionary Society commenced operations in 1871, principally on Murray Island. Native Christians from the Loyalty Islands were taken there by Re Messrs. Murray and Macfarlane, who believed that they would prove to be the better pioneers on account of the special ill-feeling of the natives toward white men, caused by the outrageous conduct of those on board of some European vessels which had touched there. Of the first band of Polynesian evangelists, some were murdered and others died from the effects of the malarious climate, and even of the second and subsequent bands some were killed.

But volunteers to take their places were numerous, not only from the Loyalty Islands, but also from Tahiti, Samoa, Savage Island, Raratonga, &c., and so eager were the native Christian teachers on these islands to go, that in some cases, it had *to be decided by lot who should stay.** The

---

* The Rev. James Chalmers says in the *Sunday at Home* for September, 1887 : " The enthusiasm was especially great when it became known among a band of newly arrived teachers that we proposed to reopen the Mission at Kalo, where the natives had massacred their teachers, with their families, in all twelve persons. The Samoans volunteered for the forlorn hope. The Raiateans, too, earnestly begged to go. The Rarotongans went privately to Mr. Gill, who had brought them from Sydney, and urged him to intercede that the post of honor and peril might not be given to others. So he said: ' As Rarotongans were martyred, let Rarotongans have the preference.' " Mr. Chalmers went with them and slept soundly the first night among the murderers, and instead of harming him or his attendants, the people were pleased at the courage shown.

Rev. Mr. Lawes went himself to the mainland of New Guinea, and he was followed ten years ago by the Rev. James Chalmers, an exceedingly able man, and a most heroic missionary, who is now generally called "The Apostle of New Guinea." The Rev. Mr. Murray, Dr. Macfarlane, and Rev. Mr. Savage have labored on the islands in Torres Straits, with headquarters at Murray Island. Already there are no less than seventy stations on the mainland of New Guinea, besides those on the islands in Torres Straits, and the baptized converts number 5,000.

The Rev. James Chalmers, who labored on other islands of the Pacific before he went to New Guinea, says : " I believe no mission connected with the London Missionary Society, or any other society, can compare with this of New Guinea in results, whether you regard it merely from a social standpoint and try to estimate the repressive influence exercised on the evil ways of the people, or judge it by direct conversions and the principles of active Christianity which the new disciples exhibit."

THE CHANGE IN TORRES STRAITS.—As a boy, one of my earliest remembrances is of being told the tragic history of the "Charles Eaton." A large merchantman of that name, bound for China, was wrecked among the dangerous reefs of Torres Straits. A raft was hastily made, on which the crew and passengers all escaped to a small island, where they were treacherously welcomed by the natives. On the first night after their arrival, the savages, having seen that all their visitors were asleep, set upon them with clubs. With the exception of one little boy, every one of the white men was killed, and the bodies were eaten. The child was carried off, with the skulls of the murdered people, to Murray Island. A schooner sent out by the British Government rescued the boy ; and finding the skulls piled as a trophy, brought them to the Cape of Good Hope, where they were buried.

The facts are impressed on my mind because an uncle of my own was one of the victims, and his death must have occurred about the same time I was born. Now, through the heroism of missionaries who, fearless of its evil reputation, and of the blood of some of their own number, persisted in occupying that ill-omened region for Christ, Murray Island is civilized; it has become an educational centre; industrial and other schools are planted there, regular reports are issued of the work carried on by native teachers, and it is a well-known place of call for traders. It is quite as safe to-day for a stranger to be wrecked in Torres Straits as in Boston Harbor; and a merchant is in more danger of being clubbed on Broadway than on those once murderous shores.—*Dr. T. Harwood Pattison, quoted in the Sunday at Home, March,* 1887.

TESTIMONIES OF LORD LOFTUS AND OTHERS AS TO THE CHANGE ON THE MAINLAND.—The London Missionary Society has recently issued a leaflet concerning its New Guinea Mission, which contains some excellent testimony as to the value of the work done among the rude savages in that distant land. Rev. Mr. Lawes, who went to New Guinea in 1871, was recently given a reception at Sydney, at which Loftus, the governor of New South Wales; Commodore Erskine, commander of the British fleet in the South Seas; Sir H. B. Loch, governor of Victoria, and Sir E. Strickland, a Roman Catholic baronet, gave the warmest testimony to the value of the work done by Lawes and his coadjutors in the vicinity of Port Moresby. Ten years ago the natives of that region were suspicious, thieving and quarrelsome. Now, these men declare that the people are orderly, attentive to religious instruction, and honest. It is pleasant to have the testimony of an eminent naval officer, in view of the fact that men of the sea have been known to disparage Christian Missions.

Commodore Erskine said he was glad to have an opportunity of informing the people of this country, as he had already informed Her Majesty's government, that he should have been totally unable to carry out the orders he had received had it not been for the influence exerted in New Guinea by Mr. Lawes. He was glad to have an opportunity, coming as he did from the scene of Mr. Lawes's labors, of testifying to the noble work and good results which had been achieved during his (Mr. Lawes's) time on the island. With regard more especially to the work he himself had been ordered to carry out, he thought the result of that work was a sufficient proof of the good work Mr. Lawes had done. Mr. and Mrs. Lawes visited the island of New Guinea some ten years ago, at which time they could not, and dared not, communicate with the people of the country. But at the time he (Commodore Erskine) visited the land—a short time ago—he found that the influence exerted by Mr. Lawes was very great, and he thought that any crowned head might be proud to exercise such influence over any people. He did not intend to go into the principles of missionary life as connected with the different sects, but he had, as a naval officer, during the last few years, seen the good work which had been done on the islands, and he was glad to testify to the good results which had been achieved at New Guinea.

Hugh Milman, a magistrate who had visited the southeast coast of New Guinea, also bore this testimony : "The indomitable courage that was required and shown by them in getting a footing on the great densely populated continent is deserving of all praise, and the benefits to the natives that have already arisen from contact with them during the short space of some seven or eight years, are immense ; inter-tribal fights, formerly so common, being entirely at an end, and trading and communication, one tribe with another, now being carried on without fear." Mr. Milman also tells of an old chief with whom he was conversing as to whether the missionaries had done them good, who gave some illustrations of their work.  Pointing to some natives from other islands who had come ashore, this chief said :  " Why, a few years ago, these people, if they had been landed here, would have been killed and eaten ; now they can land in safety, and we take care of them and send them on their way to their homes."—*Missionary Herald, June*, 1885.

A Missionary's Great Influence.—The Rev. James Chalmers, Mr. Lawes's great coadjutor, has recently visited England.  The London *Christian*, in a sketch of him and his work, says : " The influence of the tribal chiefs in New Guinea had been quite undermined by sorcerers until scarcely any are left to wield authority.  Now, however, the real power along the coast covered by the mission stations is exercised by Mr. Chalmers, and also in many places far inland, for, under the name of ' Tamate ' (teacher) he is beloved by all.  Everywhere ' maino ' (peace) follows the footsteps of Tamate.  He settles their quarrels ; often he is sent for from very long distances to act as the arbitrator among tribes which are at war.  As an English naval officer testified lately : ' Everywhere Tamate's influence is supreme ; ' he soothes their excitable minds, calms and drives away their fears with a power which to those simple people seems wonderful, so that the very name ' Tamate ' has come to signify ' peace.' "

Strange Proofs of Regard.—An old chief who was much attached to Mrs. Chalmers brought her a very dainty bit, the breast of a man, as proof of his affection.  It was laid at her feet.  She spoke kindly to her cannibal friend, gave him a present, and asked him to take with him that which he had apportioned as her share, saying that we never partake of such, and hoped he would soon give it up. I do not think the old man again tasted human flesh until the day of his death, which happened some years after. * * * *

"The old man who wished to initiate Mrs. Chalmers into cannibalism was very anxious that I should really be a chief, and said that I could not be so until I had more than one wife. He brought his daughter as a first instalment, saying to Mrs. Chalmers, "You are queen, all the others will simply be secondary and do your work; other chiefs will bring their daughters, and then 'Tamate' will be a very great chief." He received a present, and took his daughter back, but thought it very strange that we would not consent to become really great in that particular way. He once travelled with me, and on starting out said, "You will see I am a great chief, as in all the villages we visit I have a wife and home." At one village he presented me with a splendid snow-white cuscus and would take no return present for it, saying, "it was his wife's pet, and she was so glad to see him with a great white chief that she was anxious I should have it."—*From "Life in New Guinea," by the Rev. James Chalmers.*

What the Gospel of Christ has Done.—From the address of the Rev. James Chalmers, at the last annual meeting of the London Missionary Society, we take the following: "There are twelve New Guinea teachers in our Eastern Branch Mission, young men and women, five of whom were cannibals when I went to New Guinea. The others were at Port Moresby, and were what is called savages when I went there; and to-day—what? The fruit—the summer fruit already! We gather it in; they have gone up to the front to help us in this great work.

Although we have now fifty mission stations in our Eastern Branch, those are manned by those grand men, the South Sea Island teachers. Oh, they are noble men. When the news was taken to the South Seas of the Kalo massacre, of the poisoning of Eso Eso, and of the deaths of one after another, still the enthusiasm was there, and noble men and women offered themselves for service. Some who had returned on account of ill-health came back to take up the work and carry it on.

"Twelve months last December I visited South Cape, when I was left there by Sir Peter Scratchley, the first special commissioner appointed by Her Majesty to the Protectorate. He left us to go to the Australian coast to die. A man full of interest and of earnestness in the work already undertaken, who thoroughly appreciated the position in which we stood on the island, and thoroughly thanked us for doing such great things for the Master and for the government. Whilst I was there, on the first Sunday in December, I met with a large company of Christian men and women, and I sat down and partook of the Lord's Supper, administered by a native pastor—one of our South Sea Islanders. There I was united with, and shed tears of joy with, men and women who only a few years before sought our lives. What did it? It is the old story still of the Gospel of Christ."

A LETTER FROM A NAVAL OFFICER.—In a recent number of the *Mission Field* there appeared a letter written by a young officer who was with the naval force sent from Australia to proclaim the British protectorate over the southern coast of New Guinea. This officer gives his impressions of men and things met with during that expedition.

" After posting my last, we weighed from Port Moresby, where, however, I was fortunate enough to go on shore one

afternoon when an examination was going on at the mission
school, and saw all the children.   They seemed a most intelligent, bright set, and wonderfully well educated, especially in geography, which they quite enjoyed.   One day
we anchored at Kerepenu, a very large village with two
thousand inhabitants, where we found all most friendly ;
indeed, the south-eastern tribes which have been brought
under missionary influence, seem  to welcome men-of-war
most warmly.   One Sunday I had a pleasant stroll through
the village, but too late for the service held by the native
teacher, and as the latter could not speak English I learned
but little of the mission work.   That little, however, was
exceptionally good, a local English trader giving most
striking testimony in its favor.

"We have been fortunate, too, in carrying with us
Mr. Chalmers, the oldest missionary in New Guinea—a
truly noble fellow, of the Livingstone stamp.   He knows
every yard of these 500 miles of coast, roughing it in an
open boat, sleeping in any shelter, or in the open air, with
only just the luggage he can carry, making long expeditions
inland where no other white man's foot has ever trod ;
trusting himself unarmed and alone amongst the wildest
tribes, yet well-nigh worshipped by even cannibals.   That
is, indeed, a marvellous personal influence spread over such
a vast extent of savagedom, and the wildest seem to
brighten up at the sight of him.   He is a short, broad-built
man of about fifty, with hearty laugh and ready wit, and a
good story for every one, the delight of our mess, and the
hero of our lower deck, yet with a manly piety which carried great weight.   On Sunday he gave us a ten minutes'
sermon, short, pithy, and to the point, full of quaint Scotch
phrases, yet instinct with earnest pleading which touched
alike officers and men.   He sits with us talking by the
hour, with such a ready fund of anecdote, wit, and general

information that 'all hands' vote him the best companion they have ever known, neither dress nor language showing aught but the rough explorer and well-read man of the world, till some remark brings forth a reply which shows what is the source of all his happiness, and 'the hope that is in him.'"

---

## NEW HEBRIDES.

GREAT DIFFICULTIES AND MANY MARTYRS.—The missionary work in the extensive New Hebrides group has been more difficult than in any other part of Polynesia. The natives are exceedingly treacherous and cruel; the climate is very unhealthy, and the languages are numerous.

Many have been the Christian martyrs, both European and Polynesian, in this group. On one of the islands that great missionary, the Rev. John Williams, and also the Gordons, were killed, and on another, the noble and devoted Bishop Patteson.

H. M. S. "CHALLENGER" AT ONE OF THE UNEVANGELIZED ISLANDS.—The following is from "The Cruise of the 'Challenger,'" by W. J. J. Spry, R. N., 1877. "On the evening of the 17th we sighted some of the eastern islands of the New Hebrides, passing very near to Mai or Three Hill Islands, and a small cluster known as Shepherd group. The next day we were off the island of Api. * * * When a landing was effected, a large number of natives hove in sight. Among them were two bearing palm-branches, supposed to indicate their friendly intentions, but the rest of the crowd had clubs, spears, bows and arrows. They had none of their women or children with them, and that is not usually a good sign.

" The natives are very dark, almost approaching to black, and are considered as belonging to the Papuan race. They are described as hostile and treacherous in all their intercourse with the white men; therefore, although their manners seemed favorable, they were not to be trusted, and it was not considered advisable to ramble beyond the beach, or out of sight of the boats and the armed crew. In consequence, none of the villages or houses were seen. The missionaries report the islanders as being among the worst they had to deal with in the South Pacific; those who have been laboring among them during the past few years have been treacherously killed and eaten. It was considered unsafe to remain long among such people, and on the boats returning, it was decided to proceed for Torres Straits, distant 1,500 miles, and having a capital breeze after us, the land was soon out of sight."

THE OUTLINES OF A GLORIOUS HISTORY.—The Rev. Joseph Annand, of the Presbyterian Church in Canada, who has labored many years in New Hebrides, stated the following deeply interesting facts in the course of an address before the International Missionary Union, at the Thousand Islands Park, in August, 1886:

" The islands of the New Hebrides group contain a population of 70,000, speaking more than twenty languages or dialects. The mission to the New Hebrides was begun by John Williams in 1839. The third day that he was in the group, and after having settled three Eastern Island teachers there, he and James Harris were murdered and devoured by the Eromangans. The next year Mr. Heath followed in Williams' steps and settled four teachers on the group. In 1847 another determined effort to plant the Gospel resulted only in the murder of seven out of nine intrepid missionaries. But in the year 1848 the mission was established again, when Rev. John Geddie, from Prince Edward

Island, settled. After four years of patient labor, amid great difficulties and dangers, he baptized ten natives and formed the first church in Melanesia. Mr. Inglis, from Scotland, joined Mr. Geddie that year, and they labored on jointly for twenty years. The whole island (Ancityum) was brought in; cannibalism gave way to Christianity; strangulation of widows and infanticide passed away; all the horrors and depravity of paganism were changed to the joys and happiness of affectionate homes.

"Every man among the natives of these islands carries weapons: for it is impossible, owing to the feuds which divide the people, for him to go even half-way across his own island in safety. Every wife (these statements refer to the former condition of all, and that at present of the yet unevangelized islands) wore a string about her neck always, with which she was to be murdered when her husband should die. Eromanga Island had five martyrs: Rev. John Williams and James Harris, Rev. George Gordon and his wife, and James Gordon. But there have been other laborers here, and the population of the island now does not include a heathen.

"Ephati Island we lived upon three years. In 1874 Mr. McKenzie and I spent five days here; our information and experiences were interesting. We met one man who had thirty-five wives, and had eaten sixty-seven human beings! We slept in a low grass house thirty to fifty feet long, and eight feet high, with a door two and a half feet high; just outside the door was a gutter of filth ankle deep. We had cocoanut mats to sleep on. The oven was open near us, and we could not, in consequence, eat some of the food cooked there. We had a shelf on the wall to lie upon, two feet and a half high, by as many wide, for two of us to sleep on, and thin mats to cover us. The mosquitoes and fleas cannot be imagined. Each leg of our bedstead-shelf had a pig tied to it, which tugged so that we feared a great fall. An old woman, who slept on the stove, however, belabored the pigs all night to keep them quiet. In the morning we were awakened by the crowing of a cock, which was right beside us. The census of this dwelling for the night was: Thirteen pigs, seven people; rats and fowls! Four or five months later the enemies of our entertainers came down upon them, and cooked and ate every person in the family!

"Yet on that island now, one-half the people are at worship this moment. Mr. McKenzie on the southern and Mr. McDonald on the northern side have both strong churches. Let me tell you an illustration of the change in this island: In 1852 a vessel was wrecked there; the following morning the chief told the mariners that he would take them to the neighboring island; formed them into a procession, each warrior preceded and followed by a native warrior. On the way every one was killed, and their bodies were distributed and eaten! In 1878 another vessel was wrecked there, with one hundred and twenty natives on board. They were all rescued; thirty were taken to one village, thirty to another, and so on about the island, and sheltered and fed for six months, until the arrival of a convenient vessel, upon which they were all kindly provided with safe passage to Fiji.

"Nine of these islands are now occupied by missionaries. Churches are organized on seven islands. Ten languages have been reduced to print, and the work is going on well. Efate and Nynna have large Christian churches and active workers."

WOMEN IN THE HOLY WAR.—I give another story to show that women were not wanting in this holy war. I have already noted that the wives always accompanied the teachers. In Rarotonga a native teacher once expressed to his missionary his desire to get married, " akaipoipo vaine." The missionary expressed his concurrence, and asked if he had thought of any one. " Yes," he said, " I have been thinking of Maria, the daughter of another teacher." On being asked if he had made known his desire to her, he replied that he not spoken to her, but that he had been looking at her for a long time. On being told that something more than looking was necessary, he produced a letter, which ran as follows : ' I, Akatangi, have been appointed to go as a native teacher to the heathen in the dark lands westwards. I have been looking at you for a long time, and I desire that you will go with me. If you love Jesus, if you love the heathen, and if you love me, let us go together. Think of this and let me know. Blessings on you from Jesus. Amen.

" NA AKATANGI."

A deacon of the Church conveyed this letter to Maria, who, on being told whence it came, betrayed an expression of countenance which showed that his looking at her had produced no unfavorable impression, and, on reading it she was pleased to accept, with her parents' consent. They were married, went to Eromanga, the scene of the murder of John Williams, the two Gordons, and Mrs. Gordon, and lived with and converted the murderer of John Williams.—*Robert N. Cust, Esq., in C. M. Intelligencer.*

---

# NEW ZEALAND.

SUBLIME SCENERY BUT BARBAROUS PEOPLE.—New Zealand is distinguished for its rich and varied scenery, and for everything which naturally strikes the eye as beautiful or sublime ; but the European discoverers of it found that though every prospect was pleasing, man was very vile and cruel. Children were taught by their parents, and even by the priests, to be cruel, war-like, liars, thieves, and, in a word, to be guilty of almost every crime. At the time of the naming of the child, small pebbles, about the size of a pin's head, were thrust down its throat to make its heart hard and incapable of pity. The Maories loved fighting above all things, and they tortured and made slaves of their captives, or killed and ate them.

When Captain Cook visited New Zealand, the people were always engaged in intertribal wars, and they were quite ready to attack their foreign visitors. In 1772 they killed twenty-eight men belonging to a French ship. In 1782 ten sailors were seized, cooked and eaten in triumph. In 1809 the whole crew of H. M. S. "Boyd" were massacred.

GREAT SUCCESS AFTER PATIENT LABORS.—We do not suppose that these white visitors were altogether blameless. Indeed we know of one chief, Ruatara, who was cruelly deceived and ill-treated by them. The Rev. Samuel Marsden met with this chief at Sydney, was kind to him, accompanied him to his home in New Zealand; and, by his aid, succeeded in beginning missionary work there. On the night of December 20th, 1814, Marsden, through the influence of Ruatara, slept in safety on New Zealand soil, the natives laying around with their spears' heads buried in the ground in proof of their friendship. The missionary preached his first sermon on Christmas day, on the words, "Behold, I bring you glad tidings," Ruatara acting as interpreter. But the time of success was slow in coming, the natives being more anxious to get guns wherewith to fight other tribes, than to learn the truths of the gospel of peace.

Indeed years went on and no converts were made. In

1822 the Rev. H. Williams, and in 1825, the Rev. W. Williams, afterwards Bishop of Waiapu, arrived from England.  In the latter year the first conversion was made, but it was five years more before there were any further baptisms, but after this the progress was very rapid—so rapid, that when the elder Bishop Selwyn arrived in New Zealand, in 1842, he wrote: " We see here a whole nation of pagans converted to the faith. . . . Where will you find, throughout the Christian world, more signal manifestations of the presence of the Spirit, or more living evidences of the Kingdom of Christ ? "

The baptized converts connected with the Church Missionary Society's mission now number about 20,000. There are 27 native clergy and 280 voluntary workers. The missions of the Wesleyans have also been successful in New Zealand.

"THE STANDING MIRACLE OF THE AGE."—We can only glance at New Zealand.  In 1837, Marsden, its devoted apostle, paid his last visit to its shores.  At his first visit it was so cannibal and savage that no ship captain could be found adventurous enough to bring him there, so he had to purchase a brig at his own expense, and land with only a single companion.  Look at it to-day—a precious gem in the British Crown, with its native Church, its three missionary bishops ; its twenty-seven native pastors, its native church council, and, notwithstanding past wars and defections, its 20,000 Christian natives ; cannibalism unknown, heathenism well nigh extinct, and such a state of social progress attained as led Karl Ritter, the great geographer, to call it "the standing miracle of the age."— *Bishop W. Pakenham Walsh.*

BISHOP SELWYN FOUNDS THE MELANESIAN MISSION. —Besides his zealous labors among the Maories and the English colonists in New Zealand, Bishop Selwyn founded the Episcopal Melanesian Mission. Between 1848 and 1852, the Bishop visited more than fifty islands, and brought from them scholars speaking ten different languages to the school at Auckland. Under his successor, Bishop Patterson, the headquarters of the Melanesian Mission was transferred to Norfolk Island. In 1871 the noble and brave Bishop Patterson was killed by the natives of Nakapu, in revenge for the cruel wrongs they had endured from those on board some of the "labor vessels," which had visited the islands. Bishop Selwyn, the younger, is now head of the Melanesian Mission.

PERILS ENCOUNTERED.—As illustrations of the perils encountered when first visiting unevangelized islands, take the following from an English book, entitled "Under His Banner," page 255:

"In 1852 the Bishop of Newcastle accompanied the Bishop of New Zealand in his yacht, the 'Border Maid.' Visiting or sighting fifty-three islands, he was able to hold intercourse with the people of twenty-six, and from eleven of them he was allowed to take away scholars. This work was attended with many dangers. At Fate, one of the New Hebrides group, a plot was formed to cut him off and to seize his schooner, but adverse winds prevented him from approaching the island, and thus providentially his life was spared.

"At Malicolo, in the same group, the Bishop had gone ashore with a boat to procure water, leaving on board the Bishop of Newcastle, the mate and two or three sailors. Many canoes surrounded the ship, and the natives, who were very savage in their bearing, endeavored to board, but were overawed. At last they consulted together and made for the shore—the boats were lying near the beach, one man being left in each, while the Bishop and his party had gone inland. On the beach were about a hundred men fully armed; it was evidently intended as soon as the canoes reached land to seize the boats and prevent the Bishop's escape. It was an anxious moment; the Bishop of New-castle consulted with the mate, and found that, as far as material weapons went, they were powerless; the little company on board joined fervently in prayer for the deliverance of their friends, and on the island Bishop Selwyn had detected the evil looks of the people and retreated, getting into the boats amid a shower of arrows, which providentially did no harm."

MR. DARWIN AND THE ENCHANTER'S WAND.—The late Mr. Charles Darwin, in the course of his voyage round the world in H. M. S. "Beagle," visited Waimate, in New Zealand, and this is what he wrote concerning some of the results of missionary labors there : " At length we reached Waimate. After having passed over so many miles of an uninhabited, useless country, the sudden appearance of an English farm-house and its well-dressed fields, placed there as if by an enchanter's wand, was exceedingly pleasant. Mr. Williams not being at home, I received in Mr. Davis' house a cordial welcome. We took a stroll about the farm ; but I cannot attempt to describe all I saw. There were large gardens, with every fruit and vegetable which England produces, and many belonging to a warmer clime. Around the farm-yard there were stables, a threshing barn, with its winnowing machine, a blacksmith's forge, and on the ground ploughshares and other tools; in the middle was a happy mixture of pigs and poultry, lying comforta-bly together as in every English farm-yard; and at a little distance a large and substantial water-mill.

" All this is very surprising when it is considered that five years ago nothing but the fern flourished here. More-over, native workmanship, taught by the missionaries, has effected this change. The lesson of the missionary is the enchanter's wand. The house had been built, the windows framed, the fields ploughed, and even the trees grafted by the New Zealander. When I looked at the whole scene I thought it admirable. Several young men, redeemed by the missionaries from slavery, were employed on the farm; they had a respectable appearance. Late in the evening I went to Mr. Williams' house, where I passed the night. I found there a large party of children, collected together for Christmas day, and all sitting around a table at tea. I never saw a nicer or more merry group; and to think that this was the centre of the land of cannibalism, murder and all atrocious crimes! I took leave of the missionaries with thankfulness for their kind welcome, and with feelings of high respect for their gentlemanlike, useful and upright characters. I think it would be difficult to find a body of men better adapted for the high office which they fulfill."

MR. FROUDE'S STATEMENTS IN "OCEANA."—In the Diocese of Wellington there are no extensive Christian districts as in Auckland and Waiapu; but much good work is done in the south and on the Lower Wanganui; while Te Whiti is still followed by many on the upper parts of that river. It is easy, therefore, for a very partial and one-sided view of Maori Christianity to be formed in good faith, according to the particular district visited. Most English visitors see nothing of real Maori life. They only come across the waifs and strays that hang about the chief towns, and such little bands as are met with in the lake tourist district south of the Bay of Plenty, who are mostly Hauhaus; while of the numerous flourishing congregations in the far north and far east they hear nothing at all. This seems to have been the case with Mr. Froude, whose new and widely-circulated book, "Oceana," gives a sad account of the few Maori wanderers he chanced to see around the lakes.—*Annual Report of the Church Missionary Society,* 1886.

---

## NORTH AMERICAN INDIANS.

OUR NATION'S DISHONORABLE CONDUCT TOWARDS THE INDIANS.—The hundred years of our existence as an independent nation have been called "A Century of Dishonor," on account of the unjust treatment of the many Indian tribes in our wide domain. The great majority of the treaties made with the different tribes have been violated. By these treaties the vast territory of the United States has been acquired, but when the Indians yielded to the pressure brought to bear upon them, and gave up their broad lands to go on restricted reservations, it was only on the condition that the Government should compensate them by money annuities, or their equivalents in articles needed by the Indians ; by providing for the instruction of Indian children, and by keeping white intruders from the reservations. Towards many of the tribes the conditions have been almost entirely disregarded, and there are scarcely any tribes to whom they have been more than partially fulfilled.

In consequence of this, Indian wars have been numerous, and the resultant expense to the Government has been a hundred fold greater than if the conditions had been complied with, and our nation's record had been an honorable one. We are not alone in this injustice. Accounts are almost as prevalent in Canada concerning the wrong course of the authorities and the unjust treatment of the Indians, as they are here.

DR. SUNDERLAND ON THE OUTRAGEOUS TREATMENT OF THE INDIANS.—Dr. Byron Sunderland, of Washington, the president of the Indian Defence Association, has been examining the Government records, and after his investigations, in one article of a series in the *New York Observer*, he says: "The assertion is here ventured that there is not a tribe or band of Indians, however large or small, existing to-day in the country to whom the Government does not owe far more than any amount which it annually spends for their support. Pages might be filled with examples of the most outrageous treatment of most of the tribes at the hands of the Government."

A BRAVE GOVERNMENT AGENT.—Dr. Sunderland cites as a recent case the Pembina band of Chippewas, the Government agent to whom received a letter from the Indian Office at Washington, in the Spring of 1886, requiring him to impress it heavily on the minds of the Indians that "the time had come when they must either support themselves or starve." During a previous administration these Indians had been forced from the wide lands belonging to them, and cooped up in two small townships, and with only a miserable pittance of money. To the heartless and cruel announcement which the agent received, he replied in the following courageous and faithful manner :

" This reads nicely, and to parties ignorant of Indians and their condition, sounds as if the nail was being struck squarely on the head. But to me and all agents who are not ignorant as to the condition of the Indians, it sounds like a great flourish of trumpets—windy—because it requires something more than words to convince an Indian that you are in earnest when he is told that the one great object the department has now in view is his civilization, and to enable him to support himself as soon as possible. If the Indian is to become civilized and support himself by agriculture, must he not first be furnished with the necessary animals and implements before you can tell him to work or starve? It is just as consistent to tie a man up in a sack and pitch him overboard in mid-ocean, and tell him to swim ashore or drown, as it is to pen up a lot of Indians on a reservation, and tell them to work or starve, without first furnishing them the means to work with.

"Now the Indians on the Turtle Mountain reservation cannot work and support themselves for lack of means, and from what is known of them, they will not be likely to starve while there are large herds of fat cattle now grazing upon lands to which they have as good a title as any Indians ever had to lands in the United States, but which were thrown open to settlement without their knowledge or consent. Are these people to be driven to desperation by starvation and want, before anything is done to ameliorate their condition? They have time and again visited Washington to try and make arrangements to relinquish and extinguish the title to their lands in order to get the necessary assistance to support themselves in agricultural pursuits, but have not succeeded further than to hear some good promises and an advice to wait. Too bad the Indians are not the direct and lineal descendants of Methuselah, and inherit his longevity, coupled with the patience of Job, that they might live to see some of the just obligations established by precedent and treaty obligations, fulfilled by the Government!"

PRESIDENT SEELYE ON THE GOVERNMENT FAILURE TO SOLVE THE INDIAN PROBLEM.—Dr. Julius H. Seelye, the distinguished president of Amherst College, in an address at the annual meeting of the American Missionary Association in 1886, said:

"In the Report of the Commissioner of Indian Affairs for 1868, there is an estimate of the expenditure of some late Indian wars, from which we learn that it has cost the United States Government on an average one million of dollars, and the ·lives of twenty-five white men to kill an Indian. 'There is no good Indian but a dead Indian,' said General Sheridan, Lieutenant-General of our army, but the process of making the Indians good in this way is at least a costly one, and the prospect of success can hardly be considered hopeful.

"It may be doubted whether any Government efforts yet made to subdue or civilize these people have essentially improved either the Indians themselves or their relations to us. * * * I am not speaking here of what Governmental efforts should have been, or should now be, but I speak of the actual facts of the past and the present, and I say that the Governmental procedure thus far, instead of solving the Indian problem, has only increased prodigiously the difficulty of its solution. Incidents illustrative of this might be cited by the hour, but would be impertinent in an audience as intelligent as that here assembled."

THE RESULTS OF CHRISTIAN MISSIONS.—"And yet the solution of the Indian problem is not a matter of theory or of speculation, but is an accomplished fact. It has been wrought out before our eyes. Wild, savage Indian tribes, as fierce, as lawless, as intractable as any now existing, have been tamed, have been taught the arts and ways of peace, have subjected themselves to law, and are now living in orderly, peaceable, industrious communities. The Cherokees, and the Delawares and Shawnees now united with them, the Choctaws, the Chickasaws, the Creeks, and the Seminoles—who are known as the five civilized tribes—now have their constitutions and laws, their supreme courts and their district courts, their well-arranged public-school system, and indeed every provision of law and organization requisite in a State founded on the consent of the governed, controlled by officers chosen by the people, and suited to an advancing civilization." (U. S. Senate Rep., I.: XVII.)

" Pauperism among them is unknown, and, by the best reports, crime is less frequent in proportion to numbers than among the adjoining whites. The Report of the United States Senate Committee on Indian Affairs made to the Senate, July 4, 1886, says of the Cherokee nation, that ' It is difficult, after a searching criticism, to point out any serious defects in their constitution or statutes. In some respects several of our State constitutions could be amended with advantage by adopting some of the provisions of the Cherokee constitution. Their situation, and that of each of the five tribes, was full of difficulties, but they have met them skillfully." (I. : XVII.) " Fifty years ago," in the language of this same report, " these five nations—now blessed with a  Christian civilization, in which many thousands are active and intelligent workers, while the common sentiment of the whole people reverently supports their efforts, and approves their influence—were pagans."

" Fifty years ago the Sioux, now gathered at Santee and Sissiton, in Christian communities, and homes and schools, with churches enrolled on the same records as those of New York and Philadelphia, in connection with Presbytery, and Synod and General Assembly, were savage hordes, roaming through the Northwest as wild as the wildest. These savages have been changed. The facts are before our eyes. How was the transformation wrought? The answer is clear. No one can, no one does mistake it. The United States Senate Report, from which I have quoted, acknowledged these to be the results of Christian missions. Where the Government has totally failed, the voluntary efforts of the churches have been crowned with this success. The preaching of the Gospel has done this work, and it alone."—*Ibid.**

---

* From the Report of the address in the *American Missionary.*

A Few Telling Facts.—Twelve years ago the Modoc Indians were uncivilized heathen. Now they are a community of industrious farmers, with half their number professing Christians. It cost the United States Government $1,848,000 to care for 2,200 Dakota Indians seven years, while they were savages. After they were Christianized, it cost for seven years $120,000, a saving of $1,728,000. This is a fact that should tell with the political economist.

E. J. Garvie, himself one of the Sioux tribe, in a recent address, spoke with Indian eloquence of Indians whom no torture could make groan, but who weep at the story of the Cross. He said there are 2,000 living Sioux converts, and as many more who have died in the faith. A full-blooded Indian, a recent graduate of the Yale divinity school, has translated the book of Malachi into Choctaw, with an exegetical and critical commentary.

The *American Missionary* for December, 1887, contains the Report on the Indian work presented at the last annual meeting of the American Missionary Association. From it we extract the following : " The Indians are a people whom a Judge of the Supreme Court called 'a despised and rejected class of persons ; ' handicapped and hindered in all their efforts by the suspicions and hatreds developed by centuries * of injustice, robbery and cruelty † from a

---

* The injustice began early in the Colonial days.

† Similar testimony to that given in this Report, and in Dr. Sunderland's series of articles before referred to, has been borne by the venerable Bishop Whipple, who has labored so long among the Indians ; by General Harney, who has, we believe, been longer in the military service on the frontier than any other officer: by Herbert Welsh, the Secretary of the Indian Rights Association ; by Mrs. Helen H. Jackson, (" H. H.") the distinguished authoress, who resided some years in Colorado and California, and many other high authorities. In her

Government that claimed to be civilized and Christian, and also by the reservation system, which puts the missionary and the teacher under the absolute control of the Indian Agent, who may be a mere political tool and a man of no character, yet has despotic authority on the reservation. Yet in spite of all obstacles the missionaries have remained faithful amid dangers and difficulties, till, through their labors, there are now nearly 29,000 Indian church members."

For twenty-one years Bishop Bompas has been making journeys of thousands of miles on snow and ice, or in canoes, in the sub-Arctic regions of Athabasca Lake and the Mackenzie River; only once has he been to England in all that time. Since he went to northern British America 5,000 Indians have been brought into the Church in those inhospitable regions. This in the English Church Mission-

---

"Century of Dishonor," Mrs. Jackson presents the shameful facts. We remember hearing Wendell Phillips quote General Harney as saying that "he had never known the United States Government to make a treaty with the Indians which it did not violate."

In the old slavery days Thomas Jefferson said that when he thought of God and the wrongs of the slave he trembled for the future of his country. Bishop Whipple has used similar language when referring to the wrongs of the Indians. Mr. Spurgeon, the Earl of Shaftesbury, the Archbishop of York, and other eminent Englishmen, have used much the same language of their own country when referring to the terrible wrong done to China by the enforced and nefarious opium traffic. It has really seemed as if the keeping of faith with the Indians and the treating them rightly has been as much beyond the average BY.American statesman, as the acting justly toward the Chinese has been beyond the average British voter or member of Parliament. Really Christian people in both countries, and a large minority of the legislators, have been opposed to the unrighteous policies, but they have been unable to prevent the adoption of them.

ary Society's missions alone. The Canadian Methodists and Presbyterians have also been successful in the same field. If we go from the northern to the southern portion of our Continent, we find the Moravian missions very successful among the Mosquito tribe of Indians in Nicaraugua. There are 2,500 converts, and it is hoped that the whole tribe will soon be Christianized.

TESTIMONY OF COMMISSIONER RHOADS AND MR. HERBERT WELSH.—The Rev. Dr. H. L. Wayland, of Philadelphia, recently read a paper upon the Indian question before a conference of Baptists of that city. In this paper he grouped many facts, testifying to the susceptibility of the Indians to Christianization and civilization. Among other statements he said : " Dr. Rhoads, of the Indian Commissioners, stated at the Mohonk Conference that, of the 264,000 Indians in the United States, not including Alaska, 140,000 wore citizens' dress, and 70,000 know English enough to be understood. The five civilized tribes in the Indian Territory live in 16,000 houses, and outside of the territory there are 14,250 Indian houses. In the Indian Territory a prohibitory law is enforced. The Cherokees pay a higher sum for schools per child than any other community on earth. My friend, Mr. Herbert Welsh, Secretary of the Indian Rights Association, saw 700 Sioux among the Indians in Dakota gathered in one hundred families, who five years ago were blanketed savages, now living in log houses, drawing reduced rations, having each a little farm of ten to fifteen acres, supporting themselves. He saw an Indian, who was one of the band of Sitting Bull, who was in the fight in which Custer fell, who now is a Christian, civilized, helping in the elevation of his people. At Crow Creek Mr. Welsh saw a convocation of representatives of thirty-six Episcopal churches of Sioux Christians. The meetings were delightful ; during

11.

the year they have given from their poverty $1,800 toward the support of their own churches and the work of missions. Twelve years ago they were all wild savages.—*Spirit of Missions*, 1886.

THE CHANGE AT WHITE EARTH RESERVATION.— Twenty years ago we began with a small number of Indians at White Earth Reservation. They were wild folk, used only to savage life. Now there are 1,800 people living like civilized beings. They are self-supporting. It is an ordinary, law-abiding community. The laws are administered by an Indian police. This year they raised 40,000 bushels of wheat, and 30,000 bushels of oats. They have a herd of 1,200 or 1,500 cattle, several hundred horses, swine, sheep and fowls. They are proud of their homes, and are living in them like white people. They are as neat and orderly as old-fashioned Dutch housekeepers. They are excellent cooks, too; they never need to be shown twice how to cook anything. Their sewing is the most beautiful I ever saw; it is impossible to see the stitches. They have made all the carpets and bedding I have in my house. The contrast, therefore, between these White Earth people and the scattered bands of Chippewas shows plainly what can be accomplished with them by adopting right methods. The latter are utterly degraded.—*Bishop Whipple.*

"A STUDENT OF CIVILIZATION" ON BISHOP HARE AND HIS WORK.—One of the most recent pamphlets published by the Indian Rights Association is "The Latest Studies on Indian Reservations," by J. B. Harris. In it is the following mention of Bishop Hare and his work: "I know of no man who has accomplished more for the civilization of the Indians of Dakota, or for the advancement of all improving and civilizing influences in the country adjacent to the reservations, than Bishop Hare, of the Protestant Episcopal Church. Some religious workers on the frontier are

successful by means of mere rude strength or physical vigor.
They influence men all the more because of the coarseness
of taste and fibre which is common to them and to many of
the people among whom they live. But here is a man made
up of all gentle and pure qualities; at home in ' the still
air of delightful studies; ' who would be a leader among
the best anywhere; who unites to a soldier's fearlessness
and invincible devotion a spirituality so lofty and tender
that one shrinks from characterizing it while he is still in
the flesh, who is laying the foundations of Christian civilization on broad and far-reaching lines in a region large
enough to be a mighty empire. He long ago saw the need
and opportunities of the time, and answered to its call. I
am not a member of the Protestant Episcopal Church. It
is only as a student of civilization that I have written of
any of the missionary enterprises among the Indians. But
this man ought to have whatever he wants of means for
his work, with remembrance and honor from all good
men."

THE LAST LAKE MOHONK CONFERENCE.—The recent
convention of friends of the Indians, held at Lake Mohonk,
adopted a series of resolutions relative to the work of civilization now going on among them, of which the first was
as follows: " We congratulate the country on the notable
progress toward a final solution of the Indian problem
which has been made during the past year. The passage
of the Dawes bill closes the century of dishonor; it makes
it possible for the people of America to initiate a chapter
of national honor in the century to come. It offers the
Indians homes, the first condition of civilization, proffers
them the protection of the laws, and opens to them the
door of citizenship. We congratulate the country on the
public sentiment which has made this bill possible, and
the action of Congress responding promptly to a sentiment

all too tardily aroused, and to the action of the Executive welcoming the bill and the policy which it inaugurates, initiating the execution of its provisions in a just and humane spirit, and pledging its co-operation with philanthropic and Christian societies in the endeavor to prepare the Indian for the change that this bill both contemplates and necessitates."

The remaining resolutions declare the opinion of the assemblage that the Dawes bill has not wholly solved the Indian problem, but only created the opportunity for its solution ; that the work of assigning the lands in severalty to the Indians must occupy several years' time ; and that while this will change the Indian's political status it will not change his character. They assert that his character must be changed by the continued prosecution of religious work among his people, through mental education and spiritual culture.—*Spirit of Missions for November*, 1887.

AN UNPARALLELED GOVERNMENT ORDER.—The Christian friends of the Indians cannot, however, relax their vigilance and their efforts because the Dawes bill has become the law of the land, for even since the passage of this bill a very ill-advised and arbitrary order has been issued by the Indian Department of the general Government. All teaching of the Indians in their vernacular languages has been prohibited, and all schools ordered to be closed in which any language but the English is used as the medium of instruction—even those schools which are supported entirely by Christian people through their missionary societies, as well as those which are supported in whole or in part by Government funds.

Now as no nation has ever been reclaimed from superstition and barbarism except by the teaching and preaching of the Gospel of Christ in the native language, and the giving to the people the Bible and other Christian books in that language, and as this has been the course followed in the various missions among the Indians, the obstructive and tyrannical character of the order is evident. It puts an end to the only effectual way of Christianizing and civilizing the Indians.

The Rev. Dr. Samuel C. Bartlett, President of Dartmouth College, has an article in the *Independent* on the subject. He says the effort to reach and permanently benefit the great mass of any people by first teaching them all a foreign tongue is contrary to all precedent, and he doubts if any government in the civilized world would now dare to attempt such a thing, even with their conquered provinces.

"The Turks did indeed attempt to crush out the language of the Armenians in Turkey : but that was centuries ago. The Norman conquerors, though they made French the court language, did not venture to interdict the use or teaching of the Saxon tongue. The Egyptian Government does not forbid the use of Coptic in the mission schools. The Turkish Government would not be tolerated in ruling out the use of Armenian and Greek in the schools of Turkey. The Czar would not undertake to root out the native language from the schools of Poland. Such proceedings are now unknown. Christians and philanthropists encounter them nowhere among the nations. It would of course be competent for the Government of the United States to rule out the Indian languages and Indian books *from its own schools*, though it would be a grave mistake to do so. But for any functionary of the Government, or for the Government itself, to prohibit all other schools in the Indian Territory from using any book, no matter how excellent or indispensable, except in a language unknown to the great body of the people, is a stretch of power, not only unworthy of an enlightened age and a free

country, but in conflict with the first principles of wisdom
and justice. It is a wrong that requires to be speedily
rectified."

It has required the outspoken opposition of the press,
especially of the religious press, petitions to the President,
and the waiting upon him of a deputation of distinguished
men, representing the Bible and the Missionary Societies,
to get a modification, as regards the missionary schools, of
the obstructive and unbearable order of Indian Commissioner Atkins, an order which has been sustained and enforced during Mr. Atkins' absence from Washington by
General Upshaw, the Assistant Commissioner.*

THE WONDERFUL CHANGE AT METLAKAHTLA.—The
*American Magazine* for July, 1887, contains an exceedingly interesting account, by Mr. Z. L. White, of the wonderful transformation which has been effected at Matlakahtla,
in British Columbia, almost entirely through the instrumentality of one man—Mr. William Duncan. We extract
the following from it :

The Alaska tourist, steaming along the coast of British
Columbia this summer, about seventeen miles south of
Fort Simpson, may, if the weather is clear, perceive upon
a beautiful peninsula what appears to be a thriving New
England village. Unlike the Indian settlements he has
seen, which are strung along the beach with no attempt at
regularity of arrangement, the neat frame houses are built

---

* Since the above was written Mr. Atkins has ceased to be
the Indian Commissioner, and the President has caused new
orders to be issued. Though these are an improvement upon
the modifications of the obnoxious ones of Mr. Atkins, still they
are not entirely satisfactory, as there is in them the exercise,
though in a much more limited degree, of the assumed right of
the Government to interfere with the methods of instruction in
the purely missionary schools.

upon regular streets. A large salmon cannery stands upon the shore, and a church, of imposing architecture, looms up above the smaller buildings, the most prominent object in the place.

If the steamer comes to anchor, a canoe will probably soon put off to it, but while the occupants give evidence by their dusky faces and well-marked features that they are full-blooded Indians, the blankets have given place to a European costume; their hair is cut short, the paint and savage ornaments have disappeared, and they will probably hail the captain in good English, instead of in the Chinook jargon. If the tourist goes ashore, he will see on every side evidence of thrift, industry, and a high state of civilization. The houses are neat, giving evidence of having been constructed by expert mechanics, and each has its little garden attached, in which vegetables for family use are raised. These dwellings are comfortably furnished, and supplied with the conveniences of civilization. Photographs, chromos, and ornaments of home manufacture adorn the walls.

The lumber from which the village has been constructed is supplied by a saw-mill situated a few miles out in the country, and connected with the village by a telephone line. In a blacksmith shop the iron implements used in the village are made; a brickyard supplies an excellent building material, and a planing-mill and sash and door factory furnish finished lumber, doors and sashes ready for glazing. The cannery has a capacity of 10,000 cases a year, and is marketing about 6,000 cases of salmon.

Skins are tanned into leather, and that is made into boots and shoes. Ropes and many other articles are also manufactured. The women spin and weave the fleece of mountain goats into shawls, blankets and heavy cloths, for which there is a ready market among the surrounding tribes of Indians. There is a co-operative store, in which all kinds of groceries, dry goods, etc., are sold at a slight advance above cost. A small vessel takes the produce of the village—salmon, oil, furs and manufactured goods, to Victoria, and returns with such articles as are needed.

The church, which will seat one thousand people, is the largest and best in British Columbia. It was built by the people of the village, entirely from materials of domestic production, except the glass in the windows, and it cost $12,000. The school house is a commodious building, com-fortably furnished, and supplied with the necessary books and apparatus.

The young men of the village are formed into a fire company, uniformed in red shirts and appropriate hats, and armed with patent fire extinguishers. The old men consti-tute a town council, and administer the public affairs of the village. On holidays they wear green sashes as badges of their office. A brass band of fifteen or twenty pieces has been instructed by a teacher from Victoria for that purpose, and they make very creditable music. The laws are executed by a magistrate and police constabulary, and there has never been a murder in the village since its foun-dation twenty-five years ago. The village I have described is Metlakahtla; its population is about eleven hundred, and the people are full-blooded Indians—the once degrad-ed savages that Dr. Duncan found at Fort Simpson in 1857.

COMMENDATIONS OF LORD DUFFERIN AND OTHERS. —The *Missionary Review* for September, 1887, after giv-ing the testimony of the Bishops of British Columbia and Athabasca, Archdeacon Woods and others, as to the spirit-ual character of the work, and the religious earnestness and evident sincerity of the converts, says:

Lord Dufferin, when Governor-General of Canada, visited

Metlakahtla in 1876, with Lady Dufferin, and after much and careful observation, near the close of a long address, said: "Before I conclude I cannot help expressing to Mr. Duncan, and those associated with him in his good work, not only in my own name, not only in the Government of Canada, but also in the name of Her Majesty the Queen, and in the name of the people of England, who take a deep interest in the well-being of all the native races throughout the Queen's dominions, our deep gratitude to him for thus having devoted the flower of his life, in spite of innumerable difficulties, dangers, and discouragements, of, which we, who only see the result of his labors, can form only a very inadequate idea, to a work which has resulted in the beautiful scene we have witnessed this morning." Our readers should understand that the testimonies we have quoted are the merest fragment of the spontaneous commendations given by distinguished men and observers of every class and rank in society, to which may be added the book entitled "Metlakahtla," published and widely circulated by the Church Missionary Society.

MR. DUNCAN AND HIS INDIANS ARE NOW IN ALASKA.—Mr. William Duncan, to whose remarkable work among the degraded savages of Metlakahtla, in British Columbia, frequent reference has been made in our columns, has solved the difficulties of the situation by actually removing his colony over the line into Alaska.

Without stopping to discuss the merits of his controversy with the Church Missionary Society and the Dominion Government, it is enough to say that when he appeared in the United States a year ago, with his petition to our Government and to the churches for encouragement and aid in his enterprise, few regarded the scheme as at all feasible. The expense involved in transporting a thousand Indians seemed an insurmountable barrier. The loss in-

volved in forsaking a settlement which had been furnished
wtth all the appliances of civilization in schools and
churches, saw-mills, canning factories, blacksmith shops,
flour-mills, etc., was enough to stagger the faith and the
purpose of any but the most intrepid.

But the simple fact now is that Mr. Duncan and his
colony are in Alaska. By what means this has been accomplished we cannot say. We hope that wisdom will be
given to this remarkable leader, and that whatever errors
there may have been in his ecclesiastical theories may be
corrected as a result of experience and severe trial. Above
all, may the time be distant when the rush of American
enterprise shall elbow this Indian colony out of its possessions, as has been done in so many instances under that
American flag to whose protection the exiles have fled.—
*The Church at Home and Abroad, for December,* 1887.

THE NEW MISSION IN ALASKA WELCOMED BY THE
GOVERNOR.—Port Chester, on Annette Island, has been
chosen as the site of the new Metlakahtla. Governor
Swineford has welcomed Mr. Duncan and his people to
Alaska, and in company with Dr. Jackson, the Commissioner of Education for the territory, has promised assistance and co-operation. At a public meeting the Hon. N.
H. R. Dawson, United States Commissioner of Education,
addressed the people, "assuring them," as an American
lady who was present, writes, "that they should have the
protection of the United States Government, and welcoming them to American soil, where they should not be disturbed in the possession of any lands upon which they
might build their houses. The encouraging remarks were
very grateful to the Metlakahtlans, and they showed their
appreciation of Mr. Dawson's kindness by hearty applause.
One of the leaders of the people responded most fittingly
to the speech of Mr. Dawson, showing by his well-chosen

words and his excellent command of English, to what noble
manhood Christian education can raise this people."

# PERSIA.

United States Minister Benjamin on the
Growth and Power of the Missions.—S. G. W.
Benjamin, lately Minister of the United States to Persia,
in a work, published this year, entitled, " Persia and the
Persians," bears the following testimony to the value and
results of the American missions in that country :

The American missionaries have now been laboring fifty
years in Persia. There are captious persons who ask,
" Well, how many converts have they made ? would they
not do more by staying at home ? "  Although this is not a
strictly fair way to judge of the value and results of missionary effort, yet I have no hesitation in affirming that
the missionaries in Persia have made the same number of
converts as an equal number of clergymen settled in towns
of the United States during the same period.

But even if they had been less successful in this respect,
it would work no prejudice, nor serve as an argument
against the necessity and importance of missions.  For, in
the first place, years are required for breaking ground, for
acquiring the language, for translating the Scriptures and
other devotional and educational works, and for establishing schools.

But the true method for judging the result of missionary
labor is that which regards it, not like a prairie fire that
sweeps rapidly over the plains, devouring all within its
range, and so swiftly dying out, but rather as a mighty,
silent influence, like the quiet, steady forces of nature,
which carry the seed and deposit it in the soil, nursing it

with sunshine and with rain year after year, until an oak springs up and reaches out its growing arms over the sod, and in time scatters the acorns, until a mighty forest waves its majestic boughs where once were rocks and thistles. Ages passed while nature was producing this great evolution ; and they who judge superficially by the few acorns first produced might have sneered at the slow but sure results that were to come after they had mouldered in the grave.

Men do not reason about other great movements as they do about missions. Is it fair, is it just, is it sensible to make an exception in this case? American missions in Persia may be seemingly slow, but they are an enduring influence both for secular as well as for religious progress. Their growth is cumulative and their power is mighty.

COLONEL C. E. STEWART ON THE STRIKING CONTRAST IN THIRTEEN YEARS.—We have also the testimony of an eminent Englishman concerning some results of the labors of the Rev. Dr. Bruce and the other members of the Church Missionary Society's mission in Persia. We quote from the April number for 1887 of the London *Sunday at Home:* Colonel C. E. Stewart, speaking of what he had himself seen, stated that on his first visit to that country twenty years ago, he had found about 26,000 Nestorian Christians, and 25,000 belonging to the Armenian Church. These Christians were very degraded, and required missionary work among them quite as much as the heathen. In spite of the prohibition against wine he considered the Persians a most intemperate people. In six small towns there would be found no less than one hundred public houses, and it was a regular thing for the Mohammedans to resort to them and to get drunk.

When Colonel Stewart told Dr. Bruce of this at Ispahan, his reply was, "What you have told me only presents an inducement to me to go." Upon his returning there, after the Doctor had been laboring there thirteen years, the contrast was striking indeed; he had never seen such a change in his life. He found that every boy in the town could speak English, and he was perfectly astonished at the wonderful work that had been accomplished in the short space of thirteen years. A church had been built, schools had been opened, and the pupils could pass an examination equal to that of Oxford and Cambridge. There was now a school of 116 girls. The public houses had all been closed, and all the time he was there he saw only one drunken man, who was a Mohammedan.

MARK OF DISTINCTION FROM THE SHAH.—The *Echo de Perse*, a French paper published at Teheran, contains an article, of which the following is a translation, sent by one of the missionaries to the *Church at Home and Abroad* (August, 1887):

We learn with great pleasure that by imperial firman his majesty the *Shah-in-Shah* has authorized the American missionaries to establish at Teheran a hospital, where, without regard to religion or nationality, all seeking relief shall be received for treatment. Dr. Torrence, physician to the mission, has been appointed director of this establishment, which is destined to render great service to our cosmopolitan population. His imperial majesty, desiring at the same time to reward the zeal and devotion of Dr. Torrence, who for long years past has been gratuitously relieving so much suffering and distress, has named him Grand Officer of the Order of the Lion and Sun of Persia, Dr. Torrence's many friends will be gratified to hear of this high mark of distinction having been accorded him.

# POLYNESIA.

### THE FIELD GENERALLY.*

SOME OF THE GREAT RESULTS OF CHRISTIAN MIS-SIONS.—We use the word Polynesia as including all the Islands of the Pacific within the tropics east of Australia, and also the immense island of New Guinea. Seventy years ago this extensive region was entirely heathen. Now more than 300 islands are Christianized; there are more than 100,000 communicants; 500,000 adherents; hundreds of native pastors, and thousands of teachers are supported by their own people, and a large number of native missionaries are sent to still unevangelized islands, especially to New Guinea and the New Hebrides group.

These native evangelists have shown quite as much self-sacrificing devotion in the cause of Christ as any white missionary martyrs have done. Hundreds of them have been killed while at their work, and the bodies of the greater part of them have been roasted and eaten by the cannibals for whose conversion they were laboring, but the thinned ranks were quickly filled up by equally consecrated volunteers.† On the majority of the more lately evangelized islands the native missionaries were the pioneers, but white missionaries were generally on the ground while yet the perils were great, and many of them met the same fate as the Polynesian martyrs.

---

* For facts and testimonies concerning the special divisions of the great Polynesian field see under Fiji, Micronesia, New Guinea, New Hebrides, New Zealand, Samoa, Tahiti and Tonga Islands.

† The Rev. W. Wyatt-Gill, who has long labored in the Harvey group, says that no less than sixty members of his church have been killed while acting as missionaries.

Before missionaries went to the Pacific Islands there was not, nor could there be, any commerce, on account of the savage character of the natives, although the natives were not always the first offenders. Now, foreign commerce with these islands amounts to more than twenty million dollars annually. Then, the shipwrecked crews of the navigator's or whaler's ships were killed and eaten ; now, shipwrecked mariners are kindly and hospitably treated, and taken to the nearest port frequented by foreign vessels.

WHAT THE MISSIONARIES HAVE GIVEN THE NATIVES.—The progress which the Polynesians have made was really set on foot by the missionaries. They have had the greatest influence upon the civilization of the natives. They have taken their part and protected them when they could. They have further given them the fast foothold, the new, fresh object, motive and meaning of their whole existence, of which they stood so much in need.—*Russell's Polynesia*, 1840.

MISSIONS HAVE BEEN THE PRESERVATION OF THE POLYNESIANS.—Dr. Christlieb, in his " Protestant Foreign Missions," page 84, says : " The fact that we find people here at all, is the result of missions. They have been the preservation of these peoples, as the investigations of Meinicke, Waitz, Garland, Oberlander and Darwin prove, by the suppression of cannibalism, human sacrifices and infanticide, by the introduction of the rights and laws of civilization, and of less savage methods of warfare, by the elevation of the marriage state, and the like. Even travellers for pleasure, medical men seeking to obtain an insight into nature in its primitive state, in their reports, have been obliged, against their will, to become apologists of missions and of their civilizing influences."[*]

---

[*] See also, under Sandwich Islands, the testimony of the Hon. Elisha Allen on this point.

THE LIFE OF A SAVAGE.—It is often said, "Why not leave the savages alone in their primitive state? They only are truly happy." How little do those who thus speak know what that life really is! A savage seldom sleeps well at night. He is in constant fear of attacks from neighboring tribes, as well as the more insidious foes created by his superstitious mind. Ghosts and hobgoblins, those midnight wanderers, cause him much alarm, as their movements are heard in the sighing of the wind, in falling leaves, lizards chirping, or disturbed birds singing. If midnight is the favorite time for spirit movements, there is another hour when he has good cause to fear the first mentioned enemies. It is the uncanny hour between the morning star and the glimmering light of approaching day—the hour of yawning and armstretching, when the awakening pipe is lighted, and the first smoke of the day enjoyed. The following will show what I mean:

Some six years ago, the people of the large district of Saroa came in strong battle array, and in the early morning ascended the Manukola hills, surrounded the villages, and surprised and killed men, women, and children, from the poor gray-headed sire to the infant in arms. About forty escaped to Kalo, but were soon compelled to leave, as Saroa threatened to burn Kalo if it harbored the fugitives. They pleaded for peace, but without avail. Saroa said, "Every soul must die." The quarrel began about a pig.

Ah! savage life is not the joyous hilarity some writers depict. It is not always the happy laugh, the feast and the dance. Like life in civilized communities it is varied and many-sided. There are often seasons when tribes are scattered, hiding in large trees, in caves, and in other villages far away from their homes. Not long ago, inland from Port Moresby, a large hunting party, camping in a cave, were smoked out by their enemies, and all killed but one. The people at Port Moresby say that now for the first time they all sleep in peace, and that as they can trust the peace of God's Word, they mean to keep it. This is significant, coming from those who not long since were the most noted pirates, robbers, and murderers along the whole coast of the peninsula.—*Rev. James Chalmers in "Life in New Guinea."*

CAPTAIN MACDONALD ON SAFETY TO THE SHIP-WRECKED.—At a meeting in behalf of the British and Foreign Bible Society, held in 1860, at Sydney, in Australia, Captain Macdonald related the following incident:

"When I was amongst the Fiji islands I came to a place where a vessel from California had been wrecked. The passengers and crew had no fear until their vessel suddenly struck on a reef, and became a complete wreck. Their horror can hardly be described, when, in the morning, they found themselves helpless among cannibals, who were well known to regard whoever were cast on their coast as waifs and strays. Summoning all their courage they made for the shore, and went to the nearest hut, not knowing what was to become of them. On entering, the chief officer saw lying on a board a dark colored object that particularly arrested his attention. It was not a club, or barbed spear, or tomahawk; it was a Bible. 'We are safe,' he said to his companions, 'We are safe! Wherever that Book is there is no danger to be apprehended.' The fact was that some little time before missionaries had been there, and such was the change wrought among these people that they not only spared the sailors, but entertained them hospitably, until, after three weeks, I arrived and took them away."

LIVING IN A NEW WORLD.—More than a generation has passed away since the missionaries began their work in the Pacific.   In nothing is the contrast between the past and present more distinctly marked than in the matter of cleanliness.   The Hervey Islanders in their original condition were never a cleanly race.   In most of the islands fresh water is scarce; so that their sin was venial.   A saponaceous plant known as the *tutututu*, was used in the early days of Christianity for washing clothes, instead of soap.   The trunk of the tree, which grows in the interstices of the coral rock near the sea, was scraped with a piece of hoop-iron or a knife; these scrapings mixed with water make a good lather.   As commerce sprang up in the wake of Christianity, soap became plentiful and this saponaceous tree was allowed to grow unmolested.   At the beginning of our work I have known natives to wear a shirt day and night, until it fell to pieces.   These wiseacres declined to use proffered soap, lest the precious garment should wear out the sooner!   The increase of the soap trade in the Pacific is a fair index of the advance of our work on the side of civilization.   In all Protestant native communities vast quantities of soap are disposed of.   It is a pleasant thing on the Lord's day from the pulpit to survey the clean and neat appearance of the congregation in contrast with the dirt of former days.   In those early days the exclusive use of well-oiled native cloth was not favorable to cleanliness.   At times the strong scent of these garments was overpowering to European nostrils, although agreeable enough to the islanders.   To-day it seems as though we lived in a new world; so cleanly (comparatively speaking) have our converts become in respect to their persons and garments.— *Wm. Wyatt Gill, B. A., in " Jottings in the Pacific."*

CIVILIZATION WITHOUT THE GOSPEL DOES NOT CIVILIZE.—At the last annual meeting of the London Missionary Society, the Rev. James Chalmers, the " Apos-

tle of New Guinea," said: "Two years ago from this
country they sent out the British flag to that country, and
they told the natives of New Guinea that the British Queen
Victoria—God bless her!—was going to protect them.
Have you considered it? I have had twenty-one years'
experience amongst natives. I have seen the semi-civil-
ized and the uncivilized; I have lived with the Christian
native, and I have lived, dined, and slept with the cannibal. I have visited the islands of the New Hebrides,
which I sincerely trust will not be handed over to the tender mercies of France; I have visited the Loyalty Group,
I have seen the work of missions in the Samoan Group, I
know all the islands of the Society Group, I have lived
for ten years in the Hervey Group, I know a few of the
groups close on the line, and for at least nine years of my
life I have lived with the savages of New Guinea; but I
have never yet met with a single man or woman, or with a
single people, that your civilization without Christianity
has civilized. For God's sake let it be done at once!—
Gospel and commerce, but remember this, it must be the
Gospel first. Wherever there has been the slightest spark
of civilization in the Southern Seas it has been where the
Gospel has been preached; and wherever you find in the
island of New Guinea a friendly people or a people that
will welcome you there, it is where the missionaries of the
Cross have been preaching Christ. Civilization! The
rampart can only be stormed by those who carry the
Cross."

THE WONDERFUL RESULT OF A LOVING ACT.—Mrs.
Jennie F. Willing, in a late missionary address in New
York city, related a story of a missionary and his wife in
one of the South Sea Islands, where Dr. Crocker, of Michigan University, narrowly escaped being eaten by cannibals. Dr. Crocker and a companion lived to tell the story

of their adventures in England. Moved by love, and under the guidance of the Holy Spirit, a clergyman and his wife decided to go out as missionaries to that very island. Embarking on a merchant vessel, they succeeded in inducing the captain to put them ashore when none of the inhabitants were visible.

Seating themselves on a box that contained all their earthly possessions, they watched the ship spread its white sails and disappear below the horizon. When the savages, accompanied by their chief and his daughter, came on the scene, they felt the limbs of the missionary, and evidently thought that in him was material for a good dinner. The daughter ran her fingers through the long, silky hair of the lady, who, impelled by Christian love, drew the girl to her and imprinted a kiss upon her lips. That natural act won the heart of the daughter. For three days the debate on eating the unexpected guests went on, and at last was decided in the negative by the pleading eloquence of the chief's favorite child. The missionaries lived long enough to see the people of that island converted to Christ, and sending out missionaries to other islands still in heathen darkness. Thus that little act of love was the means, through God, of saving many precious souls.

CHEERING SCENES.—At a recent meeting in London, the Rev. James Chalmers, who is now on his way back to his work in New Guinea, said that he had often been cheered by what he had witnessed in the villages of New Guinea and the South Sea Islands. Just as the sun went down parents and children would assemble in their homes, and then would be heard the glad song of praise ascending to the throne of God. Speaking especially of Manikihi, he said, "The village is built round the teacher's house. This man was one of the many grand instructors these islands have supplied. When asked on one occasion by the

French Governor of Lifu, ' Who told you to come here?' he replied, ' My Master said to me, "Go into all the world to preach the Gospel." That is what brought me here.' For this reply, pronounced impudent, he was imprisoned for three days, and then sent away. This man made it a rule, just as the sun dipped into the sea, to ring a bell. Parents and children all then went into their homes, from every one of which would ascend the hymn of praise, sung to some grand old English tune, to the Father of all mankind. After about fifteen minutes devoted to reading of the Scripture and prayer, the people went into the open air and there conversed together for awhile. From that island of Manihiki some of the grandest Christian teachers have gone forth to evangelize their brethren, and many have laid down their lives for the sake of that Saviour whom as little children they learned to love.'

ROMAN CATHOLIC AGGRESSIONS.—The Roman Catholics have for some time been pursuing an aggressive, proselyting policy in the islands of the South Pacific. They have passed by whole groups of islands, and many single ones, on which were no missionaries, and have gone almost entirely to those where Protestant missions were established and flourishing. Failing in their efforts to entice many of the Christian converts to join them, or in bringing over many of the heathen, they have been persistent in their endeavors to bring these islands under the control of France and Spain, so that measures repressive of the Protestant missions might be put in force.

First they induced the French government to seize the Tahitian or Georgian group, then the Loyalty Islands, then many islands of the New Hebrides and other groups. About a year ago they persuaded Spain to take possession of the Caroline Islands, where American missionaries had been laboring for twenty-five years, and very successfully,

As soon as these islands were occupied by a foreign military force, or were in the power of a foreign fleet, the missionaries, through the influence of the priests, were either deported, or, in a great measure, silenced. Teachers were seized, Christian chiefs, and other prominent men, and Church officers were imprisoned and otherwise ill-treated, because they would not become Roman Catholics.

Exactly this was done to the English missionaries and their converts in the Georgian and Loyalty groups, and to the American missionaries and their converts in the Caroline Islands. It required the sending of English and American war vessels, and energetic action on the part of the British and American governments to get even some modification of these outrageous measures. Many and great are the hindrances and annoyances which Protestant missionaries and the native Christians on these islands still have to endure from Roman Catholic officials and priests.

This seizure of the islands still continues, one of the latest cases being that of the comparatively large one named Mare. The Rev. J. Jones, the missionary of the London Society, who had been on the island thirty-four years, was forcibly removed therefrom about a year ago. When he first went there the people were cannibals and savages of the fiercest kind. The Chief sent him word that he would come and cook him and his wife, and for years these two missionaries were in constant and imminent peril. Subsequently, this Chief became a Christian, and was one of Mr. Jones' best friends. Not only have a large number of the natives been converted, but this island has furnished many missionaries for New Hebrides and New Guinea, while Bishop Selwyn, of Melanesia, has found faithful assistants from among these men who were once such fierce cannibals.

A deputation headed by Lord Brassey, the well-known voyager and ex-First Lord of the English Admiralty, has waited upon the Marquis of Salisbury to protest against this latest outrage, and Lord Salisbury has made representations to the French government on the subject, but, as yet, without favorable result.

The Rev. James Johnston, the secretary of the late General Missionary in London, has published an account of the Roman Catholic missions, taken chiefly from Roman Catholic documents. It contains the following:

"In the South Sea Islands, no effort has been spared by the Roman Church to encroach upon ground occupied by Protestant missions, and the secular arm of France—a strange ally for a Christian Church—has been used to the utmost, not only for extending Catholic missions, but for invading the weak and defenceless islanders; and Romish priests did not scruple to take advantage of their violent and unprincipled invasion. Their conduct was a disgrace to the civilization of France, and a scandal to the Christianity of Rome. It is necessary that all should know that even temperate men, who are determined to be just, and desire to be charitable, cannot speak smoothly of such proceedings."

## SAMOA.

LA PEROUSE ON THE BARBARISM OF THE SAMOANS. —The native name of the group of ten islands often called the Navigator Islands, is Samoa. There is no one island named Samoa; the name is applied only to the entire group. The great French navigator, La Perouse, visited these islands in 1787, and, after the massacre of one of his officers and ten of his men, he writes as follows:

" I willingly abandon to others the care of writing the uninteresting history of such barbarous nations. A stay of twenty-four hours and the relation of our misfortunes, suffice to show their atrocious manners and their arts, as well as the productions of one of the finest countries in the universe."

Other navigators who visited the South Sea Islands, in the interests of science or commerce, before their evangelization, have, after enduring similar treatment, written in a similar way.

All the Samoan islands are now professedly Christian. The adherents of the London Missionary Society number 27,000, those of the Wesleyan Mission, 5,000, while the balance, 3,000, are followers of the French priests

DR. TURNER ON SOME OF THE GREAT RESULTS.— The *London Chronicle* for January contains an article of sixteen pages, by Rev. George Turner, LL.D , late of Samoa, concerning the work of the London Society in that group of Central Polynesia. These islands are about three thousand miles east of Australia, and some six or eight hundred miles north-east of Fiji. The earliest explorers found the people atrocious savages, and one place— where twelve white men were slain by the natives—is known as " Massacre Bay." The first missionaries, Williams and Barff, reached Samoa in 1830, and very rapid progress was made in the Christianization of the islands. At present heathenism is a thing of the past, and there are two hundred villages in which native pastors are supported by the people. Dr. Turner says that Samoa has a dark side, as has England. The principal difficulty has arisen out of rival claims for the chieftainship. It is affirmed that on account of these feuds, not only the great bulk of the people, but the chiefs themselves, long for foreign help and protection. These are the islands, it will be remembered, about which a stir has recently been made on account of the assumption of authority by a German warship. A more recent proposal has been made that the three principal islands of the group be given—one to Germany, one to England, and one to the United States.

The missionaries early began to translate portions of the Scriptures, and thirty years from the time Williams and Barff landed in Samoa, the people were all nominally Christian and had a beautiful octavo reference Bible in their hands. From the beginning the natives were required to pay for all their Scriptures and other books. In less than seven years after the entire Bible was printed, an edition of ten thousand copies was sold, and the British and Foreign Bible Society has received from sales the entire amount of its outlay—$15,571. After four years' revision work, another edition of ten thousand copies was printed, which has now been exhausted. At the commencement of the mission the natives had never seen a piece of money. Now there are English, French, German and American stores, and from $250,000 to $500,000 worth of native produce goes into the stores of these merchants in exchange for clothing and other necessary articles. It is pleasant to record the fact that the population, which in 1843 was 33,900, has increased somewhat, so that it now stands at 35,000. The native churches in Samoa, aside from supporting the native pastors, have within the last twenty years contributed on an average $6,000 per annum to the funds of the London Society. And yet there are some people who do not believe in foreign missions!— *Missionary Herald, March,* 1886.

CAPTAIN ERSKINE ON THE CHANGE EFFECTED.—As long ago as 1850 an English naval officer, Captain Erskine, wrote as follows concerning the change which had been effected in the character of the Samoans : " The first circumstance which must strike a stranger on his arrival, and one which will come hourly under his notice during his stay, is the influence which all white men, but in par ticular the missionaries, exercise over the minds of the natives. Among a people who from former accounts seem never to have had any definite notion on the subject of religion, a firm belief in a creating or prevailing Deity, or even in a future state, the introduction of Christianity, in the absence of evil foreign influence, was not likely to be difficult; and we find accordingly that this has been effected to a great extent, not merely in increasing the number of professed adherents, but in softening the manners and purifying the minds even of the heathen portion of the community.

" No unprejudiced person will fail to see that, had this people acquired their knowledge of a more powerful and civilized race than their own, either from the abandoned and reckless characters who still continue to infest most of the islands of the Pacific, or even from a higher class, en- gaged in purely mercantile pursuits, they must have sunk into a state of vice and degradation to which their old con- dition would have been infinitely superior. That they have been rescued from this fate at least, is entirely owing to the missionaries; and should the few points of asceticism which these worthy men, conscientiously believing them necessary to the eradication of the old superstition, have introduced among the converts, become softened by time and the absence of opposition, it is not easy to imagine a greater moral improvement than would have taken place among a savage people."—" *From Pole to Pole.*"

# SANDWICH ISLANDS.

THE EARLY NAVIGATORS ON THE SAVAGE CHARAC-
TER OF THE NATIVES —The early navigators, naval officers and others, speak of the gross immorality, cruelty,
and treachery of the Sandwich Islanders before Christian
missionaries arrived at the Island  La Perouse, remark-
ing upon their last named trait, says : " The most daring
rascals of Europe are less hypocritical than these natives
All their caresses were false  Their physiognomy does
not express a single sentiment of truth.  The one most to
be suspected is he who has just received a present, or who
appears to be the most in earnest in rendering a thousand
little services "

HON. RICHARD H DANA ON THE REMARKABLE
CHANGE.—And yet so long ago as 1860, the Hon. Richard
H. Dana, a distinguished lawyer of Boston, while on a
visit to the Islands, was able to write : " Whereas the
missionaries found these islanders a nation of half-naked
savages, living in the surf and on the sand, eating raw
fish, fighting among themselves, tyrannized over by feudal
chiefs, and abandoned to sensuality; they now see them
decently clothed, recognizing the laws of marriage, going
to school and church with more regularity than our people
do at home, and the more elevated portion of them taking
part in the constitutional monarchy under which they
live."

MISS GORDON-CUMMING ON HAWAII WITHOUT AND
WITH THE GOSPEL. — Miss C. F. Gordon-Cumming
made an extended visit to the Sandwich Islands, and
published a work on them entitled " Fire Fountains."
In one of a series of articles on the same group, in the
London *Sunday Magazine,* she says :

" All they * knew of the Isles was that they were engaged in incessant inter-tribal wars; that the gigantic stone altars reeked with the blood of human victims; that the life of a commoner was liable to be sacrificed to the merest caprice of his feudal lord, whose word was law, and who might at any moment seize everything belonging to his vassal; that infanticide prevailed to an extent unparalleled, even in the Society Isles, where the majority of the women made a common practice of putting their own offspring to death. But whereas there the little innocents were disposed of as soon as possible, the Hawaiian women frequently spared the babies for a few weeks or months, and then, on the smallest provocation, suffocated them, and buried them beneath the earth-floor of their own homes. These were a few of the details of the social life of Hawaii, which the mission party determined to try and remedy, though expecting to meet with the most vehement opposition from the priests and the chiefs. * * *

In the year 1868 it was computed that a total of about fifty thousand persons had joined the Church of Christ since the commencement of the mission in 1820. Marvellous, indeed, was the change which had been wrought. A race of thievish, sanguinary savages had been transformed into a community of remarkably honest, neighborly people. Throughout the Isles there was not a cottage which did not possess its Bible and hymn book, and in which daily family prayer and the custom of thanksgiving at every meal and a highly moral code in daily life were not invariable. The majority of the people could read and write. They had some notion of geography and mathematics, taught them by students at Lahaini College, which had already sent forth about eight hundred men. Some were

---

*The first band of missionaries from Boston, U. S.

fairly started in secular professions, as surveyors, lawyers, and even judges.

In short, the work done in fifty years had been so effectual that the parent society in Boston decided that Hawaii could no longer be considered as a mission field, but must be treated as an independent, self-ruling Christian community. It has given the best possible proof of vigorous life by its zeal for foreign missions to the isles still lying in darkness. Actually, one-fourth of the total number of Hawaiians who have been ordained to the ministry are now working as missionaries in various parts of Micronesia and in the Marquesas. Only thirty years elapsed from the day when the first American missionary set foot in Hawaii, ere a "Society Promoting Foreign Missions," was formed at Honolulu by the very men who had themselves so recently offered loathsome sacrifices on idol altars, and now each congregation throughout the isles makes its monthly collection in support of the said missions.

SUMMARY OF A GREAT WORK.—Statistics of Christian work accomplished in the Sandwich Islands have been heretofore given in various places, but the following facts brought together by Rev. Mr. Forbes, Secretary of the Hawaiian Evangelical Association, will be of interest. The first Hawaiian pastor was ordained in 1849. Since that time ninety-five Hawaiians have been ordained, of whom thirty-eight are at present pastors in the home field, and nine in foreign service, making forty-seven native Hawaiians who are now either pastors or missionaries in active service. Since 1852, when the first Hawaiians went to Micronesia in company with Messrs. Gulick, Snow and Sturges, not less than seventy-five Sandwich Islanders have gone as foreign missionaries—thirty-nine of them males ; thirty-six females. The total sum contributed at the islands for foreign missions has been $170,149.44. Of this amount $133,015.86 was contributed by native Hawaiian churches, the remainder by foreign churches and individuals at the island. The contributions of the Hawaiian churches for all purposes from the beginning, so far as can be ascertained, amount to $818,270.25. This record should awaken our gratitude and stimulate our faith.— *Missionary Visitor, November*, 1887.

HON. ELISHA H. ALLEN ON THE MISSIONARIES SAVING THE NATION.—We learn from the *Missionary Herald* that the Hon. E. H. Allen, the Hawaiian Minister to the United States, in a letter dated Bangor, Maine, Sept. 26, 1882, gave the following strong testimony to the exceeding value of the services of the missionaries of the American Board in the Sandwich Islands :

"I have a very high appreciation of the great work which the Board has accomplished. No one can fully appreciate it unless by a visit to the country which has been blessed by its labors. I went to the Sandwich Islands in 1850, and resided there till 1877, with occasional visits to the United States on special missions for the government. I was for twenty years Chief-Justice and Chancellor of the Kingdom, and had occasion to visit often the different islands of the group. I became intimately acquainted with the missionaries and the people in their charge. They were a self-denying and devoted class of men, and the ladies of the mission rendered great aid in the good work.

"The mission was established at a fortunate period. The islands, from their geographical position, have always been a favorite calling place for vessels which visit the North Pacific. It required this moral power to instruct the natives, and to resist the immoral influences which often prevail in those distant seas where there is no government. Undoubtedly many good men engaged in commerce and other pursuits were there; but it required a distinct class whose whole duty it was to educate the natives, and to be an example and teacher to the foreigners. They had great trials and great labor in the first years of their mission. They went to carry the gospel to a people of whose language they had no knowledge, and whose ideas, habits, manners and customs were, in many respects, abhorrent to their Christian civilization. You can imagine how slow this progress must have been, and the almost special grace required to prosecute the work. It was a great triumph to have saved the nation, and to have brought it within the family of nations, which was so important to Christian civilization, and to the commerce of the world, and more especially of the United States."

MR. M. D. CONWAY'S EXPERIENCES IN HONOLULU. —One cannot help being amused at reading a letter of Mr. Moncure D. Conway's, the "Liberal" preacher of London, describing his experiences at Honolulu, at which port the steamer touched which was carrying him from San Francisco to Australia. The vessel stopped there only over a Sabbath, and the disgust of this traveller at the strictness with which the people kept the day is very great. He expected on landing to witness " merry scenes, islanders swimming around the ship in Arcadian innocence, the joyous dance and song of guileless children of the sun," but his anticipations were rudely destroyed by finding a " silent city," " paralyzed by piety." " Never in Scotland or Connecticut have I seen such a paralysis as fell upon Honolulu the first day of the week." This traveller found the stores shut, and in a druggist's shop they would not even sell him a glass of soda. No one being willing to show him the sights of the place, he was compelled to go to church in order to look upon the people. He was impressed by what he saw there, especially at the Chinese church under the care of Mr. Damon, whose work in elevating the people he cannot help praising. But, after all, he can enjoy little where the Sabbath is kept so strictly, and complains bitterly of the "pietistic plague" which prevails on the island. This testimony to the success of Christian efforts in the Hawaiian Islands is undesigned, but not the less valuable.—*Missionary Herald, February,* 1884.

## SIAM.

THE HON. DAVID B. SICKLES ON THE GREAT WORK WHICH HAS BEEN ACCOMPLISHED.—The American Baptist and Presbyterian missionaries in Siam have not only accomplished a great work through the blessing of God, but they are also popular with all classes of foreigners, and also of the natives, from the King downwards. Not long since the King gave $1,000 to aid the work, and he has repeatedly contributed liberal sums before. He has also presented to Dr. Dean, the patriarch among the missionaries, a gold medal, as "the special mark of the royal high favor and regard." The *Foreign Missionary* for May, 1886, quotes the following testimony of Hon. David B. Sickles, who had been for five years United States Consul at Bangkok :

"The American missionaries in Siam, whom I have observed for several years, have accomplished a work of greater magnitude and importance than can be easily realized by those who are not familiar with its character and with the influence which they have exerted upon the Government and people. Largely through their influence slavery is being abolished, the degrading custom of bodily prostration, although still practiced, is not now compulsory. Wholesome and equitable laws have been proclaimed, criminals have been punished by civilized methods, literature and art have been encouraged by the King and Ministers, an educational institution has been established by the Government, reforms have been inaugurated in all its departments, and Christian converts have been permitted to enjoy the same liberty of conscience that they do in our own land.

A few months before my departure from that country I visited the mission stations in the interior, and was highly gratified with the substantial evidences that I witnessed of the success of Christian work among the people. The missionaries themselves in Siam are, as a class, the most consistent, devout and diplomatic people among all the foreign residents in the kingdom. Although sincerely and energetically engaged in their work, they do not hold themselves so much aloof from the men of rank and the educated foreign residents as to make themselves unpopular. On the contrary they are the general favorites in the entire community, and I never heard, during my residence in Bangkok of nearly five years, the expression of an unfavorable opinion in regard to their character or their work. At the palace they are more popular than any other foreign residents, and in the homes of the merchants of other nationalities they always find a welcome. *Before I went to the far East I was strongly prejudiced against the missionary enterprise and against foreign missionaries ; but, after a careful examination of their work, I became convinced of its immense value.*

THE FAVOR OF THE KING AND QUEEN.—A letter from Petchaburi,* in the New York *Evangelist*, dated Feb-

---

*An important town in the interior of Siam.

13

ruary 18, indicates a remarkable state of affairs in the relation of the government toward Christian missions. Dr. Thompson, of the Presbyterian mission, had rendered good service to several men injured in the explosion of a Japanese gunboat, and the king, through the prime minister, sent his thanks to Dr. Thompson. Later the king visited Petchaburi, with hundreds of princes, nobles and soldiers, and asked for a report of mission work, and called the missionaries to an interview. The princes had a prolonged conversation with Messrs. Thompson and Cooper about Jesus and his mission on earth. When the audience room of the king was reached he held a full and free conference with his guests about their work and his own plans as to a system of free schools, which he hoped to establish at an early day. He spoke of his high appreciation of the excellent and generous work accomplished by the Christian missionaries for the good of his people. He promised to always encourage their work, and calling the minister of education into his presence, he directed him to grant freely whatever aid the missionaries should apply for. An evidence that these utterances were sincere was furnished by two letters handed the missionaries as they retired, one from the queen to the ladies of the mission, and the other from the king to the gentlemen of the mission; the former containing a gift amounting to $960, and the latter a gift of $1,440 for the purpose of enlarging the mission hospital building. The king's letter concluded with these words: "His Majesty asks that you labor to complete this work, and that it may be finally established and ever prosper."—*Missionary Herald, July,* 1887.

Secretary of State Bayard lately received a dispatch from the United States minister at Bangkok, reporting that the Siamese king and queen, who have lately returned from a visit to Petchaburi, express much gratification at the

course pursued by the American missionaries there. Their
majesties gave liberally of money to the hospital and to
the missionary schools, and manifested in several other
ways their high regard for the work which the American
missionaries are doing in Siam.

---

# SIBERIA.

The Work of Dr. Lansdell and Others.—
Henry Lansdell, D.D., M.R.A.S., F.R.G.S., has visited
Siberia several times, and has traversed the whole of
this extensive country. He has circulated 60,000 copies
of the Holy Scriptures, besides other books and tracts,
among the Russian convicts, the Buriat natives, and
others. The Russian Government does not permit the
permanent residence of any missionaries except those of the
Russo-Greek Church, even among tribes in which this
Church is doing nothing. Dr. Lansdell, in *Harpers' Magazine* for August, 1887, says :

"The Buriats in 1886 numbered 260,000 souls, the
largest native population in Siberia, and the only one
amongst whom the English missionaries have been allowed
to labor. In the first quarter of the present century three
men went out to Selenghinsk and Verchne Udinsk, where
they translated and printed the New Testament in the
Buriat language. They had also a school, and tokens of
success were not wanting. But the work was stopped by
the Russian Synod, the members of which were jealous of
foreign interference, and found an occasion of dismissing
all foreign missionaries from the Russian dominions, under
the pretext that the Synod wished to do all its own
mission work for its own heathen. The Englishmen,
therefore, about 1840, had to quit the country, leaving

behind them, however, a sacred enclosure I visited in Selenghinsk, where lie the bodies of five members of their families, whose graves silently tell their own tale of British labor and Christian self-denial."

DR. LANSDELL'S LATEST BOOK. — Some years ago Dr. Lansdell published " Russian Siberia," a work which received the highest praise. This year he has issued " Through Central Asia," in which he recounts his experiences and observations during his latest and most extensive travels and explorations. A notice of it in a London paper of Nov. 25th says :

" In making preparations for such an enormous journey (it included Russia, Western Siberia, Bokhara, Khiva, Turkestan, and other governments and provinces), the first consideration involved the carriage of over thirty boxes of books, &c., for distribution among hospitals, mines, prisons, educational institutions, and so forth. In other words, his prime motive for travelling in foreign lands was a combination of missionary and philanthropical duty. The spirit of the traveller naturally evoked reciprocal favors. Even the rigid ecclesiasticism of dignitaries of the Greek Church softened under the influence of the literary gifts offered to them, consisting of Bibles, or parts of it, printed in Russ, Sclavonic, Hebrew, Chinese, Mongolian, Kirghese, Arabic, Turkish, Polish, German, and French, thus meeting the wants of all classes, bond or free. We must also give the Russian government every credit, as well as grateful thanks, for providing their travelling guest with a Crown podorjona, or authority, to have the first claim on all animals and vehicles *en route* throughout Russian Asia. No less than a thousand horses and camels were thus utilized by him in a journey of 8,000 miles. * * * * * * *

" Perhaps the most important individual Dr. Lansdell

met with in Asia was the late Emir of Bokhara. To get
into Bokhara alive was one thing, to get out alive was a
problem which few Englishmen ever solved. In the days
of a former Emir, Dr. Wolff, the missionary, narrowly
escaped with his life; Colonel Stoddart and Captain
Conolly were put to death. So that Bokhara has a terrible reputation. Still 'Bokhara the Noble' came in the
way, and a successful visit would repay any amount of
misfortune to effect such a *desideratum*. Hence the entry
into Bokhara, the stay there, and how he got out again
form one of the most interesting portions of the book.
Nearly everything turned out most auspiciously; but, of
course, much circumspection and tact were always needed.

"Everything in the remarkable city of Bokhara is full
of interest. The mosque services, the strange buildings,
and that strangely ubiquitous people, the Jews, commanded the particular attention of Dr. Lansdell.

"'Through Central Asia' is extremely well illustrated,
no less than seventy-four engravings being given of places,
persons and important buildings. A splendid map is also
included amongst the many good things. If there were no
other merits belonging to the volume than that of being a
record of lasting work done in the Master's service, it is
worthy of the highest praise; but considering that Dr.
Lansdell has described in his works wide tracts of country
unknown, or little known, before, and in every department
—whether historical, geographical or personal—has given
the plain record of what he has seen and heard, we must be
grateful to him for his interesting work."

A LETTER FROM THE CONVICTS.—A correspondent of
the *Pall Mall Gazette* writes as follows: " Some time ago
I came across an enormous official-looking document which
had been sent from Siberia, and in which a number of
convicts had expressed, in touching words, their gratitude

for the pamphlets and portions of Scripture which the Religious Tract Society had sent out to them. At the foot of the neatly-written letter a long string of the names of the convicts appeared. Some were written in a firm, clear hand, many more faintly and illegibly, while not a few of the condemned men had put the mark of the illiterate, which seems to be an x all the world over.

"Those who have seen the detachments of prisoners making their weary way along the endless high road which leads northward from St. Petersburg, who have watched the gloomy, sullen, helpless looks of the gray-coated men, whom the immense cross of orange cloth on their backs stamps as convicts, going to be buried alive in the Siberian mines and quarries, will understand that it is no mere formula when in their humble letter the convicts state that having lost all hope for this life, a new hope for the future one is brought to them by the leaflets and Scripture portions from the Tract Society."

---

# TAHITI.

ADMIRAL WILKES ON THE VALUE OF MISSIONARY LABORS.—Tahiti was one of the first of the South Sea Islands to be reached by missionary efforts, and as long ago as 1840, Admiral Wilkes, of the United States Exploring Expedition, was able to write of Tahiti: " As a proof of the value of missionary labors, my experience warrants me in saying that the natives of Tahiti, once given to perpetual internecine broils and the worship of idols propitated by human sacrifices, are now honest, well-behaved and obliging; that no drunkenness or rioting is seen, except when provoked by white visitors, and that they are obedient to the laws and to their rulers."

FAITHFUL NATIVE CHRISTIANS.—The population of the island to-day is about 10,000 natives, Europeans and Chinese. The eighteen Protestant Churches have 2,337 native communicants, and the ten Roman Catholic Churches, most of which have been established since the French assumed the Protectorate of the island, have not more than 200 native members. Nearly all the native Protestant communicants resist the efforts of the proselyting Roman Catholic priests, and the hold which true religion has over them is spoken of as wonderful. Against the baneful example of the foreign population, and surrounded with manifold temptations, these native Christians are living faithful, prayerful and godly lives.

The other islands of the group, Huahine, Porapora, Raiatea and Tahaa, are also Christian, having about two thousand communicants, and almost all the other people being adherents. The native Christians on all these Tahitian or Society islands not only support the native ministers and teachers, 225 in all, pay for church and school buildings and other local expenses, but they have also for many years given a large sum annually to the funds of the London Missionary Society.

MR. CHARLES DARWIN ON THE MORALITY AND RELIGION OF THE TAHITIANS.—Here is what the late Mr. Charles Darwin wrote in his "Journal of Researches into the Natural History and Geology of the Countries visited during the voyage of H. M. S. 'Beagle' round the world, under the command of Captain Fitzroy," 1839 :

"Thus seated, it was a sublime spectacle to watch the shades of night gradually obscuring the last and highest pinnacles. Before we laid down to sleep, the elder Tahitian fell on his knees, and, with closed eyes, repeated a long prayer in his native tongue. He prayed as a Christian should do, with fitting reverence, and without the fear of ridicule or any ostentation of piety. At our meals, neither of the men would taste food without saying beforehand a short grace. Those travellers who think that a Tahitian prays only when the eyes of the missionary are fixed on him, should have slept with us that night on the mountain side. * * *

" One of my impressions, which I took from the two last authorities, was decidedly incorrect, viz. : that the Tahitians had become a gloomy race, and lived in fear of the missionaries. Of the latter feeling I saw no trace, unless, indeed, fear and respect be confounded under one name. Instead of discontent being a common feeling, it would be difficult in Europe to pick out of a crowd half so many merry and happy faces.

" On the whole, it appears to me that the morality and religion of the inhabitants are highly creditable. There are many who attack, even more acrimoniously than Kotzebue, both the missionaries, their system, and the effects produced by it. Such reasoners never compare the present state with that of the island only twenty years ago, nor even with that of Europe at this day ; but they compare it with the high standard of gospel perfection. They expect the missionaries to effect that which the Apostles themselves failed to do. Inasmuch as the condition of the people falls short of this high standard, blame is attached to the missionary, instead of credit for that which he has effected. They forget, or will not remember, that human sacrifices, and the power of an idolatrous priesthood — a system of profligacy unparalleled in any other part of the world—infanticide, a consequence of that system of bloody wars, where the conquerors spared neither women nor children — that these have been abolished ; and that dishonesty, intemperance, and licentiousness have been greatly reduced by the introduction of

Christianity. In a voyager to forget these things is base ingratitude : for should he chance to be at the point of shipwreck on some unknown coast, he will most devoutly pray that the lessons of the missionary may have extended thus far."

TESTIMONY OF CAPTAIN HARVEY.—Captain Harvey, master of a whaling vessel, who visited Tahiti in May, 1839, gave the following testimony to the good effects of missionary labor on the island : "This is the most civilized place that I have been at in the South Seas. It is governed by a queen, daughter of old Pomare, a dignified young lady about twenty-five years of age. They have a good code of laws. No spirits whatever are allowed to be landed on the island, therefore the sailors have no chance of getting drunk, and are all in an orderly state, and work goes on properly. It is one of the most gratif ing sights the eye can witness on a Sunday in their church, which holds about 5,000, to see the Queen near the pulpit, and her subjects around her decently apparelled, and in seemingly pure devotion. I really never felt such a conviction of the great benefit of missionary labors before. The attire of the women is as near the English as they can copy."

## TERRA DEL FUEGO.

EUROPEAN GOVERNMENT REPRESENTATIVES COMMEND THE WORK. — The South American Missionary Society of the Church of England, was formed for the purpose of carrying the gospel, not only to the degraded Fuegians, but also to the Patagonians and other aborigines of South America, and also to the neglected foreign communities on that continent. The society now has many stations scattered from Terra del Fuego to Panama. The present headquarters of the mission is on Stanley Island, one of the Falkland group, and the bishop is the Rt. Rev. Waite H. Stirling, D.D., who was formerly a missionary in Fuegia and Patagonia. His work, and that of his colleagues, has recently been very highly commended at a meeting in London Mansion House, by representatives of France, Germany, and Italy, for the change that has been brought about in the treatment of wrecked crews by the Fuegian natives.

ADMIRAL SULLIVAN WRITES TO DARWIN ON THE WONDERFUL CHANGE.—Admiral Sullivan, of the English navy, found the transformation of character so great that he informed Darwin of the change in the natives who had been under the influence of the mission. As an illustration, he said that during eleven years the mission fowl-houses had remained unlocked and not one egg had been stolen. Darwin replied that he " could not have believed that all the missionaries in the world could have made the Fuegians honest." Darwin had once maintained that all the pains bestowed on them would be thrown away, but he now acknowledged his mistake, and became a regular subscriber to the funds of the South American Missionary Society.*

LIEUTENANT BOVE'S TESTIMONY.—In the Fall of 1882 the Antarctic Expedition, commanded by Lieutenant Bove of the Italian army, was wrecked in Sloggett Bay,

---

* Writing to the Secretary of the Society in 1870, he says : " The success of the Terra del Fuego Mission is most wonderful, and charms me, as I always prophesied utter failure. It is a grand success. I shall feel proud if your Committee think fit to elect me an honorary member of your Society. I have often said that the progress of Japan was the greatest wonder in the world, but I declare that the progress of Fuegia is almost equally wonderful."

off the coast of Terra del Fuego. The officers and crew were not drowned, neither were they robbed and cruelly massacred by the natives, as the crew of the " Roseneath" were on the West Coast a few months before. They were happily rescued by the efforts of the crew of the " Allen Gardiner" and mission yawl, and by the Rev. Thomas Bridges and his Christian natives. Lieutenant Bove, in a recently published narrative, says: " The presence of English missionaries in Terra del Fuego has undoubtedly modified the character of a great part of the inhabitants of the Beagle Channel. So rapid is the improvement, so great are the sacrifices which the good missionaries impose on themselves, that I believe we shall in a few years be able to say of all the Fuegians what is now said of Palla-laia; he was one of the most quarrelsome, the most dis- honest, the most superstitious of the inhabitants of Terra del Fuego, and now he lives under the shadow of the Cross, a model of virtue, and a pattern of industry." The Italian Government decided to present to the South American Missionary Society a gold medal and an official letter of special thanks. The medal contains a likeness of the King and a record of the occasion.

A CHRISTIAN FUEGIAN VILLAGE.—The mission sta- tion at Ooshooia, on the north shore of Beagle Channel, has become a Christian village, the natives having their cottages, gardens, and roads, while polygamy, witchcraft, wrecking, theft, and other vices have been abolished in the vicinity. In September, 1885, an English squadron arriv- ed at Ooshooia, and a distinguished naval officer reports that " a crew of six natives came out, the men as well dressed and well trained as the sailors of our seas." He describes the climate of Oooshooia as healthy and agreea- ble, the slightly undulating land as " covered with good grass and producing good potatoes, turnips, cabbages, pears, apples, roses, pinks, violets," etc.

---

## TONGA ISLANDS.

THE RESULTS OF A LONG AND PERILOUS STRUG-
GLE.—The Friendly Islands, as Captain Cook designated them, or the Tonga Islands, as they are now generally called, consist of 150 smaller, and 32 greater islands, the chief of which is Tongatabu, or Sacred Tonga, which contains about 7,500 inhabitants out of a total population of 25,000. In 1822 the work of evangelization was begun by the Wesleyan Methodists, and after a lengthened and perilous struggle with the savage paganism of the inhabit·ants, it was crowned with success. There are at present more than 8,000 communicants, and more than 19,000 adherents.

King George, the principal chiefs, and the majority of the people, have separated from the Wesleyan Church, and have organized the Tongan Free Church, which is Methodist in theology and church government. The King and his prime minister, Mr. Baker, were guilty of acts of violence in effecting this separation, which led to the appoint·ment by the English Government of a High Commissioner to examine into affairs. This Commissioner, Sir. C. Mitchell, has made his report in a parliamentary paper. The Commissioner acquits the Wesleyan churches of fault, and shows that the king and his minister had violated the constitution, and recommends that the king grant amnesty to all prisoners and that he make proclamation that all men are free to worship as they please. The king accepts these recommendations, but Mr. Baker is not to be removed at present. Solemn promises are given that no persecution shall be allowed.

The London *Christian*, for Nov. 25, 1887, says: " Sir Charles Mitchell's detailed report to Sir Henry Holland on the troubles in Tonga tells very decisively against Mr. Shirley Baker. The report makes it clear that there was persecution of a very persistent and cruel kind. The law was violated, and the most cruel outrages practiced in order to compel the Wesleyans to abandon their Church. Sir Charles Mitchell adds that "the patience with which the Wesleyans endured the brutal ill-treatment, accompanied with robbery, to which they were exposed, astonishes me, and I can only attribute it to the good influence of Mr. Moulton."

THE FEARLESS ENERGY OF THE NATIVE CHRISTIANS.—Miss C. F. Gordon-Cumming gives, in the London *Sunday Magazine*, the following account of the fearless energy and sanctified zeal of the native Christians of the Tonga islands:

" The fierce cannibals of Fiji owed their first impressions of a holy faith and life to the bold energetic islanders of Tonga—a powerful race both bodily and mentally. When these men received the foreigners, whose words brought them a new revelation of life, their own strong conviction of the truth seems to have impelled them to proclaim it everywhere. They were then, as they are still, a race of fearless sailors, finding their way to many distant isles.

" Thenceforth, whenever they travelled, they preached the new religion, and expounded the scriptures to all who would listen. Moreover, their own entirely changed lives spoke volumes In place of the wild orgies of olden days, the arrival of a Tongan boat was now marked by frequent meetings for prayer, by the singing of sweet unknown hymns, very different from their licentious heathen songs ;

and the people listened in wonder, and many believed.

"The bold, fearless energy of the Tongans had always secured to them great influence amongst the neighboring races, notably amongst the Fijians, and a strong Tongan colony had established itself on one of the Fijian Isles—a colony of the very wildest spirits of Tonga, who here found an atmosphere of more unbridled license than Tonga could endure even in heathen days. So desperately bad were the lives of these men, that even their cruel cannibal hosts were afraid of them, and spoke with awe of their evil deeds.

"When the Great Light had dawned on Tonga she bethought her of her sons at Lakemba (in Fiji), and soon canoes sailed thither, on which each sailor was a preacher of righteousness  These men told their brethren of the changes wrought in Tonga, and a conviction of the truth came home so forcibly to these prodigals, that many arose and returned to their own land, while others (repenting of the evil they had done in the far country) not only reform ed their own lives, but went about explaining to their Fijian friends and neighbors the reason of their doing so."

## TURKISH EMPIRE.

SUMMARY OF THE MISSIONS OF THE AMERICAN BOARD.—The summary of the missions of the American Board is as follows : Missionaries from the United States, 156, of whom 52 are ordained , stations, 18 ; out stations, 281 ; native pastors, 66 , native preachers, 91 , teachers and other native helpers, 455 ; churches, 105, with a membership of 8,259, of whom 598 were added in the year 1884–5 ; colleges and high schools, 26, with 1,003 pupils ; girls' boarding schools, 19, with 815 pupils ; common

schools, 345, with 11,973 pupils; total number under instruction, 14,740.—*Historical Sketch of the Missions of the
American Board in Turkey*, 1886.

SIR AUSTEN LAYARD ON THE JUDICIOUS AND EAR-
NEST EFFORTS OF THE MISSIONARIES.—Sir Austen
Layard says (*Nineveh and Babylon*, p. 404) : "A change
of considerable importance, and which it is to be hoped
may lead to the most beneficial results, is now taking place
in the Armenian Church. It is undoubtedly to be attri-
buted to the judicious, earnest and zealous exertion of the
American missionaries. Their establishments, scattered
over nearly the whole Turkish empire, have awakened
amongst the Christians, and principally among the Armenians, a spirit of inquiry, and a desire for the reform of
abuses, and for the cultivation of their minds, which must
ultimately tend to raise their political as well as their
social position in the human scale."

LORD REDCLIFFE ON THEIR DISCRETION TEMPERED
WITH ZEAL.—When Lord Stratford de Redcliffe, who
was for a long time the British Ambassador at Constantinople, was about to return to England, the missionaries
presented him with a farewell address in which they
thanked him for the protection he had afforded them, and
their helpers, and they commended his efforts in behalf
of civil and religious liberty. In his reply to the address
Lord Redcliffe said :

"Among the testimonies of approving kindness which I
have recently received, from those with whom my functions
in this country long brought me into frequent and intimate
relations, there is none more gratifying than the address
which you did me the honor of placing in my hands a few
hours ago. The cordial expressions by which you have
identified my course of conduct with the progress of your
labors in a great and good cause, may well awaken some

feelings of satisfaction, and even of pride, in my heart. At the same time, I fervently join with you, in tracing our mutual endeavors to that surer and higher Source, whence all wise counsels and all corresponding results originally proceed. But while I accept with pleasure your kind recognition of my services here, it is only just that I should bear witness to your constancy in seeking to afford to all classes of the population in this vast empire, means and opportunities of approaching more nearly the pure foun- tains of our common faith. I have noted with deep inter- est, the discretion which, almost without an exception, has invariably tempered your zeal; the happy consequences which, in many important respects, have attended your exertions; and the still happier prospects which, though slowly, are nevertheless perceptibly opening for your en- couragement, in a most difficult, and at times most hazard- ous field of duty."—*Missionary Herald, Jan.* 1859.

THE EARL OF SHAFTESBURY ON THE COMMON SENSE AND PIETY OF THE MISSIONARIES.—One of the most delightful instances of Christian magnanimity was displayed in England about this time. The financial troubles of 1857 in America had embarrassed the Board and threatened serious embarrassment in this mission. Noble Christians in England, of all evangelical communions, including ministers of the Church of England, came at once to the rescue. They formed the " Turkish Mission Aid Society," invited Dr. Dwight to present our cause to England, and raised money thenceforward, not to found missions of their own in Turkey, but to aid ours. At an anniversary of the Society in 1860, the Earl of Shaftes- bury crowned this magnanimity of deeds by an equal mag- nanimity of words. He said of our missionaries in Turkey : " I do not believe that in the whole history of missions, I do not believe that in the history of diplomacy, or in the history of any negotiation carried on between man and man, we can find anything to equal the wisdom, the soundness, and the pure, evangelical truth of the men who constitute the American mission. I have said it twenty times before, and I will say it again, for the expression appropriately conveys my meaning—that they are a marvellous combination of common sense and piety."—*Historical Sketch.*

THE MISSIONARIES DESERVING OF UNLIMITED PRAISE.—The English "Turkish Mission Aid Society" still exists. At the last annual meeting, in the absence of the Earl of Aberdeen, who had gone to India, the chair was occupied by Robert Needham Cust, LL.D., a member of the committee of the Church Missionary Society. Some handsome compliments were paid to the American missionaries. Reference was made to the fact that the special field in which the society was interested was the very field which had been consecrated by the labors of Paul and Barnabas and other apostolic preachers, and from which the gospel came to western countries. To this field we owe a debt of gratitude, and it would be a disgrace to Protestant Christendom if it were neglected. The American missionaries, the report stated, besides deserving unlimited praise for their own efficiency, have also the advantage that political motives cannot be imputed to them. Great Britain, France, and Germany are believed to be always ready to annex portions of the Turkish Empire, but no one ever supposes Americans to have any such designs. The record of American missionaries in the East has been to the last degree honorable. It was stated that the committee had remitted funds to forty-four different portions of the field.

THE HON. GEORGE P. MARSH ON THE VAST SIGNIFICANCE OF THE FACTS.—The Hon. George P. Marsh, LL.D., was the United States Minister to the Sublime

14

Porte, from 1849 to 1853. In a letter in reply to an invitation to be present at the annual meeting of the Board in 1855, he gives the following testimony to his estimate of our missionary work :

" Although I could have added nothing to the facts of which the Board and the religious public are already possessed, yet I would have taken special pleasure in bearing testimony, as an eye-witness, to the value and importance of the missionary efforts in the East, and the eminent piety, zeal, learning, and ability of the immediate agents of the Board in that great enterprise. The success of these efforts to carry back to their original source the lights of Christianity and civilization is not to be measured by the results apparent to distant observers; and however familiar American Christians may be with the statistical data of missionary movements in the Turkish Empire, the vast significance of those facts can only be appreciated by a personal acquaintance with the field of operations. The action of the missionaries has, I believe, thus far, not been impeded by the events of the war. If that action were now to be suspended, still the seed already sown could not fail to yield a harvest that would amply repay the sacrifices it has cost to American liberality and American devotion. *    *    *    *    I have not the slightest doubt that the keen-sighted Layard is right in assigning to this manifestation of the tendencies of American institutions in the East, a prominent place among the occasions of the political and military movements which have shaken Asia and Europe since 1853.—*Missionary Herald.*

TESTIMONY OF GENERAL LEW WALLACE.—In the Brocton (Mass.) *Daily Enterprise*, of December 21, 1886, there is an account of addresses made before the Old Colony Congregation on last Forefathers' Day. Among the speakers was General Lew Wallace, late United States

Minister to Turkey, who gave emphatic testimony to the
work and worth of the missionaries in Turkey

" When abroad in the East, I have found the best and
truest friends among the missionaries located in Constantinople, and among those good people, those of the Congre-
gational denomination seemed to predominate. I have
often been asked: ' What of the missionaries of the
East ? Are they true, and do they serve their Master ? '
And I have always been a swift witness to say—and I say
it now, solemnly and emphatically - that if anywhere on
the face of this earth there exists a band of devout
Christian men and women, it is there. I personally know
many men and women, and the names of Dr. and Mrs.
Riggs, the names of Woods, Bliss, Pettibone, Herrick,
Dwight, and others, spring up in my memory most
vividly."

GENERAL WALLACE'S PREJUDICE CHANGED TO HIGH
REGARD.—General Lew Wallace, United States Minister
to Turkey, author of " Ben Hur," was in the city a few
days ago, and, in the course of conversation, said that
when he went to Turkey he was prejudiced against missionaries, who constitute nearly all the American residents in the
country. But his views of them and their work had
completely changed. He had found them to be an admirable body of men, who are doing a wonderful educational
and civilizing work outside of their strictly religious work.
—*Missionary Outlook, Toronto, July*, 1887.

LIEUTENANT COLONEL MARK S. BELL AS A WITNESS.
—Lieutenant-Colonel Mark S. Bell, of the United Service
Club, Simla, India, in sending a check, May 8, for £10
to Mr Peet, treasurer of the mission, Constantinople,
gives this very important testimony: " I have been
travelling in Eastern Turkey and Persia, and the routes
taken led me through many of your chief missionary

stations.  To all interested in the welfare of the East, the inestimable value of your Society's labors cannot fail to be appreciated.  Nothing can be done to reform Turkey without setting before her living models ; and among those the moral, educational, and civilizing models, sent through the labors of your Society, cannot be considered to be the least, and America is to be highly congratulated on the success which, as a traveller, I have seen to have already attended her efforts to raise the peoples of Turkey."—*Missionary Herald*, 1886.

WHAT THE BRITISH CONSUL AT ALEPPO WRITES. —Mr. Skene, Her Britannic Majesty's Consul at Aleppo, writes : "Aintab is the metropolis of Oriental Protestantism—here the reformation worked out by the American missionaries has its headquarters, and is represented by no less than fourteen hundred persons.  The Church of Killis numbers one hundred members; that of Birijek, fifty ; Marash, one thousand; Diarbekir, four hundred ; Urfa, forty ; Aleppo, thirty ; Beitias, one hundred ; Kissab, five hundred, and Yekolook, one hundred ; in all, three thousand seven hundred and twenty in North Syria alone.  Education, as well as preaching the Gospel, has been spread to a great extent, schools having been established by the American missionaries in every considerable place in the province.  Besides these, which are merely elementary, there are theological classes for the preparation of natives for the ministry, upper-schools affording classical and scientific tuition, and a girls' boarding-school, under the enlightened charge of American ladies."

MRS. CHARLES ON THE ENTIRE CONSECRATION OF THE MISSIONARIES.—Mrs. Charles, the author of "The Schonberg-Cotta Chronicles," in her introduction to the book entitled "The Romance of Missions," (1885,) says : " A few words of most reverent and affectionate sympathy with the noble Christian work of American missionaries in the East, I feel it a delight and an honor to have an opportunity of giving. I have seen and known men and women devoted to those Oriental missions who seemed to me to come as near to the first type and the last idea of Christian life as any I hope to know—lives laid down for the Master and the brethren with such entire consecration, and simplicity, and joy, that when at last, from one of these* the life was demanded, and laid down in death, we felt that it was scarcely a fresh sacrifice, but merely the natural fulfilment of all that had gone before."

Sir Thomas Tancred on the Missions in Asia Minor.—Sir Thomas Tancred, Bart., C E., whose name is well known in connection with the famous Forth Bridge, contributes an article to the *Sunday at Home*, for November, 1887, under the title of " A Peep at Asia Minor." In it he refers as follows to the missions at Marash, Aintab, and other places in Asia Minor :

" Upon nearing Marash, which is built upon the slope of the hills forming the northern boundary of this plain, we sent forward our Zaptieh to look for quarters. We gave him one or two letters we had to native merchants; these individuals, however, seemed difficult to find, so he betook himself to the American schools, and, upon our arrival in the outskirts of the town, we were met by some pupils who escorted us to headquarters.

" Here we were most kindly received, and spent two most enjoyable days, learning a great deal about that part of Turkey. As for the schools themselves, they are no doubt doing thoroughly good work in a most judicious and praiseworthy manner. By the kind assistance of the Rev. Henry Marden, one of the missionaries there, we were in-

---

* Rev. Augustus Walker, of Diarbekir, Mesopotamia.

troduced to the Governor of Marash, a Turkish official who is very much interested in anything that affects the welfare of his province. We met with him a large number of the principal merchants, and conversed with them as to the desires and necessities of the people. The great complaint, as elsewhere in Asiatic Turkey, is the want of communication. It took the mission over four months, we understood, to bring up their harmonium from Alexandretta, only one hundred and twenty miles distant.

" Leaving our hospitable friends at Marash, we set out for Aintab, with letters to Dr. Trowbridge, who is the principal of the Central Turkey College at Aintab. From this gentleman and his friends we met with similar acts of courtesy and kindness. As regards the neighboring country, we were astonished to find so many evidences of population, and of wealth, which, if given a fair chance, could be enormously developed."

Although these missions have not received any special rights under Imperial Firman, the Turkish Government recognize the general usefulness of the schools and institutions; and at all times the governing body have been assisted by H. E. Munif Pasha, the minister of Education at Constantinople.

The work of the American missionaries at Aintab was begun in 1846, mainly through the efforts of a medical missionary, the Rev. Azariah Smith, M.D. A short time before the arrival of Dr. Smith, another missionary had been driven from the city with much violence by a mob of native Armenians, aided by Turkish officials; but the arrival of a well-educated medical man, led the people to give him, at first a reluctant, but eventually a very hearty welcome. Gradually schools were established at Aintab, and in adjoining towns and villages congregations were gathered, books were distributed, and newspapers circulated. Other missionaries were placed at Marash, Oorfa, Aleppo, Antioch, and other places throughout the region, and the work has grown to its present wide dimensions. There are now thirty-two well-organized evangelical churches where there was not one in 1846.

Many of these churches are wholly self-supporting, having well-educated native pastors over them. They have, too, their own common and high schools, supported wholly or in part by themselves. There are thousands of women connected with them who have learned to read, and many of whom have been educated as teachers, in the girls' seminaries at Marash and Aintab.

A theological seminary for the training of young men for the ministry has been established at Marash, and a well-organized college at Aintab. This college was opened in 1876, and has recently issued its tenth annual report. From this report it appears that there were one hundred and twenty students in the institution at the end of the last college year. These students come from distant places, and many of them from the western and eastern as well as from the southern and central parts of Asia Minor. In the hospital, which is connected with the medical department, large numbers of patients from all nationalities, are successfully treated.

MISSIONS OF THE CHURCH MISSIONARY SOCIETY IN PALESTINE. — The English Church Missionary Society has stations at Jerusalem, Nazareth, Salt, Nablus, Jaffa, Gaza, and in the Hauran. There are nine ordained European missionaries, one lay teacher, and one female teacher; fifty male native Christian teachers, and thirteen female; four hundred and fifteen communicants, sixteen hundred and thirty-three native baptized Christians, thirty-five schools, fifteen seminaries, sixteen hundred and sixty-five scholars. A native Church Council has been formed for

Palestine on the plan of those which have worked so well in India.  In the annual report of the Society, made in May, 1886, it is said:

" The success of the Society's schools in Palestine has had the effect of rousing the Turkish authorities to energetic action against the attendance at them of Moslem children.  Some of the mission schools are being peremptorily closed; while, all over Palestine, Mohammedan schools are being opened.  But, as the Rev. C. T. Wilson says, " Until Bishop Gobat opened schools, nothing whatever was done for the education of the young.  Alarmed by success, Greeks and Latins, aided by Russian and French money, opened schools, followed now, at length, by the Turkish Government.  One result of all this will be that the rising generation will be better educated, and from this we, as missionaries, have nothing to fear and everything to hope."

THE MORAVIAN HOSPITAL FOR LEPERS AT JERUSALEM.—The Moravian missionaries are pre-eminent for self-denying zeal, and for their willingness to go to the most difficult and trying fields.  They are found in Greenland, Labrador, Alaska, Australia, Thibet, South Africa, West India Islands, Nicaragua, and Surinam, and in most of these countries they have numerous converts.  In the last named country, for instance, they have no less than twenty-three thousand church members.

The Moravian brothers and sisters have been noted also for their compassion for the forlorn and pitiable condition of the lepers, and they have hospitals for them, and missions to them, in South Africa and Jerusalem.  Referring to what has been done at Jerusalem, *The Christian* (London) of December 16th, 1887, says :

" The work has been carried on, not without spiritual blessing, for twenty years.  Last Spring, a breakdown in the nursing staff necessitated a call for volunteers, and an immediate response came from twelve Christian women in Germany and England. The three selected from these are now assisting Mr. and Mrs. Muller, the self-denying and indefatigable missionaries in charge of the Home."

A new hospital was opened last April. To this the patients of the old hospital have been transferred, and others have since been received. But with the most careful housekeeping, the ability to admit more of these incurables involves enlarged expenses of maintenance, nor is the cost of the new building entirely defrayed.

A letter received from Mr. Muller gives some idea of the terrible character of the disease which he and his helpers are seeking to alleviate. He says:

" A few days ago one of these unfortunates, named Musa, died in our house. He had been here for ten years. On arrival he was quite active and comparatively strong, notwithstanding his fearful infection. Later his strength forsook him, and loathsome sores began to appear on his arms and legs. In spite of medicine and the application of salves, these spread more and more, gradually consuming the flesh, until, in many places, the bones could be seen. At last the sufferer was entirely confined to bed, and this for months. There he lay — a living skeleton—groaning and moaning piteously to be released from his torment. We were filled with indescribable horror and pity whenever we looked at him. Six days before his death he could no longer eat, his throat appearing to be completely closed. We could afford him no relief—the only thing to do was to pray the Saviour to release him from his suffering.

" We have seen many die of this terrible disease, some afflicted more and others less. At present we have twenty-two lepers in the Home. They have all to be bandaged daily, and must be nursed like children. Some of them have neither fingers nor toes, the leprosy having done its work. It pervades every portion of the body, but as soon as the throat is affected, death is sure to follow : because starvation ensues.

"'The misery of the leper outside our walls is enhanced by the cruelty of his relatives. He is utterly forsaken by them and must die alone in some cave or hole, his only refuge. This would not be the case if he were willing at once to come to the Leper Home ; but too frequently he is tardy to acknowledge the fact of his leprosy, considering it a shame and disgrace to be in such a loathsome condition. No real remedy for leprosy has yet been found, but good nursing and Christian treatment go a great way towards alleviating these frightful sufferings."

The mission to the lepers in South Africa has been carried on for fifty years, and though the average term of life of those who serve in the hospital is only seven years, yet there are always other missionaries ready to take the places of those who fall victims to the loathsome disease, or die from other causes. This is Christian heroism of the highest type. Hundreds of the terribly afflicted Africans have been won to faith in Christ, and to the blessed assurance that their sufferings on earth would give place to the eternal bliss of heaven, by God's blessing on the efforts of His faithful servants. Many lepers in India are ministered to by missionaries of the Church of England, and by Scotch and American Presbyterian missionaries, and some others.

THE PRESBYTERIAN MISSION IN SYRIA.—Formerly the American Presbyterians united with the Congregationalists in the support of missions in Syria, but lately this field has been given up entirely to the Presbyterians, who now have in it 14 male missionaries, 23 females, including the wives of missionaries, 36 native pastors and preachers, 143 native teachers and other helpers, 19 churches, 1,440 members, 5,574 pupils in schools, and the annual contributions are about $7,000.

The whole Bible has been translated into Arabic by the Rev. Drs. Eli Smith and Van Dyck of this mission, and copies of this translation are circulated not only in the Turkish Empire, Persia, Arabia and Egypt, but also in all parts of the world in which there are any followers of the false prophet, applications coming from missionaries in countries as far east as Sumatra, as far west as Sierra Leone, and as far south as Zanzibar. Large editions of this Bible and of other books in Arabic, and also in other oriental languages are printed at the Mission Press in Beirut.

THE SYRIAN PROTESTANT COLLEGE.—The Syrian Protestant College at Beirut, founded in 1865, and connected with this mission, has always been noted for its very able professors, its thorough equipment and its wide influence. Writing concerning it, a correspondent of *The Church at Home and Abroad,* for December, 1887, says :

" Its graduates are employed as preachers, teachers, medical missionaries, translators, physicians of hospitals and muncipalities, merchants, and government officials in all parts of Turkey, in Egypt, Morocco, Sierra Leone, Aden and Zanzibar. They have infused into the body politic of these important strategic regions, wider apart than Alaska and Maine, the germs of a new intellectual and political life.

Two of the graduates of the college, Messrs. Sarruf and Nusir, conduct the *Mugtataf,* an Arabic scientific journal of a high order, which has a circulation over the whole eastern world, and is without question the leader of scientific thought in all those wide regions.

Another graduate of the college, Dr. Shibly Schmeil,

of Cairo, publishes the leading medical journal of the Arabic-speaking world. It is carried on in the highest scientific spirit, and is an immense stimulus to the large number of medical men who are being educated in Arabic-speaking lands.

The theological seminary of the mission was established in as close relations as possible with the college without organic connection. The commodious building forms part of the group around the college campus, and the students are as far as possible, drawn from the college classes. The atmosphere of the college proves a stimulus to the habits of the theological students, while the presence of such an institution keeps ever before the minds of the undergraduates one of the chief ends for which the college was established—to aid in the training of a native ministry.

The situation of the college, in an Arabic-speaking and Bible land, has attracted students from England and America, who came to enjoy in its halls the advantages of a comfortable and economical home, where they could pursue studies in the biblical languages and archæology. The gradual development of this opportunity has led to a plan for making the college a centre for biblical study, available to students from all lands who may wish to pursue a course of study in the Arabic, Hebrew, Syriac, and other oriental languages, as well as to work up the archæ- ology, geography and customs of the East."

Other distinguished laborers in this field besides Drs. Smith and Van Dyck are the Rev. Drs. W. M. Thomson, (author of "The Land and the Book," and other works,) Henry H. Jessup and Daniel Bliss. These names, and some others, are as familiar to the friends of missions as are those of the Rev. Drs Goodell, Dwight, Hamlin and Riggs, at Constantinople, and Bishops Gobat and Barclay,

and the Rev. Messrs. Wolters and Zeller, at Jerusalem.
Of the venerable Dr. Thomson, who is now in the United
States, a correspondent at Beirut writes :

"No other missionary has been privileged to labor so
many years in Syria. No other one has travelled so widely through the land and made his influence so extensively
felt. He was born to be a pioneer missionary. His resources for planning and suggesting new channels of effort,
and extricating the mission from trouble in times of opposition, were boundless. His body and mind seemed insen-
sible to fatigue. His brain thought out the Syrian Protestant College, and the Dodges, father and son, made that
thought an actual and splendid reality."

# APPENDIX.

# APPENDIX.

## THE ENRICHMENT OF OCCIDENTAL SCIENCE BY THE MISSIONARIES.

ONE of the reflex benefits of Foreign Missions is the enrichment of science and literature by the contributions of the missionaries. An octavo volume of over 500 pages has been prepared by the Rev. Dr. Laurie, and published by the American Board, to show the services of the missionaries to Geography, Geology, Mineralogy, Natural History, Archæology, Philology, Ethnography, Music, Religious Beliefs, History, Education, Medical Science, Commerce, the Arts, &c.

The volume was undertaken at the desire of, and the expense of its publication was provided for, by the late Hon. Alfred B. Ely, of Newtown, Mass., who believed that the contributions of the missionaries to the various branches of knowledge were greatly under-estimated. The work is not confined to these incidental services of the men whom the American Board has sent out, but it is mainly devoted to them ; and if so much can be said concerning the agents of one society, what may not be said concerning the workers sent forth by all the societies? We append some of the testimonies of distinguished scientists and others contained in the book.

Professor Whitney, the distinguished Orientalist, says : "I have a strong realization of the value of missionary labors to science. The American Oriental Society has been much dependent on them for its usefulness. There would hardly be occasion for the society at all, but for them." The late Rev. Dr. Wm. Adams, of New York, said : "I believe that more has been done in philology, geography and ethnology, indirectly, by our missionaries than by all the royal and national societies in the world that devote themselves exclusively to these objects."

One writer says : "Missions enable the German in his study to compare more than two hundred languages ; the unpronounceable polysyllables used by John Elliot, the monosyllables of China, the lordly Sanskrit and its modern associates, the smooth languages of the South Seas, the musical dialects of Africa, and the harsh gutturals of our own Indians."

"It would be impossible," said Professor Silliman, "for the historian of the islands of the Pacific to ignore the important contributions of American missionaries to science;" and Professor Agassiz testified: "Few are aware how much we owe them both for their intelligent observation of facts, and for their collecting of specimens. We must look to them not a little for aid in our efforts to advance future science."

"In the Oriental Translation Society of London, Sir A. Johnson, former Chief-Justice of Ceylon, moved, and Sir W. Ousely seconded, a vote of thanks to our mission in Ceylon for such service to science. Dr. Harris also speaks of the value of the aid furnished by missionaries for proving the common origin of the race—a conclusion endorsed by Schlegel, the French Academy, and others."

TESTIMONY OF MR. G. M. POWELL.—In a paper read before the American Institute, Mr. G. M. Powell, of the Oriental Topographical Corps, presented testimony of his own and of others to the immense amount of valuable contributions to knowledge made by missionaries. He said : " Probably no source of knowledge in this department has been so vast, varied and prolific as the investigations and contributions of missionaries. They have patiently col·lected, and truthfully transmitted much exact and valuable geographical knowledge, and all without money and without price, though it would have cost millions to secure it in any other way."

" Carl Ritter, 'the prince of geographers,' confesses he could not have written his vast works 'Erdkunde' and others without the aid of material collected and transmitted by missionaries."

" Professor Whitney of Yale College, Secretary of the American Oriental Society, writes : ' Religion, commerce, and scientific zeal rival one another in bringing new regions and peoples to light, and in uncovering the long buried remains of others, lost or decayed ; and of the three, the first is the most prevailing and effective.'

" ' I have seen,' says Warren, ' a letter from the celebrated astronomer, Herschel, expressing thanks to a missionary in Persia, Rev. D. T. Stoddard, for important meteorological discoveries. He pledged to Mr. Stoddard a vote of thanks from the Royal Society.'

" Champion's essays on the Botany and Geology of South Africa, in Silliman's Journal, and on the topography of that region, in the ' American Journal of Science,' are a few only among the works of that talented and cultured gentleman, who gave his fortune as well as his life to one of the most difficult missions in the world."

" Balbi, one of the greatest of encyclopediaists, is most hearty in his acknowledgment of the value of the scientific researches of missionaries.

" My own intercourse with missionaries—looking at this work with the eye of a business man—when in Northern

15

Africa and Western Asia, for the Oriental and Topograph·
ical Corps, fully corroborates the testimony cited in this
paper, as has also my subsequent correspondence with them
in the same connection."

---

### ENRICHING THE ORIENT WITH TRUE SCIENCE AND PHILOSOPHY.

While the missionaries have been thus enriching the
science of the Occident, they have at the same time
been still more enriching the Orient with science and true
philosophy. While from a literary point of view, they
have given their greatest attention and their best efforts to
translating the Word of God into the various languages
of Asia, and the preparation in them of books on the religious life, Christian Evidences, Church History, and Syste-
matic Theology,* they have also rightly deemed it their
duty to combat the false science and false philosophies
prevalent in Turkey, Persia, India, China and Japan, by
works in the vernaculars on astronomy, chemistry, ethnolo
gy, geography, geology, history, moral science, natural
history and philosophy. Missionary physicians have
published books on anatomy, physiology, *materia medica*,
and therapeutics  The missionaries, too, in all lands to
which they go, are the makers of elementary and advanced
school books, grammars, phrase-books, dictionaries, and
books of folk-lore.

If it is a fact in the Occident that "true science is the
handmaid of true religion," how much more is it the case
in the Orient, where the false religions are so interwoven
with false science and false philosophies. Sir Richard

---

* Of course all the Missions prepare a Hymn Book, and the
Episcopal Missions a Liturgy also, for use in public worship.

Temple bears testimony to the high character of the educational and scientific books prepared by the missionaries in India. He says that many of them are of " lasting fame and utility." More than one hundred scientific books have been written or translated by the missionaries in China, and about thirty thousand volumes are sold annually there at the cost of their production; and as the Chinese government has ordered that all candidates for government offices shall be examined in certain departments of Western science, the demand for these books will be immense. The New York *Evangelist* of March 8, 1888, contains an article by the Rev. Dr. George E. Post, in which there is the following remarkable exhibit of the contributions of the American Mission in Syria to the religious and scientific literature of the many lands in which the Arabic language is used :

" It would take a long list to exhaust the religious, literary, and scientific contributions to the Arabic language from the missionaries in Syria. They include the translation of the Scriptures and the stereotyping of the same in numerous styles; the preparation of a Scripture guide, commentaries, a Concordance, and a complete hymn and tune book; textbooks in history, algebra, geometry, trigonometry, logarithms, astronomy, meteorology, botany, zoology, physics, chemistry, anatomy, physiology, hygiene, materia medica, practice of physic, surgery, and a periodical literature which has proved the stimulus to a very extensive native journalism. The Protestant converts of the mission, educated by the missionaries, have written elaborate works on history, poetry, grammar, arithmetic, natural science, and the standard dictionary of the language, and a cyclopædia which will make a library by itself, consisting of about twenty volumes of from six hundred to eight hundred pages each."

## THE AWAKENING IN THE EAST.

THE extensive American Missions in the Ottoman Empire, with their numerous religious, scientific and other books in the vernaculars, and Robert College at Constantinople, the Syrian Protestant College at Beirut, and the educational establishments in Asia Minor and elsewhere, are exerting a vast and wide-spread influence. They are the main sources of that awakening and progress now so manifest in the East. We have given some proofs of this under Turkish Empire, in this book, but there are other evidences. High authorities state that the progress in so many respects in Bulgaria is mainly owing to the fact that many of the leading men in the country were educated at Robert College or by American missionaries resident in Bulgaria.

United States Minister E. F. Noyes, reporting in 1880 on the relations of his country and the Ottoman Empire, wrote as follows:

" The salutary influence of American missionaries and teachers in the Turkish Empire cannot possibly be over-rated. By actual observation I know that wherever a conspicuously intelligent and enterprising man or woman is found in the East, one imbued with the spirit of modern civilization, it is always found that he or she was educated at an American school or college in Constantinople, Alexandria, Cairo, Asyoot, or Beirut. And with the educational influences comes a demand for the refinements and comforts of civilized life. The Arab youth who has graduated at the college in Beirut, is no longer contented to live in a mud-pen, to clothe himself in filthy rags, or not at all, and to live on sugar-cane. He aspires to live as do his teachers, who came from the Great Republic on the other side of the Atlantic Ocean. He tells his family and friends something of what he has learned; and an ambition, a longing for something better than they have known is inspired in them."

When the missionaries first went to Beirut, it was a malodorous town of only 15,000 inhabitants; now it is a fine city of 80,000 people, and it is lighted, paved, and drained like an occidental city. Schools abound, and there is much spiritual and intellectual life, while manufactures and commerce are flourishing.* There is also moral and material progress at Jaffa, Haifa, Cesarea, Tiberias, Nablous and Jerusalem. At the last two cities, and at ·Bethlehem and Nazareth very efficient and successful work is being done by the missionaries of the English Church Missionary Society. Agents of the London Society for promoting Christianity among the Jews, and a few Missionaries of other European organizations, are also doing a good work in Jerusalem.

Turkish intolerance and Moslem fanaticism are not what they once were, though there are still outbursts of Mohammedan bigotry in some portions of the huge Ottoman Empire; the government of the Sultan has recently, and somewhat unexpectedly, granted its imprimatur to the

---

* Beirut, in Syria, is called "the crown-jewel of modern missions." It is to-day a Christian city, with more influence upon the adjacent lands than had the Berytus of old, on whose ruins it has risen. Stately churches, hospitals, a female seminary, a college, whose graduates are scattered over Syria, Egypt, and wherever the Arab roams, a theological seminary, a common-school system, and three steam-presses, throwing off nearly a half-million pages of reading matter a day; a Bible-house, whose products are found in India, China, Ethiopia, and at the sources of the Nile; these are the facets of that "crown jewel" which the missionaries have cut with their sanctified enterprise. —*Missionary Review for December, 1888.*

religious and other books printed at the extensive mission printing establishment at Beirut; men of worthier character are sought to fill official stations; there are more Christian officials in the employ of the Government, and they are not now required to wear the Turkish fez; the bells of the churches in Jerusalem, after being silenced for a long time, are permitted to be rung again; and, better than all, the Word of the Lord is having more free course, and is being glorified in the enlightenment and conversion of an ever increasing number of the descendants of Abraham and of Ishmael, the followers of the False Prophet, and others of the diverse peoples and religionists of the East.

---

## THE STATESMANSHIP OF MISSIONS.

In *The Missionary Review* for December, 1888, there is a remarkable article by J. M. Ludlow. D D , on "The Statesmanship of Missions" In it occurs the following on the great missionary, Rev. Christian Frederick Schwartz:

"One of the most beautiful monuments in India was built by Sarfogee. the Rajah of Tanjore, to the memory of Schwartz, who died in 1798. These lines may be taken from the epitaph which the Rajah composed:

'To the benighted, dispenser of light,
Doing and pointing to that which is right;
Blessing to princes, to people, to me,
May I, my father, be worthy of thee.'

Well might the Rajah call Schwartz his father, for when the old Rajah, his real father, was dying, he called for the missionary, and, putting his hand upon his son's head, said: 'This is not my son any longer, but thine, for into thine hands I deliver him.' By his practical counsel, Schwartz really kept the crown upon the young prince's head. He quieted revolts among his people, as when 7,000 rebels, who had refused to hear the government, said to the missionary: ' You have shown us kindness. . . . We will work for you day and night to show our regard.' When famine desolated Tanjore, and the people were taking their revenge upon their rulers by refusing to sell them provisions, and when no threats from the authorities availed, Schwartz was able to secure, within two days, 1000 oxen and 8,000 measures of grain. The British resident wrote home : ' Happy indeed would it be for India if Schwartz possessed the whole authority.' "

At the time that this great and good pioneer missionary labored, the British ruled over only a small part of India. Since their sway has been gradually extended over the whole of that vast country, Christian missionaries have been, by their influence and their untiring efforts, as we have shown under "INDIA," the means of abolishing tremendous native evils, and much foreign misrule.

Through this, and by their faithful preaching of the Gospel of Christ, furnishing a Christian literature in the various languages of India, establishing Christian schools, colleges, orphan asylums, hospitals, and leper asylums ; by their ministrations of mercy to the poor, the fever-stricken, and the famine-stricken ; by kindness and courtesy to all classes of the natives, and by being among them as those who serve, and not, as many foreigners are, masterful and overbearing towards them ; by religious services for the benefit of foreign residents and visitors, where there is no chaplain ; and by ever seeking the Divine blessing upon all branches of the work, and upon themselves, that they may have more of the mind of Christ, and walk more closely in His footsteps, they have been, as Sir Rivers Thompson, an ex-Governor of Bengal, says, " The salt of the country and the true saviors of the Empire." Lord John Lawrence, who is acknowledged to have been the greatest of all the English Viceroys of India, said at a public meeting in London:

"Notwithstanding all that the English people have done to benefit India, the missionaries have done more than all other agencies combined. As a body they are remarkably popular in the country."

And what is true of India is true of all countries in which Christian Missions have been established, as we have proved in this volume, by the testimony of many eminent, and, for the most part, independent witnesses. Dr. Benson, the Archbishop of Canterbury, states that Professor Drummond, since his return from visiting various mission stations in Africa, has remarked: "Mission reports are said to be valueless; they are not half so valueless as anti-mission reports."

The large amount of testimony given in this book is mainly from non-missionary sources, and it would seem as if every candid reader of it must agree that Archdeacon Farrar was right when he said that "to talk of the failure of Foreign Missions is to talk at once like an ignorant and like a faithless man."

# INDEX OF PERSONS.

Aberdeen, Earl of, 209.
Adams, Rev. Dr. Wm., 224.
Aitcheson, Sir Chas., 25, 96, 101.
Akbar, Emperor of India, 93.
Allen, Hon. Elisha H., 175, 190.
Augell, President J. B., 27, 61.
Annand, Rev. Joseph, 145.
Arnold, Rev. Dr., 83.
Ashmore, Rev. Dr., 56.
Auckland, Lord, 81.

Bainbridge, Rev. W. F., 18.
Baker, Shirley, 204, 205.
Balbi, Prof., 225.
Barclay, Bishop, 220.
Barth, Dr. Heinrich, 1.
Bartlett, Rev. Dr. S. C., 165.
Baxter, Rt. Hon. W. E., 96.
Bayard, Hon. Thomas F., 194.
Behari, Lal Chandra, 89.
Bell, Lieut.-Col. Mark S., 21, 211.
Benjamin, Hon. S. G. W., 171.
Benson, Archbishop, 232.
Bird, Miss Isabella, 115.
Bismarck, Prince, 132.
Bliss, Rev. Dr. Daniel, 14, 220.
Bloomfield, Bishop, 92.
Bridges, Rev. Thomas, 203.
Boardman, Rev. Dr., 83.
Bove, Lieut., 202, 203.
Bompas, Bishop, 160.
Boone, Bishop W. J., 112.
Brassey, Lord, 183.
Bright, John, 83.
Brinkley, Capt. R. A., 21, 121.
Brooke, Rajah, 50.
Brown, Dr. Robert, 22, 78.

Brownlee, Charles, 41.
Bruce, Rev. Dr., 172.
Burdon, Bishop, 5.
Butler, Rev. Dr. Wm., 81, 109.

Caine, W. S., 94.
Calvert, Mrs., 73.
Calvert, Rev. James, 72, 177.
Cameron, Commander V. L., 22, 25, 32.
Canning, Lord, 106.
Carey, Felix, 52.
Carey, Rev. Dr. William, 80, 91, 102.
Carlton, Rev. M. M., 110.
Castelar, Senor, 133.
Chalmers, Rev. James, 134, 136, 137, 140, 141, 143, 177, 178, 180.
Chamberlain, Rev. Dr. Jacob, 88, 107.
Charles, Mrs., 212.
Christlieb, Rev. Dr. Theodore, 48, 111, 175.
Clarke, C. B., 90.
Clive, Lord Robert, 80, 81, 86.
Coilliard, M., 39.
Comber, Rev. J. T., 37.
Cook, Captain, 149, 204.
Conway, Moncure D., 191.
Crocker, Dr. 179.
Cumming, Miss C. F. Gordon, 26, 56, 57, 69, 72, 73, 187, 205.
Cust, Robert N., LL. D., 22, 23, 33. 209.

Dalhousie, Lord, 82, 106.

(233)

Dana, Hon. R. H., 2, 187.
Darwin, Charles, 2, 8, 22, 29, 152, 199, 202.
Dawson, Hon. N. H. R., 170.
Dean, Rev. Dr., 192.
De Morgan, Professor, 85.
Denby, Colonel Charles, 21, 27, 60, 61.
Doane, Rev. E. T., 132, 133, 134.
Donavan, J. P., 2, 59.
Draper, Rev. Dr. Gideon, 44.
Drummond, Professor, 232.
Duff, Rev. Dr., 169.
Dufferin, Lord, 21, 106, 168.
Duncan, William, 166, 168, 169, 170.
Dwight, Rev. Dr., 208, 220.

Edwardes, Major-General, 21, 84, 85, 86, 87, 93, 95.
Ellenborough, Lord, 81.
Ellinwood, Rev. Dr., 19.
Ellis, Rev. Dr. W., 31.
Elouis, J. J. H., 92.
Ely, Hon. Alfred B., 223.
Emin Bey, 25, 33.
Ensor, Rev. George, 4.
Erskine, Captain R. N., 73, 74, 185.
Erskine, Commodore, 22, 138, 139.

Falding, Rev. Dr., 16.
Farler, Archdeacon, 26, 46.
Farrar, Archdeacon, 4, 232.
Feng, General, 67.
Ferguson, Bishop S. D., 37.
Fletcher, Miss, 132.
Forbes, Rev. Mr., 189.
Foster, Bishop R. S., 19.
Frere, Sir Bartle, 98.
Froude, James A., 29, 153.

Geddie, Rev. John, 145, 146.
George, King, (Tonga), 204.
Gill, Rev. T. Wyatt, 136, 174, 177.
Gobat, Bishop, 216, 220.
Goldsborough, Commodore, 22.
Goodell, Rev. Dr., 229.

Gordon, Rev. George, 145, 146.
Gordon, General, 25, 33.
Gordon, Sir Arthur, 71.
Gore, Admiral, 22.
Gowan, Colonel, 109.
Gracey, Rev. Dr. J. T., 53, 110.
Graves, Hon. N. F., 126, 128.
Gray, Rev. J. H., 92.
Griffin, Sir Lepel, 24.
Griffis, William Elliott, 2, 10, 114.

Haig, Major-General, 21, 44.
Haines, Sir Frederick, 106.
Hamlin, Rev. Dr., 220.
Hannington, Bishop, 6, 26, 43, 44.
Happer, Rev. Dr., 63.
Hare, Bishop, 162.
Harnam Singh, Prince, 88
Harney, General, 159.
Harris, J. B., 162.
Harvey, Captain, 201.
Hastings, Warren, 83.
Henry, Rev. B. C., 12.
Hepburn, Dr. J. C., 114.
Herrick, Dr., 211.
Herschel, Sir John, 225.
Hiraiwa, Rev. Y., 123.
Hole, Canon, 90, 91.
Holland, Sir Henry, 205.
Hornaday, W. D, 50, 51.
Hubbard, Hon. R. B., 123.
Hübner, Baron, 41.
Hume, Rev. Robert A., 11.
Hunter, Sir William, 103, 104.

Jackson, Mrs. Helen H., 159, 160.
Jay, Narain, Rajah, 185.
Jefferson, Thomas, 160.
Jeremiassen, Dr., 67.
Jessup, Rev. Dr. Henry H., 220.
Johnson, Sir A., 124.
Johnson, Mr. H. H., 9.
Johnston, Rev. James, 183.
Jones, Admiral Gore, 130.
Jones, Rev. John, 182.
Judson, Rev. Dr. Adoniram, 52, 80.
Judson, Mrs. Annie, 52.

Kane, Dr. Elisha, 22, 76, 77, 78.
Kerr, Dr. (Canton),65, 125.
Keshub, Chunder, Sen., 106.
Kiernander, Rev. Mr., 81.
Kincaid, Rev. Dr., 53.
King, Mrs. M. D., 68.
Knight, Alfred T., 120.
Knight, Rev. T. 121.

Lansdell, Rev. Dr. Henry, 195, 196, 197.
La Perouse, 183, 187.
Laurie, Rev. Dr., 223.
Lawes, Rev. Mr., 137, 138, 139.
Lawrence. Lord John, 21, 83, 97, 106, 231.
Layard, Sir Austen, 207.
Lenz, Dr. Oscar, 5, 8, 25, 46.
Liggins, Rev. John, 112.
Li Hung Chang, 63, 68.
Li, Lady, 68
Limburg-Hirum, Count, 16.
Livingstone, Rev. Dr. David, 6, 25, 31, 38.
Lloyd, Rev. Llewellyn, 56.
Loch, Sir H. B., 138.
Loftus, Lord, 21, 138.
Longfellow, the Poet, 10.
Lowell, James Russell, 6.
Ludlow, Rev. Dr. J. M., 230.
Lyth, Mrs., 73.
Lytton, Lord, 106.

Macdonald, Captain, 177.
McDougal, Bishop, 49, 50.
Macfarlane, Rev. Mr., 136, 137.
McGregor, William, 75.
Mackenzie. Bishop, 25.
Maclay, Arthur Collins, 1, 117, 118, 119.
McLeod, Sir Donald, 96.
Main, Dr. Duncan, 67.
Maitland, Sir P., 92.
Marden, Rev. Henry, 213.
Marsden, Rev. Samuel, 149, 150.
Marsh, G. P., LL.D., 22, 209.
Martin, Col. W. J., 109.
Martin, Rev. Dr. W. A. P., 63.
Medhurst, Consul W. H., 27, 58, 69.

Mitchell, Sir Charles, 205, 206.
Milman, Hugh, 139.
Moffatt, Rev. Dr. Robert, 6, 25, 38.
Morgan, Lewis H., 22.
Muir, Sir William, 98.
Muller, Rev. Mr., 217.
Munif, Pasha, 214.
Miller, Dr. Hugh, 109.
Murchison, Sir Roderick, 76.
Murdoch, Rev. Dr., 88, 91.
Murray, Rev. Mr., 136, 137.

Na Aaktangi, 148.
Nana Sahib, 85.
Napier and Ettrick, Lord, 21, 97.
Northbrook, Earl of, 21, 95.
Noyes, Hon. E. F., 228.

O'Neil, Consul Henry E., 32.
Ousely, Sir W., 224.

Pallalaia, 203.
Palm, Dr. (Japan), 115, 116.
Patteson, Bishop, 6, 144, 151.
Pattison, Dr. T. Harwood, 138.
Perkins, Commissioner H. E., 109.
Phelps, General J. W., 21, 131.
Phillips, Wendell, 160.
Powell, G. M., 224.
Prime, Rev. Dr. Eusebius, 19.

Rama, Rev. T., 109.
Ram, Chundra, 85.
Randle, Rev. Horace, 69.
Reade, Winwood, 25.
Redcliffe, Lord, 27, 207.
Rein, Prof. J. J., 2, 116.
Rhoads, Dr. (Indian Commissioner), 161.
Richards, Rev. W. J., 110.
Riggs, Rev. Dr., 220.
Ripon, Marquis of, 106.
Ritter, Karl, 29. 150, 225.
Rowley, Rev. Henry, 31.
Ruatara, 149.

Saker, Rev. Alfred, 2.

Salisbury, Marquis of, 183.
Sarfogee, Rajah, 230.
Schmeil, Dr. Shibley, 219.
Schmid, Dr. H. Ernest, 112.
Schwartz, Rev. C. F., 81, 230.
Scratchley, Sir Peter, 142.
Schweinfurth, Dr. George, 22, 25. 32.
Scott-Stevenson, Mrs., 28.
Seelye, Dr. Julius H., 156.
Seymour, Consul Charles, 125.
Selwyn, Bishop, 6, 150, 151, 182.
Shackleford, General, 27.
Shaftesbury, Earl of, 68, 83, 208.
Shaw, Rev. G. A., 31.
Sheridan, Gen. Philip, 157.
Shumway, A. L., 124, 125.
Sibree, James, 130.
Sickles, Consul David B., 192.
Skene, Consul, 212.
Silliman, Professor, 224.
Smith, Rev. Azariah, M. D., 214.
Smith, Rev. Dr. Eli, 219, 220.
Smith, Dr. George, 102.
Smith, Samuel, M. P., 94.
Smith, Sir Thomas, 121.
Speke, Capt. R. A., 25, 31.
Spry, Capt. W. J.. R. N., 135, 144.
Spurgeon, Rev. Charles, 160.
Stack, Rev. Matthew, 79.
Stanley, Henry M., 25.
Steere, Bishop, 25.
Stevens, Rev. Dr. Abel, 20.
Stevenson, Rev. Dr. W. F., 18.
Stevenson, Mrs. Scott, 28.
Stewart, Col. C. E., 21, 172.
Stewart, T. McCants, 37.
Sterling, Bishop W. H., 202.
St. Julian, Sir Charles, 71.
Stock, Eugene, 21.
Stoddard, Rev. D. T., 225.
Strickland, Sir E., 138.
Sullivan, Admiral, 22, 202.
Sunderland, Rev. Dr. Byron, 154, 155, 159.

Swineford, Governor, 170.

Tancred, Sir Thomas, 29, 213.
Taylor, Rev. J. Hudson, 69.
Taylor, General, (India), 21.
Taylor, Canon Isaac, 21.
Temple, Sir Richard, 11, 79, 99, 100.
Tenney, Rev. Charles, 63.
Terrero, Emilio, 132.
Thompson, Sir Augustus Rivers, 96.
Thomson, Dr., Archbishop of York, 16.
Thompson, Rev. Dr. (Siam), 194.
Thomson, Mr. Joseph, 8.
Thomson, Rev. Dr. W. M., 14, 220, 221.
Thurston, J. B., 76.
Torrence, Dr. (Persia), 173.
Trowbridge, Rev. Dr., 214.
Tucker, Judge, 13.
Turner, Rev. Dr. George, 184.

Upshaw, General, 166.

Vanderkemp. Rev. Dr., 48.
VanDycke, Rev. Dr. C. V. A., 14, 219, 220.
Vidal, Bishop, 35.
Vinton, Rev. Dr. J. B., 53.

Walker, Rev. Augustus, 213.
Wallace, Alfred Russell, 22, 55.
Wallace, General Lew, 21, 210, 211.
Walsh, Bishop W. P., 150.
Warren, Sir Charles, 32, 39.
Washburn, Rev. Mr., 14.
Wayland, Rev. Dr. H. L., 161.
Weeks, Bishop, 35.
Welsh, Herbert, 159, 161.
White, Z. L., 166.
Whipple, Bishop, 155, 162.
Whitney, Professor, 223, 225.
Wilberforce, William, 81.
Wilkes, Admiral, 22, 70, 198.
Williams, Rev. C. M., 112.

Williams, Rev. John, 144, 145, 146, 184.
Williams, Bishop, W., 150.
Willing, Mrs. J. F., 179.
Wilson, Rev. C. T., 216.
Wilson, Rev. Dr. (Bombay), 107.

Wilson, Rev. Leighton, 31.
Wilson, Sir Charles, 21.
Wolff, Rev. Dr., 197.
Wolters, Rev. T. F., 221.

Zeller, Rev. John, 221.
Ziegenbalg, Rev. Mr., 81.

# UNDER FRENCH SKIES;

## Or, Sunny Fields and Shady Woods.

By Madame de GASPARIN,

*Author of "Near and Heavenly Horizons."*

**16mo, Cloth, $1.25.**

---

This is a new work by the author of "Near and Heavenly Horizons," which, when published some years ago, attained such popularity that the Countess Gasparin's latest publication will probably be eagerly sought for. The author's love of nature, the depth of her religious feeling, and the rare quality of her literary skill, give her works a charm and grace which secure to them an assured place in literature.

"We have seldom read a professedly religious book so thoroughly free from dogmatism, so sympathetic in its tone, and so wholesome in its spirit of wide and truly Christian charity, or one in which the author so evidently wrote from the fullness of the heart. Considered merely as a literary production, Madame de Gasparin's work is equally deserving of praise. There is about it an amount of care and of finish which are not amongst the least proofs of the writer's earnestness and sincerity."—*Glasgow Herald.*

"This collection of *historiettes* by Madame de Gasparin has to do, in the way of scene, chiefly with the Jura borderland district on the Swiss and French frontiers. It has a type of beauty of its own. Its modest mountain heights contrasted with the magnificent panorama of the Bernese Oberland within view, its wealth of dark pine forest, its pastoral highlands of intense green, have great attractions for many, not least for the authoress herself. And this district, known and loved as it is by the writer, is here peopled with a number of actors who come forward in the various tales contained in the volume. Raoul and Marjolaine, the happy young couple in their mountain cottage and bit of farm, Pierre the woodman, Silvio and Serinette, the loves of Victor and Louise ; these, and many more, form the *dramatis personæ* that appear in the pleasant pages of the book."—*London Bookseller.*

---

*Sent, postpaid, on receipt of the price, by*

# THE BAKER & TAYLOR CO

## 740 and 742 Broadway, New York.

# MODERN CITIES

## AND THEIR RELIGIOUS PROBLEMS.

### By Rev. SAMUEL LANE LOOMIS.

With an Introduction by Rev. JOSIAH STRONG, D.D.

#### 12mo, Cloth, $1.00.

---

" For all who love their fellow-men, this book will be a stimulus and a guide. It presents clearly and forcibly the increasingly difficult problem of the modern city, and will prove to be a storehouse of information to all workers in this field. Like 'Our Country,' by Rev. Dr. Strong, this book is one of the most marked books of the current year. Every worker in city or country should read and inwardly digest this suggestive volume."—Rev. A. F. SCHAUFFLER, D.D.

" This volume is in point and substance the *companion volume to be read in connection with ' Our Country,'* by the Rev Josiah Strong, D.D. The author's sociology is sound. The chapters on methods of philanthropic endeavor, and especially those which show what has been done, are wise and helpful. We commend the book heartily to our readers."—*The Independent.*

" This is an important little volume, and a fit companion to place side by side with the remarkable work by Dr. Strong. entitled ' Our Country.' It is a book which will startle many and convince all who read it. It ought to go into every household in the land."—*Christian at Work.*

" The author has reached more nearly to the true cause of the difficulty, and the proper manner to remove it, than any other author with whose works we are acquainted."—*Hartford Post.*

"A striking and sensible book—one of the clearest and best things ever written on this live and stirring current question."—*Michigan Christian Advocate.*

"A timely book, well written, sensible, practical. A book that deserves reading."—*Springfield Union.*

" The present volume is directly to the point, wise, timely, and earnest."—*Christian Sanctuary.*

" This is a very able book."—*Baltimore Sun.*

---

*Sent, postpaid, on receipt of the price, by*

## THE BAKER & TAYLOR CO.,

### PUBLISHERS.

### 740 AND 742 BROADWAY, NEW YORK.

# Two Books of National Interest.

The very general attention attracted by the publication, under the title of "National Perils and Opportunities," of the Discussions of the General Christian Conference held at Washington, D.C., Dec. 7-9, 1887, under the auspices of the Evangelical Alliance, has induced the publishers, in the hope of finding a still larger circle of readers, to issue, in two uniform cheap volumes, certain of these noteworthy papers, grouped under the two following titles, which describe the divisions into which the work of the Conference naturally fell:

**PROBLEMS OF AMERICAN CIVILIZATION:** Their Practical Solution the Pressing Christian Duty of To-day. By Presidents MCCOSH and GATES, Bishop COXE, Rev. Drs. PIERSON, DORCHESTER, MCPHERSON, and HAYGOOD; Hon. SETH LOW; Prof. BOYESEN; Col. J. L. GREENE, and Rev. SAMUEL LANE LOOMIS. (Uniform with Co-operation in Christian Work.) 16mo. Paper, 30 cents; cloth, 60 cents.

The topics are: "Immigration," by BOYESEN; "Misuse of Wealth," by GATES; "Estrangement from the Church," by PIERSON; "Ultramontanism," by COXE; "The Saloon," by HAYGOOD; "The Social Vice," by GREENE; Relation of the Church to the Capital and Labor Question," by MCCOSH and LOW; "The City as a Peril," by DORCHESTER, MCPHERSON, and LOOMIS.

**CO-OPERATION IN CHRISTIAN WORK:** Common Ground for United Interdenominational Effort. By Bishop HARRIS, Rev. Drs. STORRS, GLADDEN, STRONG, RUSSELL, SCHAUFFLER, GORDON, KING, and HATCHER, President GILMAN, Professor GEO. E. POST, and others. (Uniform with "Problems of American Civilization.") 16mo. Paper, 30 cents; cloth, 60 cents.

The topics are: "Necessity of Co-operation in Christian Work," by STORRS, HARRIS, GLADDEN, and POST; "Methods of Co-operation in Christian Work," by STRONG; "Co-operation in Small Cities," by RUSSELL; "Co-operation in Large Cities," by SCHAUFFLER; "Christian Resources of Our Country," by KING, GILMAN, and HATCHER; "Individual Responsibility Growing out of Perils and Opportunities," by GORDON, and others.

*Sent, postpaid, on receipt of the price, by*

## THE BAKER & TAYLOR CO.,

### 740 and 742 Broadway, New York.